THE KINGDOM

by Rav Sha'ul

The Kingdom

Of Yahuah

The Kingdom

Of Yahuah

by
Rav Sha'ul

Rav Sha'ul

I would like to thank my wife Stephanie you are the love of my life and my gift from Yahuah. I dedicate this book to my children Stephanie Yates, Ashley Black, Alexis Fox, and Dane Sides, may you all walk the path of righteousness, and be granted a place in the Kingdom.

Special thanks to Susan my dear sister in Yahuah, thank you for your labors to edit this book to the Glory of His Kingdom!

Copyright © 2015 by Rav Sha'ul

All rights reserved. No part of this book may be reproduced, scanned, or distributed in any printed or electronic form without permission.

First Edition: June 2015

Printed in the United States of America

ISBN: 978-1514159590

Table of Contents

Introduction 1

Chapter 1

The "Keys" to studying the Kingdom of Yahuah

The Central Theme of Scripture... the 'Kingdom' 2

The Kingdom *of Yahuah* is not of this World 3

We Must Be Qualified to Enter *the Kingdom of Yahuah* 5

Training Aids 6

The Text Book 7

The Course 7

The Obstacle 8

The Urgency 9

What is the Kingdom of Yahuah? 10

The Outline of this Book 13

Introduction 15

What is the True Word of Yahuah? 17

Covenants 19

What is a Covenant? 19
All Covenants are still active and valid 21
The Kingdom progressively revealed in covenants 23

Study Aids or "Keys" to Understanding *the Kingdom* 24

Progressive Revelation / Progressive Disclosure 24
Physical to spiritual parallels 25
Transposition 27
Example of physical to spiritual parallels, and transposition ... 28

The 7 Covenants of Yahuah 31

A Tour of all 7 Covenants between Yahuah and Man 36

The Sabbath Covenant 36
The Edenic Covenant/ Adamic Covenants 37

The Noahic Covenant 38

  The Abrahamic Covenant 38

  The Mosaic Covenant 39

  The Davidic Covenant 40

  The Yahushaic Covenant 40

Terms and Conditions 43

  The Law is the *'Terms and Conditions'* of every covenant 45

Summary 47

Introduction 52

Yahuah's Purpose 56

The Universe is Our Inheritance 58

This Life is Training in His Law 60

  We are being trained as priests and kings 61

  We are in "Torah Training" 62

  The Kingdom will rule the Universe for eternity 64

The Purpose - Summary 65

Hope - The Fall of Creation by Design 66

The Mystery of the Ages 71

We are Held in Bondage to the Fear of Death 74

Progressive Revelation of the Realm 82

- Edenic Covenant 82
- Adamic/Noahic Covenants 82
- Abrahamic Covenant 85
- Mosaic Covenant 87
- The Davidic Covenant 88
- Yahushaic Covenant 88

Introduction 92

Yahusha, the Ruling High Priest (*Melchizedek*) 95

- The King's Training 97
- The King's Qualification 99
  - Yahusha was the Second Adam 100
  - Yahusha was the Messiah ben Joseph 101
  - Messiah ben David 105
  - Yahusha demonstrated the love of a true King 107
  - Yahusha had to demonstrate he could be trusted with great wealth 108

Yahusha mastered Yahuah's Righteousness............................ 112

Yahusha possessed the Seal of Yahuah's Kingdom 115

Yahusha faithfully carries "the standard"................................ 116

Yahusha was obedient to the ritual of Yahuah called "Mikveh" 117

Yahuah is My Strength – the Creation of the King! 122

"You (Yahusha) will say in that day (you are created) YAHUAH ELOHIM is my strength!" 124

Yahusha was a human being, who repented before John at his Mikveh (baptism) 128

Isaiah 12 picture of Yahusha 136

Yahusha "came into being in his mother's womb"! 137

"From my mother's womb, you are my strength" 143

What does "come in the flesh" and "according to the flesh" mean? 146

In that day you will say "Behold! Yahusha" 149

Yahusha was TRANSPOSED into *the Kingdom of Yahuah* 153

The Mediator and the "New Bride" 156

The Plan of Salvation through a Mediator 159

Qualified to Mediate the Covenant and Atone for Our Sins as Eternal High Priest 162

The Witness of Yahuah that Yahusha is the Messiah 166

Yahuah and Yahusha Enter into an Adoption Covenant 169

Yahuah Chooses a New Bride for His son 174

How did Yahusha Defeat Death? 180

    Every one dies for their own sin! 185

The Law of Sin and Death vs. The Law of the Spirit of Life 189

    The Law of Sin and Death 190

    The Law of the Spirit of Life 191

Yahusha Sends *the Comforter* 195

If Yahusha was "God"... We are Dead in Our Sins! 197

The Messiah had to be 100% Human!.... 202

How Could a Man Do All the Work of Salvation? 204

Human Sacrifice or Love Offering? 207

Human sacrifice forbidden.. 207

Shedding blood to consummate covenants is required......... 209

Yahusha's life pleased Yahuah 209

The Capital City of the Kingdom of Yahuah 211

Biblical Description of Yahuah Shammah 212

Gates 213

Geometry of Yahuah Shammah.. 214

Introduction.. 216

The Physical Design of the Temple of Solomon 217

The 3 chambers of the Temple of Solomon........................... 218

The Human Portrait in the Temple of Solomon 220

The High Priest as Temple Man 220

Transposition of the Temple of Yahuah.. 225

The Sons of Yahuah are Living Arks of the Covenant 227

Introduction 230

Transposition of the Altar of Yahuah 231

    The Physical Altar Metaphor 238

The Transposition of Sacrifices on the Altar 240

Transposition of the Law that Governs the Sacrifices 244

    Passover the true sacrifice for sin 245

    True sacrifices in the Spiritual Kingdom of Yahuah 249

Introduction 253

The Meaning of Frontals 259

The False Seal or Mark of the Beast 264

They who don't have the mark could not buy or sell 271

the Kingdom

Introduction 276

The Scriptural Truth concerning the Sabbath 277

Breaking the Everlasting Covenant of the Sabbath 278

> Only Sabbath Keepers inherit Yahuah's Creation 278

We are to Obey Yahusha's Sabbath Keeping Example 281

Only Sabbath Keepers Enter Yahuah's Kingdom of Rest 284

Don't Keep the Sabbath? You do not Know Yahuah! 287

Sunday is the Standard or Ensign of the 'Beast' 291

Yahuah Raised Yahusha on the Sabbath Day! 298

Introduction 303

Yahuah's Plan to Fulfill His Promises to Abraham 305

The History of the Nation of Israel 307

The Birthright Blessing vs. The Scepter Blessing 307

Remnant Israel 309

Replacement Theology?   Not in my Bible! 312

Sha'ul Taught the Prophets and Yahuah's Plan 314

The Re-Unification of the Nation of Israel 316

The House of Israel is Only *"Called"* Gentiles 318

Yahusha came only for the Lost Sheep of the House of Israel 321

What does "the way of the Gentiles" mean? 322

The Apostle Sha'ul's Dilemma 326

How Did Sha'ul Know the House of Israel? 331

Remnant Israel a subset of Israel 334

The Gifts of Yahuah to Remnant Israel 338

Sha'ul's letter to the Ephesians 344

Summary 346

Introduction.. 348

How is the Yahushaic Covenant "New"? 354

The Plan of Salvation is *conditional* on keeping the Law... 357

The Law is a gift of Yahuah to His Sons... 361

The Spirit of Error and the Spirit of the False Messiah 362

The *'Transgression'* of Desolation is the Abolishment of the Law.......................... 370

Transgression of Desolation vs. the Abomination of Desolation 372

Hebrew/Aramaic Scriptures vs. English Translations 375

The Meaning of Italics in the English Translations of the Bible 375

English Words ADDED to the Book of Daniel 376

Hebrew Word translated "Daily" mistranslated................. 378

Proper Implication of "Tamiyd" is Michael not Sacrifices .. 379

The Law is the Governing Constitution... 384

Law Breakers thrown out of *the Kingdom of Yahuah* 387

Transposition of *the Law of Yahuah* 392

4 States and 3 Transpositions 393

4 States of the Law 394

3 Transpositions of the Law 394

The Law existed prior to Adam 395

First Transposition of Law 401

Second Transposition of the Law 403

Third Transposition of the Law 406

Yahusha *Strengthened* the Law 408

Yahusha the Nazarene 409

Yahusha came to restore the Torah and Prophets 409

The Apostle Sha'ul Taught the Law Properly 416

Sha'ul taught the transposition of the Law 418

The Apostle Sha'ul – Leader of the Nazarenes, follower of Yahusha 420

The Apostle Sha'ul's view of the Law: Abolished or not?........ 421

Summary 428

Introduction.. 433

Yahuah's Appointed Festivals 436

The Meaning of the Fall and Spring Festivals 442

The Spring Festivals – Fulfilled in the First Coming 442

PASSOVER AND FEAST OF UNLEAVENED BREAD (Leviticus 23:4-8) 442

FIRSTFRUITS (Leviticus 23:9-14) 445

FEAST OF WEEKS (Leviticus 23:15-22) 445

The Fall Festivals – Fulfilled in the Second Coming 447

FEAST OF TRUMPETS (Leviticus 23:23-25) 447

DAY OF ATONEMENT (Leviticus 23:26-32) 448

FEAST OF TABERNACLES AND CLOSING ASSEMBLY (Leviticus 23:33-36) 449

The Feast Cycle is Based on the Message Written in the stars! 450

The Annual Wedding Portrait 452

The Physical Shadow of Greater Truths 453

xvii

The Festivals of Yahuah are Kept in the Future Kingdom of Yahuah 457

The Meaning of the Weekly Sabbath 460

Yahusha and His Disciples Kept the Festivals of Yahuah... 466

The 'Battle of the Ages' continues... 473

- Book 1: Creation Cries Out! 475
- Book 2: Mystery Babylon the Religion of the Beast 476
- Book 3: 'Christianity and the Great Deception' 477
- Book 4: 'The Antichrist Revealed!' 478
- Book 5: 'The Kingdom' 479
- Book 6: 'The Yahushaic Covenant Volume 1 - The Mediator' 480
- Book 7: 'The Yahushaic Covenant Volume 2 -   The Law and the Pauline Doctrine' 481
- Book 8: 'The Yahushaic Covenant Volume 3 - Melchizedek and the Passover Lamb' 482
- Book 9: 'The Narrow Gate' 483

the Kingdom

Introduction

The Central Theme of Scripture... the *'Kingdom'*

The central theme of The Bible is **the Kingdom of Yahuah** and that message is called **The Gospel**.

> Matthew 10:5-6
>
> These twelve Yahusha sent out after instructing them: "Do not go in *the* way of *the* Gentiles, and do not enter *any* city of the Samaritans; ⁶ but rather go to the lost sheep of the house of Israel. ⁷ And as you go, preach, saying, '<u>**the Kingdom of Yahuah is at hand**</u>.'

Most of us have probably sat in the pews of our Christian Church our entire life listening to our preacher and have come away thinking The Bible's central theme is

> "The Revelation of God on Earth in the incarnation of Jesus H. Christ"

Not only is the Messiah's name **not** Jesus H. Christ but the true Messiah Yahusha was **not** Yahuah in the flesh! Moreover, that is not at all the central theme of The Bible. We all need to go back to the drawing board here and start over or we are going to miss entrance into **the Kingdom of Yahuah**!

Granted, one of the most important aspects of **the Kingdom of Yahuah** is the High Priest and King (Melchizedek) who rules over it. Melchizedek was the topic of my book **Melchizedek and The Passover Lamb**. While Melchizedek (The Ruling Zadok) may be paramount in Yahuah's Kingdom (as Kings tend to be in all kingdoms), it is not all that is revealed concerning **the Kingdom of Yahuah**. In fact, it is **the Kingdom of Yahuah** that Yahusha came to reveal...

The Kingdom *of Yahuah* is not of this World

> **John 18**
> 36 Yahusha answered, "*My kingdom is not of this world*. If My kingdom were of this world, My servants would fight, so that I should not be delivered to the Jews; but now My kingdom is not from here."

The Kingdom **of Yahuah** is not "of this physical world" but rather a spiritual kingdom. You see, this physical creation that surrounds us; which we interact in... that which we can see, feel, touch, and taste is but a "veil" pulled over our eyes to hide true existence. True existence is in the realm of the spirit. Yahuah's Kingdom is... a spiritual kingdom and Yahuah is a spiritual being (the Creator) whom we cannot "see, feel, hear, smell, or taste" in this physical realm. Therein is the challenge! How can we learn of such a kingdom that is outside our realm of existence? The challenge for Yahuah (if there is such a thing) was:

> "How to reveal a spiritual kingdom to His sons <u>effectively,</u> so that it could be <u>fully understood</u> BEFORE giving His sons access to it?"

Why do we need to understand this spiritual kingdom before we have access to it? Simple: the promises that Yahuah makes to

His sons are literally <u>unbelievable</u>.   Yahuah simply cannot risk granting us full son ship and access without *training* because <u>we could not handle it</u>.   Once we are begotten in His Image through resurrection, we then are <u>His literal sons</u> with all His attributes and we are eternal!

Think about that statement and try and comprehend it if you can.

We Must Be Qualified to Enter *the Kingdom of Yahuah*

If Yahuah is not careful to train us properly <u>BEFORE</u> giving us that power and eternal nature... well He might end up with the same situation that exists now with the Angelic Realm... the Angels were created directly into that spiritual kingdom and given authority to rule and they later rebelled **and they are eternal**! Even Yahuah cannot destroy that which He has created eternal. So now the rebellious Angels are an <u>eternal problem</u>.

No... Yahuah made sure when procreating His literal family (which will be even higher in power and authority than the Angels) that only those *qualified* and *trustworthy* would be granted that power, authority, and eternal nature.   Yahuah promises to beget those qualified and trustworthy in His spiritual image as "gods"; His literal offspring with all the power, authority, and omnipotence that implies.   Then He would organize those chosen sons of His into a government and set them over His Creation to rule it.   Before He fulfills that promise to those so chosen, He has determined to ensure those chosen are very well

trained, disciplines, and qualified to have such power **_and can be trusted with it_**.

This life is the training ground and we must meet the qualifications
---

So instead of just building His spiritual family from the start in the spiritual realm and placing them directly in the position of power and authority, He has wisely chosen to first put His future sons through a physical life on Earth.   It is through this physical life that He then introduces us to His spiritual kingdom through what is called physical shadows, physical portraits, and physical rehearsals contained in covenants.   Together, these physical training aids teach us of spiritual counterparts or *Truths*.

This is called teaching through **physical to spiritual parallels**. Then over an extended period of time (6,000 years per **the Sabbath Covenant**) Yahuah gradually introduces each aspect of His kingdom little by little and establishes it <u>in the physical realm</u> over 6 Covenants.   This process is called *progressive revelation*.

Each covenant building on the one before until His kingdom is fully defined <u>physically</u>. Then in the final 7th Covenant, Yahuah transposes that kingdom to its final spiritual reality.   This is called **Transposition**.

Training Aids

Remember these terms as they are "keys" or training aids in studying **the Kingdom of Yahuah**:

- Physical to spiritual parallels
- Progressive Revelation/Disclosure
- Transposition

I will clearly define each one of these "keys" in this book and employ them to define **the Kingdom of Yahuah**.

The Text Book

Yahuah has delivered into our hands the "text book" in the study of His kingdom.   All 7 Covenants each progressively disclosing Truth over time and teaching us through *physical to spiritual parallel*s His kingdom in detail.   That text book is **The Bible** and we must understand how to read it!

The Course

The Kingdom *of Yahuah* has always existed, in eternity past and in the eternal future.   Yahuah revealing that kingdom to humanity (His sons specifically) is a process that takes time in context of a physical realm.   It also requires physical bodies with which to interact with that physical realm.

Time, if fact, is just another part of that great "veil" and exists only within the context of this physical realm.   There is, however, a very specific "timeframe" allotted within this physical realm whereby to teach and then transpose **the Kingdom of Yahuah**. That timeframe was revealed in the very first covenant... **the Sabbath Covenant**.

We should understand the spiritual kingdom of Yahuah at this time as we are at the end of the allotted timeframe.   If we do not, we have failed in our responsibility to seek His kingdom. That is the purpose of this book, to clearly define that kingdom so we can move forward and understand our role in it.   Then we can set about to achieve His purpose in us in this life.   We can also truly fulfill **The Great Commission** and spread the true Gospel that **the Kingdom of Yahuah** is within our reach.

The Obstacle

We are all trapped in some way in the "religious system" that evolved out of Babylon that is specifically designed to:

- Hide His Holy Name "Yahuah" behind the title LORD which is English for Ba'al the Babylonian sun god.
- Keep us from keeping His Sabbath, the very SIGN we are His son and destroy us through keeping the Babylonian day of the sun god Ba'al.   That day is **Sun**day worship.
- Keep us from righteousness by teaching us <u>disobedience to His Law</u> and that His Righteousness (defined in the Law) has been abolished.
- Prevent us from our atonement through the true Messiah by having us put our faith in the Babylonian celebration of "Easter" instead of putting our faith in Passover.
- Keep us in the highest form of idolatry by elevating an image of a man in the form of Jesus H. Christ (Hesus Horus Krishna) as "God" in our hearts.   Causing us to commit both **The Transgression of Desolation** and **The Abomination of Desolation**.

If you haven't already, I highly recommend (rather I insist) that you first read the first two books in this series **The Mystery Religion of Babylon** and **Christianity the Religion of the Beast**. You will need a solid foundation in The False Religion in order to even stomach what I say in this book. In this book I am going to do my best to shed the blinders so that we can overcome this false religious lie.   We need to transcend our past, our traditions, <u>and</u>

our teaching. We must develop the *Spiritual Eyes* required to see **the Kingdom of Yahuah** because **the Kingdom of Yahuah** has now been fully defined. Moreover, that Kingdom even now has been elevated (transposed) to its final spiritual state! But have we been properly prepared for it by the Christian Church? No. Have we been properly instructed in each element of it? No...

> We have been completely misled by another gospel, and we have followed The False Messiah Jesus Christ who came in his own name, not the name of Yahuah.

The Urgency

We are on the verge of the second coming of Yahuah's chosen King who will rule by proxy over that Kingdom that has been revealed. Will you partake in it? You may if you finish this book series! You will have the tools to effectively overcome **The Great Deception** and the opportunity to accept the Truth **and act on it**. What you then do with this information will determine if you are a chosen son destined to rule in **the Kingdom of Yahuah**.

What is the Kingdom of Yahuah?

The Kingdom *of Yahuah* is no different than the physical kingdoms on Earth as they are but "imperfect physical shadows" of the perfect spiritual kingdom.   Like all kingdoms, Yahuah's kingdom:

- was established by Yahuah with a purpose
- has a defined "realm" over which it exercises authority and dominion
- is ruled by a sovereign king
- has a capital city
- has a "castle" or "temple" in this case
- has an altar
- has a seal
- has a standard or sign carried by Ensigns
- contains citizens and requirements for citizenship:
    - must display the sign or raise "the standard of the kingdom"
    - must bear the seal or "mark of the kingdom"
    - must be delivered from **the Law of Sin and Death**, and live by **the Law of the Spirit of Life**

- - must pledge allegiance to The King and enter into covenant with him to serve **the Kingdom of Yahuah**
  - must be awarded **The Gifts of Yahuah** as a son… one of which is eternal life
- has various hierarchical positions under The King:
  - councilors
  - judges
  - priests
  - governors
  - an army
- is governed by a defined set of laws which clearly define:
  - what is right i.e. *Righteousness*
  - what is wrong i.e. *Sin*
  - penalties for breaking the law
  - mercy
  - justice
  - atonement
- has days set aside for celebration (Holidays or rather Holy Days)
- has seasons in which to "plant or sow" and then to "reap the harvest"

His Kingdom is a fully functional kingdom in every respect! All of these aspects of **the Kingdom of Yahuah** are clearly laid out in The Bible. This book could be the *"Cliff Notes"* to that text book (the Bible) on **the Kingdom of Yahuah**.

The Outline of this Book

In this book I am going to clearly define:

- The Keys to study – Covenants, Progressive Revelation, *Physical to spiritual parallel*s, and Transposition

- The Purpose of Yahuah in creating **the Kingdom of Yahuah**

- The Realm governed by **the Kingdom of Yahuah**

- The Sovereign King of **the Kingdom of Yahuah**

- The Capital City of **thee Kingdom of Yahuah**

- The Castle or Temple of **the Kingdom of Yahuah**

- The Altar of **the Kingdom of Yahuah**

- The Seal of **the Kingdom of Yahuah**

- The Standard or Sign of **the Kingdom of Yahuah**

- The Citizens of **the Kingdom of Yahuah**

- The Constitution of **the Kingdom of Yahuah**

- The Holy Days in **the Kingdom of Yahuah**

- The Abomination of Desolation that denies entrance into **the Kingdom of Yahuah**

Let us begin our journey and may Yahuah give us "eyes to see" into that spiritual kingdom.

Chapter 1

The "Keys" to studying the Kingdom of Yahuah

Introduction

In our study of the textbook of **the Kingdom of Yahuah**, The Bible, we must know how to approach it. We have all been taught very damaging lies that cripple us from being able to study this text book effectively.

Lie #1 – there are two "testaments"

Lie #2 – one of the testaments is "old" and no longer relevant

Lie #3 – the church replaced "Israel"

Lie #4 – fulfillment means "abolishment"

Lie #5 – the physical shadows and rehearsals have passed away

Lie #6 – all 6 covenants, prior to the 7th "New Covenant", are no longer valid

The above list is just a short list. The list of lies told by the false religion of Christianity is much larger. In fact; there is no truth in the religion of Christianity, it is a lie.

There are not "two testaments" but rather one revelation of Yahuah to mankind from Genesis to Revelation. That revelation came in the form of covenants between Yahuah and man. Seven covenants to be exact, each covenant building on the ones that came before it culminating in **The 7th Yahushaic Covenant.** The 7th Covenant is the renewing and final transposition from the physical realm to the spiritual realm of all previous 6. The 7th

Covenant "fulfilled" all previous 6 covenants; meaning it brought them to their "***fullest meaning, intent, and measure <u>spiritually</u>***".

> In no known universe does fulfill mean to destroy or abolish!

Each covenant must be studied from the standpoint of **physical to spiritual parallels** in order to "understand" spiritual truths found in **the Kingdom of Yahuah**.   All 7 Covenants are still in effect. Each covenant is, in most, cases an "addition" to the previous covenants as Yahuah progressively builds His kingdom over time.

In isolation, outside of the previous 6 covenants, Yahusha would have no authority to rule nor would he have the authority to serve as High Priest; as authority is given and defined in previous covenants.   We must approach Yahuah's revelation to man, The Bible, from the understanding that EVERY WORD that proceeds out of His Mouth is alive, active, and sharper than a two-edged sword.

The "New Testament" is the documented life of The Messiah (the Gospels/Revelation) and the rest of the books in the NT are *inspired* <u>commentary</u> on how The Messiah fulfilled (brought to the fullest meaning) the previous 6 covenants.

What is the True Word of Yahuah?

We must be careful what we call **The Word of Yahuah**. The actual "Word of Yahuah" is limited to:

- the Torah (first 5 books of the so-called Old Testament) which Yahuah <u>literally</u> wrote down for Moses.

- The Prophets (Isaiah, Jeremiah, Ezekiel, Daniel, etc.) who spoke for Yahuah

- The Words of the Messiah found in the Gospels and in Revelation (who was the greatest Prophet of all).

We have elevated the <u>commentary</u> of the New Testament writers to the level of "Words of Yahuah" when they are <u>no such thing</u>. These men were not prophets and never claimed to be. Many times they disagreed among themselves.

The writers in the New Testament were eye-witnesses to the life of The Messiah. In Sha'ul's case, a trained professional in the Torah (a **LAW**yer) qualified to teach the *physical to spiritual parallels* in scripture (the Torah and Prophets). So while being inspired writers, witnesses, and teachers... they never claimed to speak as prophets of Yahuah and therefore their words are not His. They did not close their teachings with *"thus saith Yahuah"*. I'm not saying they do not have tremendous value to us today because they absolutely do. We should study these writings and many more left out of The Bible by the Catholic Church. We, however, have to be extremely cautious with our English translations, because they have been altered, doctored up, words added and subtracted, and grossly mishandled over the years. What I am saying is that at any time if their writings (or rather our understanding of their writings) contradict the Torah, The Prophets, and The Messiah then either the way we understand their writings are wrong or they must be declared... false teachers.

Covenants

The Bible is a text book to **the Kingdom of Yahuah** and this kingdom is introduced slowly over time by Yahuah as He established covenants with mankind.   As these covenants progress over time we learn more and more about His kingdom through **physical to spiritual parallels**.   So the first step in studying The Bible in order to understand **the Kingdom of Yahuah** is to identify the covenants through which that kingdom was revealed.

What is a Covenant?

First we need to firmly comprehend what a covenant is and what every covenant contains.

cov·e·nant

1. General definition

an agreement, usually formal, between two or more persons to do or not do something specified (in the terms and conditions).

2. Biblical definition

    a. the conditional promises made to humanity by Yahuah, as revealed in Scripture.

    b. the agreement between Yahuah and His people, through a signatory or chosen representative, in which Yahuah promised to protect them if they kept His law (terms and conditions) and were faithful to Him.

We see above in **2.b** that covenants are intimately connected with **the Law of Yahuah**. From the above definition we see that a covenant is the same today as it was back then; we now just call them "agreements" today for the most part. They are between two or more people to do or not to do something specified. The "something specified" is called today the **Terms and Conditions** of the agreement/covenant. The "two or more persons" are called today the **signatories** to the agreement/covenant. If the covenant was between Yahuah and a group or nation of people, one person was chosen by Yahuah to represent them as the *signatory*. The covenant came to be known by the name of that chosen representative.

For example; *Mosaic Covenant named after the signatory Moses who represented the Israelites.* The covenants in the Bible are known by the name of their chosen human representative (all but one, **the Sabbath Covenant**, as it was between Yahuah and Creation and was made for man not with man).

In The Bible, there are 7 covenants:

1. The **Sabbath Covenant** – between Yahuah and creation; it is Yahuah's stamp over His creation as The Creator

2. **The Edenic/Adamic Covenant** – between Yahuah and humanity, Adam the chosen signatory

3. **The Noahic Covenant** – Renewed the Adamic Covenant, Noah the chosen signatory

4. **The Abrahamic Covenant** – between Yahuah and His chosen bloodline, Abraham the signatory

5. **The Mosaic Covenant** – between Yahuah and the sons of Yahuah known as Israel, Moses the chosen signatory

6. **The Davidic Covenant** – between Yahuah and His chosen royal bloodline, David the signatory.

7. ***The Yahushaic Covenant*** (The New Covenant) – between Yahuah and His chosen REMNANT sons, Yahusha the signatory.

All Covenants are still active and valid

As I stated earlier, there are very damaging lies we have been taught that cripple our ability to understand ***the Kingdom of Yahuah***. Lie #6 is that we are under a totally "New Covenant" and all previous covenants are no longer valid.   We don't really need much "wisdom" to overcome that lie.   Just a little common sense.

> Does creation still exist in a fallen state and does death still reign (6,000 years we labor under the curse of Adam then a 1,000 year rest)?   Do we still keep a 7 day week looking forward to entering into His Rest?   Yes.   <u>**The Sabbath Covenant is still in effect**</u>.
>
> Is man still created in the image of Yahuah and does humanity still have dominion over the Earth?   Yes.   <u>**The Edenic Covenant is still in effect.**</u>

Do men have to work for a living and women have pain in childbirth? Do you still step on sticker weeds when you walk outside? Yes. **The Adamic Covenant is still in effect.**

Are there still Rainbows that grace the skies after a rain? Yes. Has the Earth been destroyed by a flood since the flood of Noah? No. **The Noahic Covenant is still in effect.**

Are the offspring of Abraham through Isaac and then Jacob still the chosen sons of Yahuah and a blessing to all the Earth? Yes. **The Abrahamic Covenant is still in effect.**

Is Righteousness vs. sin still defined by *the Law of Yahuah*? Yes. **The Mosaic Covenant is still in effect.**

Does Yahusha sit on the Throne of David and is Jerusalem still the seat of government? Yes. **The Davidic Covenant is still in effect.**

The facts above are very simplistic illustrations **that all covenants are still in effect.** I will break each covenant down as it relates to the progressive revelation of *the Kingdom of Yahuah* in this book to further illustrate, in detail, the importance of each covenant.

The Kingdom progressively revealed in covenants

What we must understand at this point is that ***The Plan of Yahuah*** was revealed to humanity through those 7 covenants.   It is in these 7 covenants that Yahuah literally built and established His kingdom... ***the Kingdom of Yahuah***!   This process is called *Progressive Revelation* where Yahuah progressively built on each of the previous covenants over time until He fully disclosed who He is, what His plan is, what His kingdom is, who His Messiah is, and what defines those chosen as His sons!   The Bible cannot be understood outside of this truth and the study of progressive revelation through covenants.

Study Aids or "Keys" to Understanding *the Kingdom*

Now that we know the covenants in The Bible whereby Yahuah introduces **the Kingdom of Yahuah** we can begin studying them to learn what that kingdom is.   But before we can do that, we must know "how" to study these vital covenants between Yahuah and man.

Let me define a few terms at this point:

Progressive Revelation / Progressive Disclosure

This is the process of progressively (little by little) revealing more and more over the duration of time.   Yahuah employs this concept and with each covenant Yahuah reveals more and more about His kingdom.   Every aspect of **the Kingdom of Yahuah** is progressively revealed over time through the covenants He established with man.   We will approach the covenants in The Bible from the standpoint that each and every one is still valid. We will examine each covenant to discern the aspects of **the Kingdom of Yahuah** that are revealed in them.   We will carry each covenant over into the next covenant as each one builds on the previous one.

Physical to spiritual parallels

Isaiah 48
³ I foretold the former things long ago, my mouth announced them (to my prophets) and I made them known (through physical shadows); then suddenly I acted, and they came to pass (Spiritually).

Colossians 2:17
These are (physical) shadows of the things that were to come; the (Spiritual) reality, however, is found in *The Yahushaic Covenant*.

The use of the physical world that surrounds us to teach us concepts in the spiritual realm is called ***physical to spiritual parallels***. Yahuah establishes physical examples that correlate to spiritual truths, and uses those physical examples to help us understand His spiritual kingdom.

> Yahuah establishes physical rehearsals (such as keeping the Sabbath and Passover) to help us understand spiritual principles.

These physical shadows help define His kingdom, the purpose of His Messiah, and His Plan of Salvation.

We will examine the physical requirements of each covenant to understand the Spiritual Truths they are intended to teach us concerning **the Kingdom of Yahuah**.

Sha'ul understood the concept of *physical to spiritual parallel*s and their importance in understanding **The Spiritual Kingdom of Yahuah**:

1 Corinthians 13
¹² For now we (physically) see only a reflection (of spiritual reality) as (if we were looking) in a mirror; (but when resurrected) then we shall see (clearly) face to face (the spiritual realm directly). Now I know in part (through *physical to spiritual parallel*s); then I shall know fully, even as I am fully known.

Hebrews 5:12-14 - *Spiritual Immaturity*
12 For though by this time you ought to be teachers (of the Torah and Prophets, there was no such thing as the New Testament when he wrote this), you need someone to teach you again the first principles of the oracles of Yahuah (that is the Torah); and you have come to need milk and not solid food. 13 For everyone who partakes only of milk is unskilled in the word of righteousness (Righteousness is Keeping the Law so "word of righteousness" is the Torah), for he is a babe. 14 But solid food belongs to those who are of full age (mature sons with minds set on Spiritual Law written on their hearts), that is, those who by reason of use (keeping the Feasts/Torah/Sabbaths) have their (spiritual) senses exercised (trained through *physical to spiritual parallel*s) to discern both good and evil (which is defined by the Law of Yahuah, good is obedience to His Commands, evil is breaking them).

Transposition

Transposition is the transfer of position from one state to another without changing the meaning and intent. One of the terms I use most in this book is **Transposition**. I use this term because it is the word chosen by the Apostle Sha'ul to describe the "change" that occurred in both the physical Law and Priesthoods. Sha'ul used the Greek word "***metathesis***" in Hebrews 7:12 when explaining how the Law and the Priesthood of Levi in **The Mosaic Covenant** "changed" in **The Yahushaic Covenant**. I will cover this in detail in this book.

> Metathesis means "transposition" or "transfer of position". Transposition is the "key" to understanding **The Yahushaic Covenant**.

Today the word transposition is used in music and the musical application beautifully and very accurately illustrates the point. "Transposition" in music is the shifting of a melody, a harmonic progression or an entire musical piece to another key, <u>while maintaining the same tone structure</u>.

This is exactly what happened with the Law and the Priesthood from **The Mosaic Covenant** to **The Yahushaic Covenant** and in fact all of Yahuah's commandments and ordinances. They were first given orally, then transposed to "written in stone", and ultimately transposed to "written in our hearts" while maintaining their structure and validity.   They went through **a transfer of position** (transposition) from oral to written to spirit.

Nothing established by Yahuah has ever been "abolished" other than the decrees found within the Law for violating His commands.   Even those decrees were not "abolished" they were covered by the blood of the Passover Lamb for those who believe and keep Passover as commanded.   They are still active for those who do not believe and who do not keep Passover and will condemn anyone not covered by the blood of The Passover Lamb; they have not been "abolished".   So actually, nothing Yahuah has ever done has been "abolished" by anyone or anything.   No one has that authority.

Example of physical to spiritual parallels, and transposition

It would probably help if I quickly show a very solid example of the "Keys" to understanding scripture being actively employed. Let's look at the Apostle Sha'ul, as he employs progressive revelation, *physical to spiritual parallels*, and transposition.

We see these "keys" employed by Sha'ul, as he makes the point clearly in the book of Hebrews, that the Levitical Priesthood was a physical teaching tool to help us understand the role of Melchizedek.   Sha'ul explains that both the Law and the Priesthood of Levi were transposed to serve Yahusha as High Priest.   Sha'ul says there was a "change" in the Law. Unfortunately, our English translations are not very accurate and translated the word "change" poorly.   Sha'ul used the Greek word "metatheses" when describing what happened to the Law.

Below is the proper translation of the word "metathesis" that was translated "*change*" that occurred in the Law in Hebrews 7:12. The word translated "*change in the Law*" in Hebrews 7:12 is the Greek word #3331 in Strong's. If you look this word up, the proper translation and meaning of this word is NOT *change* as in *abolished* as taught by Christianity but rather it is "***transferred to Heaven***"... ***transposition***.

| 3331 | metathesis met-ath'-es-is | from - metatithemi 3346; transposition, i.e. transferral (to heaven), disestablishment (of a law from physical to spiritual):--change to, removing, translation. |

Sha'ul is speaking of ***physical to spiritual parallel***s as he illustrates that the Levitical Priesthood was given to help us understand physically what Yahusha would do spiritually as High Priest before Yahuah (***physical to spiritual parallel***s). And given the final High Priest has come and taken His position as Melchizedek... the human priesthood of Levi was TRANSFERRED over to Melchizedek and so was the Law by which the priesthood has authority to make sacrifices and offerings! Neither of them was abolished but rather underwent a transfer of position from physical to spiritual. Below is how Hebrews 7:12 should have been translated:

> **Hebrews 7:12**
> "for when there is a transfer of the priestly office (of Levi to Melchizedek), out of necessity there is ALSO A TRANSFER of the LAW of the priesthood (by which the Priesthood has authority)"

In other words, Sha'ul is explaining that the Law that defines the priesthood and sacrifices had to be transferred with Yahusha "out of necessity".   <u>Yahusha would have no authority as High Priest without the Law that defines the High Priesthood.</u>   the Law was not abolished, it was transposed.

Now Yahusha is the Spiritual High Priest and has all the duties and authority provided him by **the Law of Yahuah** concerning sacrifices and atonement. Both the High Priesthood and the Law were "transferred to heaven" or transposed spiritually from the physical realm to the spiritual realm as **the Kingdom of Yahuah** had arrived in the 7th Covenant.

This is just one example of how to employ the "keys".   Sha'ul was demonstrating that Yahuah had progressively revealed the role Yahusha would play as High Priest by first giving us the Levitical Priesthood in **The Mosaic Covenant**.   And by studying the physical sacrifices and atonement required of the Levitical Priesthood, we could come to a better understanding of the Spiritual Sacrifices and Atonement made by Melchizedek before **The Altar of Yahuah** in the spirit.   Then, after progressively disclosing the role of Melchizedek and teaching us Spiritual Truths of the role of Melchizedek (using the physical priesthood of Levi). Sha'ul teaches us that the Law, which gives the priesthood authority and the priesthood itself, was TRANSPOSED to The Spiritual Kingdom of Yahuah.

Sha'ul clearly understood how to study scripture!   That is what we are going to do in this book.

The 7 Covenants of Yahuah

Let's take a more detailed look at each covenant and demonstrate how each one builds on the other through **Progressive Revelation**.

> We are going to learn as Yahuah teaches the vital aspects of His kingdom through *physical to spiritual parallel*s.

We are going to witness the Law being transposed 3 times from 4 different states as it is established as the constitution of **the Kingdom of Yahuah** and transferred from the mind of Yahuah to the hearts of His sons. We are going to see that the Law is the **Terms and Conditions** of all 7 Covenants between Yahuah and man.

As a quick review, we learned in the last chapter that each covenant came to be known by the name of that chosen representative i.e. Mosaic Covenant named after the signatory Moses. The covenants in the Bible are known by the name of their chosen human representative (except the Sabbath Covenant as it was with creation not a man).

Scripture defines 7 major covenants, through which the Kingdom is defined:

1. **The Sabbath Covenant** – between Yahuah and creation

2. **The Edenic/Adamic Covenant** – between Yahuah and humanity, Adam the chosen signatory

3. **The Noahic Covenant** – Renewed the Adamic Covenant, Noah the chosen signatory

4. **The Abrahamic Covenant** – between Yahuah and His chosen bloodline, Abraham the signatory

5. **The Mosaic Covenant** – between Yahuah and His chosen bloodline, Moses the chosen signatory

6. **The Davidic Covenant** – between Yahuah and His chosen royal bloodline, David the signatory.

7. *The Yahushaic Covenant* (the Christian Church calls the New Covenant) – between Yahuah and His chosen bloodline, Yahusha the signatory.

Christianity has promoted an entirely false doctrine of "two covenants; one old and one new" and **in error** divided **the Word of Yahuah** into two volumes: the Old Testament and the New Testament. There is no "Old Testament and New Testament" there is ONE testament of Yahuah to mankind by which He progressively disclosed His Kingdom *through covenants*!

The Word of Yahuah is actually contained within the Torah (first 5 books written by the Hand of Yahuah and given to Moses), the Prophets (words spoken directly by Yahuah through the mouths of His chosen prophets), and then the words of His greatest prophet of all Yahusha the Messiah in the Gospels and in the Book of Revelation.

> Together they (*Torah/Prophets/Words of the Messiah*) make up "***the Word of Yahuah***".

We have again erred in elevating the writings of the Apostles and Disciples to the level of "***Words of Yahuah***". These men, including the Apostle Sha'ul, were not prophets. They were inspired and very knowledgeable men who wrote commentaries and teachings on the Torah, Prophets, and words of the Messiah. At times they argued among each other in disagreement.

I say this because we have literally misunderstood and **mistranslated** the words of the Apostle Sha'ul in our Christian Churches. We then elevated *our misunderstandings* of what he said as "***the Word of Yahuah***" and establish these lies and teach false doctrines that contradicts the actual Words of Yahuah. We do this to justify our doctrines; such as "*Jesus nailed the Law to the cross and abolished it*" which completely contradicts everything written in the Torah, the Prophets, and literally declared by the Messiah Yahusha! If you believe Sha'ul said such a thing then you must label him a false teacher for contradicting the rest of the Bible and specifically contradicting Yahusha and Yahuah's words concerning the Law.

In fact, Sha'ul did not say "the Law" was nailed to the stake, he said the "decrees against us"; meaning the "death decrees" found within the Law were nailed to the stake. I'll explain this is detail in this book. The reason I bring this point up now in this chapter is because the Law is the *Terms and Conditions* of every covenant... especially **the Yahushaic Covenant**.

> To know Yahuah fully, and to understand *the Yahushaic Covenant,* we must realize that every covenant is still valid, each one building on the one before as they evolved into a complete definition of *the Kingdom of Yahuah.*

Covenant upon covenant; each one adding something new or further defining the previous until all aspects of **the Kingdom of Yahuah** were fully defined to those chosen to rule in that coming kingdom. All 6 covenants leading up to the final **7th Yahushaic Covenant** were given to define His kingdom physically. Then Yahusha would bring them all to their fullest meaning and application (real meaning of fulfillment) and literally "usher in **the Kingdom of Yahuah**" through transposition (the transfer of position from physical to Spiritual)! That is what this book is about and *the Law* plays a vital role as it is the foundation of **the Kingdom of Yahuah.** It is the very expression of His Holiness.

> One of the main focuses of this book will be **the Law of Yahuah** and its relevance in **the Kingdom of Yahuah.** We (*as Christians*) have been taught that "Jesus" nailed the Law to the "cross". Then we lump the entire Torah/Prophets/Writings together and call it all "Old" (*Old Testament*) and abolish the literal Word of Yahuah! We abolish His Law, His Covenants, and thereby <u>**we abolish His Kingdom**</u>.

Before we can even address the question "has the Law been abolished?" we must understand covenants. The real question isn't "has the Law been abolished?" but rather **has the Mosaic Covenant been replaced by the New Covenant and does the Law play a role in The New Covenant.** I will address these questions in detail in this book as we restore the Law to its rightful place in **the Kingdom of Yahuah** as the constitution of the coming Divine government.

A Tour of all 7 Covenants between Yahuah and Man

Let's take a brief tour of the covenants in The Bible. Next, I summarize each covenant to demonstrate how each one progressively revealed vital aspects of **the Kingdom of Yahuah** (this is a simple overview not intended to be an in depth study of these covenants):

The Sabbath Covenant

The Sabbath Covenant established Yahuah as The Creator. It is between Yahuah and His Creation and the basic revelation in that covenant was:

- The Sabbath Covenant was defined as 6 days then a Sabbath Rest on the 7th Day <u>specifically</u>. This 7-day portrait is a **Physical to spiritual parallel** that established the timeframe by which Yahuah would introduce His Kingdom through covenants and progressive revelation. The "days" are prophetic days where 1 day = 1 thousand years. So the Sabbath Covenant establishes a 6,000-year timeframe by which Yahuah would train His sons by putting them through a life on Earth. It is during this life that Yahuah would purchase their salvation to serve Him in His Kingdom. At the end of 6,000 years Yahuah would establish His Kingdom on Earth and further train His sons to rule under the authority of Yahusha the Messiah. At the end of 7,000 years His Kingdom would be complete, His sons trained to rule, and **the Kingdom of Yahuah** would then expand to govern all of His Creation for eternity... Yahuah blessed and sanctified the Sabbath (7th Day) and made it Holy.

- The Sabbath would serve as a "sign" between Yahuah and His chosen sons for eternity in all covenants and those who keep the Sabbath are set apart from His Creation with Him.   It is the Sabbath that is "the Standard of **the Kingdom of Yahuah**".   Keeping the Sabbath weekly is expressing faith and hope in the coming **Kingdom of Yahuah**.

The Edenic Covenant/ Adamic Covenants

Yahuah reveals in these first covenants with man:

- He has given His sons the authority to rule creation.
- Yahuah discloses His intent to choose a human King/Messiah through the "seed of a woman" who would crush all those opposed to Yahuah's Authority.
- Yahuah establishes the "system of training" used to train His chosen.   A system of "right" and "wrong" defined as "obedience to Yahuah's commandments" known as the Law.
- It is the Law that is the foundation of and constitution of His Divine Government.
- The Law in the Edenic/Adamic Covenants was active but unknown to man as it was in the Mind of Yahuah.   It was

slowly being **transposed** from the Mind of Yahuah to man orally.

The Noahic Covenant

Yahuah renewed the two previous covenants with Noah after destroying the remnant seed of the Nephilim (Satan's sons from the seed of women) from the face of the earth.   In this covenant:

- Yahuah made a promise not to destroy this planet again by flood.   The rainbow is the sign of this promise.

- The Noahic Covenant is a continuation of the previous two covenants and all aspects of the Edenic/Adamic Covenants are still in effect nothing changed, it just needed to be renewed as mankind started over with Noah.

The Abrahamic Covenant

Yahuah reveals His chosen bloodline among the sons of men.   In the Abrahamic Covenant Yahuah reveals:

- The bloodline would run through Abraham/Isaac/Jacob and be called "Israel".

- It is from within this bloodline that Yahuah would introduce His chosen family to His creation, train them through a life on Earth, and prepare them for His coming Kingdom.

- It is through this bloodline that Yahuah would bring forth "Yahuah's Salvation" which is what the name *Yahusha* means in Hebrew.

- Yahuah also reveals the ***physical to spiritual parallel*** of the Promised Land and His promises to His sons of inheritance.
- The Abrahamic Covenant contains all the terms and conditions of the previous 3 covenants with the addition of the chosen bloodline and promises to that bloodline.
- ***the Law of Yahuah*** was then fully ***transposed*** to Abraham orally and the Oral Law was passed down from generation to generation.

The Mosaic Covenant

The Mosaic Covenant builds on all the previous covenants as Yahuah:

- ***Transposed*** His Law from oral to written down in stone as He reveals the "Constitution of His Kingdom" in detail. The instructions to His sons on how to be righteous before Him known as ***the Law of Yahuah***.
- Yahuah firmly establishes <u>in stone</u> that His Kingdom <u>is a kingdom of law</u>.
- Yahuah establishes and defines various "cabinets/positions" within His Kingdom such as High Priests, Priests, Judges, Kings, etc.
- Yahuah chose specific bloodlines within "Israel" to serve Him as Priests (Levi) and High Priests (Aaron). These priesthoods served as physical examples of what Yahusha would do spiritually as Melchizedek.

- Yahuah reveals specific seasons i.e. Holy Days which were to serve as training aids (**Physical to spiritual parallels**) to help His chosen know the Messiah when he came/comes again.

The Davidic Covenant

The Davidic Covenant builds on all previous covenants as Yahuah:

- Established a physical righteous King to serve as an example of the coming Spiritual King (**Physical to spiritual parallels**).

- It was established that the Throne of David would be the throne and bloodline through which the Messiah and King would come to govern His Kingdom for eternity.

- Yahuah established His Throne, Capital City, Temple, and Altar in detail physically as **physical to spiritual parallels**.

The Yahushaic Covenant

The Yahushaic Covenant builds on all previous covenants and "fulfills" them all by transposing them to their fullest spiritual application. The Yahushaic Covenant is "new" in that the Law is now written on our hearts.

The "intent" behind the "letters" supersedes the physical act. Up to this point, Yahuah had fully defined His coming Kingdom through **physical to spiritual parallels** so that we could understand the Yahushaic Covenant.

All previous 6 physical covenants are **TRANSPOSED** to Spiritual Reality in the Yahushaic Covenant:

- (**Sabbath Covenant**) – Yahusha fulfills the Sabbath Covenant when he returns to reign as King of the 7th Millennium and gives us "rest".

- (**The Edenic Covenant**) – Yahusha is given all authority over creation and trains the sons of Yahuah to rule creation. **the Kingdom of Yahuah** is set up on a smaller scale over the Earth during the 7th Millennium and "Eden" is restored.

- (**The Adamic Covenant**) Established the system for training His sons to rule and foretold of His coming Messiah/King that would crush all rebellion against Him – Yahusha is that prophesied king who is born of a woman and crushes the head of the enemy.   As the first born of the resurrection and first son to be **TRANSPOSED** to **the Kingdom of Yahuah**; Yahusha is called "the Second Adam" and "forefather of everlasting life".

- (**The Mosaic Covenant**) Yahusha **TRANSPOSES** the Law from written in stone or "the letter" to the Spiritual intent of your heart.   the Law is transposed from **the Law of Sin and Death** to **the Law of the Spirit of Life** as Yahusha's blood covers the decrees in the Law that demand our death for disobedience.   The Priesthood is **TRANSPOSED** to the Spiritual Kingdom under a new eternal High Priest... Melchizedek.   the Law that defines the role of the priesthood is **TRANSPOSED** to the Spiritual Kingdom of Yahuah to give Yahusha authority to make the proper sacrifices and atonement as High Priest.

- (***The Davidic Covenant***) Yahusha is the Spiritual Righteous King from the line of David and sits on the Throne of David for eternity. Yahusha TRANSPOSES the Temple, the Altar, and the Capital City to the Spiritual Kingdom of Yahuah. Yahuah's Temple is our body, His Altar is in our hearts, His Capital City is made up of all of the sons of Yahuah; Yahusha the cornerstone. All the physical metaphors, examples, rehearsals, shadow-pictures find their fullest expression Spiritually as Yahusha "fulfills" them all and ushers in **the Kingdom of Yahuah**.

As we can see with each new covenant the previous covenants are still valid. Each covenant adding to the Law, defining new elements of **the Kingdom of Yahuah**, and progressively disclosing new physical shadows that parallel Spiritual Truths.

Terms and Conditions

Even today every covenant (agreement) between two parties contains what is called the "**Terms and Conditions**". These *Terms and Conditions* govern the covenant and spell out in detail what is required of both parties to fulfill the covenant. The covenants in the Bible are no different. All 7 covenants between Yahuah and man <u>contain the same Terms and Conditions</u>. The only things that changed going from one covenant to the other were the signatories and the <u>detail of the Terms and Conditions</u>. the Terms and Conditions grew as Yahuah progressively disclosed His Law that would govern **the Kingdom of Yahuah**.

> The Terms and Condition of every covenant is <u>the Law of Yahuah</u>.

Contrary to what is taught in our Christian Churches today, **the Yahushaic Covenant** far from abolished the Law; the Yahushaic Covenant is defined by one thing <u>and one thing only</u>.... **the Law of Yahuah**.

> **Hebrews 10:16**
> This is the covenant I will make with them after that time, says Yahuah. I will put my laws in their hearts, and I will write them on their minds.

Sha'ul is quoting from Jeremiah 31:33 where Yahuah foretells of **the Yahushaic Covenant** and defines that covenant in context of His Law! Yahuah tells us His intent in the final covenant is to TRANSPOSE His Law from written in stone to Spiritual intent of the heart. In this way, His sons will be qualified to govern in all

Righteousness by their very nature. We, who enter that Kingdom, will all be LAWYERS! One thing is certain, to make it into **the Kingdom of Yahuah** you will not have bought into the false doctrine that His Law was "nailed to the stake" and abolished. You will instead have a deep love and "heart for His Law".

The Christian Church has literally grouped the entire kingdom of Yahuah defined in the first 6 covenants into what they call "the Old Testament". Then the Christian Church <u>summarily abolished the entire kingdom of Yahuah including the constitution that governs it</u>. By doing so, they have left their Roman demi-god Jesus H. Christ (Hesus Horus Krishna) standing alone with no authority, no government, no constitution, no priesthood, no throne... **nothing**. He is nothing more than a "false Messiah" who will be destroyed by the testimony of Yahusha the coming King who stands with all authority given him by all covenants in the Bible. Yahusha is granted all the promises in all 6 covenants because he faithfully fulfilled the terms and conditions of them. He fulfilled the Law and the Prophets!

Yahusha was very well aware that **the Law** was the foundation and Terms and Conditions of his covenant with Yahuah:

> **Matthew 5** - *The Fulfillment of the Law*
> 17 "Do not think that I have come to abolish the Law (Torah) or the Prophets (the Torah and Prophets are true scripture, they are not "old"); I have not come to abolish them but to fulfill them (bring them to their fullest meaning and Spiritual application through transposition). 18 For truly I tell you, until heaven and earth disappear, <u>not the smallest letter, not the least stroke of a pen, will</u>

by any means disappear from the Law until everything is accomplished. 19 Therefore anyone who sets aside one of the least of these commands and teaches others accordingly will be called least in the kingdom of heaven (that is if such a person even enters the Kingdom), but whoever practices and teaches these commands (the Law) will be called great in the kingdom of heaven (the Law will be alive and active in the Kingdom of Yahuah). 20 For I tell you that unless your righteousness (defined as obedience to the Law) surpasses that of the Pharisees and the teachers of the law, you will certainly not enter the kingdom of heaven (there it is, if you abolish the Law you don't enter the Kingdom of Yahuah. By this, Yahusha meant the Law would be strengthened to attitude not the act, as we would be held to a higher standard. By applying the Law to Spiritual Intent, we can surpass the outward righteousness of the Pharisees who kept only the letter of the law outwardly but their intent was selfish pride)

The Law is the *'Terms and Conditions'* of every covenant

The single most misunderstood fact about every covenant of Yahuah is that His Commandments or the Law are the "Terms and Conditions". Christianity teaches us that the Law/Commandments came into existence at the time of Moses some 430 years after the promise to Abraham. This is simply not true. What "came into existence 430 years after the promise" was *the transposition of the Law from oral to written in stone*.

The WRITTEN LAW is what Sha'ul is referring to in Galatians. I will cover the Law and all the false doctrines of the Christian Church concerning Sha'ul's writings later in this book and in detail in my upcoming book *the Law of Yahuah*. What I want to do in this book is to simply illustrate that the Law always existed and was active and was the Terms and Conditions of every covenant.

Summary

In this chapter I have introduced a few of the vital keys to understanding the Bible.   We have to approach **the Word of Yahuah** from the standpoint it was intended.   Yahuah progressively disclosed **the Kingdom of Yahuah** over time through covenants.   He gave us (in each covenant) physical examples, shadow pictures, portraits, and parallels that teach us of corresponding Spiritual Truths found in the spiritual kingdom.

The Spiritual Truths I will explain in this book are not for everyone to know.   The mighty men of old in the Torah and Prophets were not given this knowledge, they were not given the wisdom, or they were commanded to be silent if they were.   We see that many mysteries of Yahuah were sealed up... Daniel **was not** given the keys; they were hidden until the time of the end.   We are now in that timeframe and it is time the sons of Yahuah stand up for **the Kingdom of Yahuah**.

> **Daniel 12:4**
> [4] "But you, Daniel, **shut up the words, and seal the book until the time of the end**

Yahusha spoke these Spiritual Truths through parables/riddles/idioms because it was not given to the masses to understand but only to those with spiritual "eyes to see and ears to hear" or rather **Remnant Israel;** the true spiritual sons of Yahuah:

> **Matthew 13:10-17**
> [10] And the disciples came and said to Him, "Why do You speak to them in parables?" [11] He answered and said to

them, "Because it has been given to you to know <u>the mysteries</u> of *the Kingdom of Yahuah*, but to them it has not been given... ¹³ Therefore I speak to them in parables, because seeing (trying to apply these things physically not understanding *physical to spiritual parallel*s) they do not see (into the Spiritual Realm), and hearing they do not hear, nor do they understand....¹⁶ But blessed *are* your eyes for they see, and your ears for they hear; ¹⁷ for assuredly, I say to you that <u>many prophets and righteous men</u> <u>desired to see what you see</u>, and did not see *it,* and to hear what you hear, and did not hear *it.*

The Apostle Sha'ul would not speak of what he saw in the 3rd heaven when he was almost stoned to death (Acts 14:19) and then sworn to silence about what he witnessed in **the Kingdom of Yahuah**. It was his thorn in the flesh:

2 Corinthians 12
¹ It is doubtless not profitable for me to boast. I will come to visions and revelations of Yahuah: ² I know a man (speaking in the 3ʳᵈ person) in covenant with Yahusha who fourteen years ago—whether in the body I do not know, or whether out of the body I do not know (he didn't know if he was dead or alive), Yahuah knows—such a one was caught up to the third heaven. ³ And I know such a man—whether in the body or out of the body I do not know, Yahuah knows— ⁴ **how he was caught up into Paradise and heard <u>inexpressible words</u>, <u>which it is not lawful for a man to utter.</u>**

John was silenced during his vision of things found in *the Kingdom of Yahuah*...

> ### Revelation 10
> ⁴ Now when the seven thunders uttered their voices, I was about to write; but I heard a voice from heaven saying to me, "**Seal up the things which the seven thunders uttered, and <u>do not write them</u>**." <u>**And they were hidden until the VERY END OF TIME and given to men of Wisdom risen up for the appointed time!!!**</u>

It simply wasn't the appointed time for Yahuah to disclose *the Kingdom of Yahuah* in full detail.   It wasn't time to reveal the False Messiah.   They still had 2,000 years to go before the end of the 6,000 years when the Kingdom would be established on Earth for the Sabbath Rest.   That time is now; we are on the verge, literally, of Yahusha's return and *the Kingdom of Yahuah* to be established on Earth.   Those "men of wisdom" that Yahuah has ordained during these times to have "eyes to see His Kingdom", "ears to hear His voice", and the "understanding" to know the mysteries of His Kingdom are now among us.   The question is: "who will stand up and have the voice to declare what they have seen and heard?" and stand against the false religion of Christianity and the False Messiah Hesus Horus Krishna?

> "I will!
> Here am I...
> *send me.*"

Chapter 2

The Purpose - Yahuah's Family

Introduction

> **Romans 8:28**
> ²⁸ And we know that all things work together for good to them that love Yahuah, to them who are called **according to *Yahuah's* purpose**.

Before we continue in defining **the Kingdom of Yahuah**, an understanding of Yahuah's *purpose* is necessary. ==It is Yahuah's purpose to "procreate" Himself and beget a "family of gods". It is with this purpose in mind that Yahuah created the Universe and destined it to be governed by His kingdom in righteousness according to His Law.==   Only with a clear picture of this purpose in mind can we fully understand **the Kingdom of Yahuah**.

You see, **the Kingdom of Yahuah** is just that... A kingdom!   It is an organized government that has a specific purpose...

The purpose of His kingdom is to govern Yahuah's creation in His Righteousness for all eternity.

Yahuah has literally **_purposed_** to "train" His future sons through a life on Earth to serve (as literal sons of Yahuah or gods) in that kingdom that is destined to rule His Creation...

> **Psalm 82**
> 6 I have said, you are gods; and all of you are children of the Most High.

Yahuah's purpose for His future sons is to train each and every son through this physical life for the ultimate goal of being conformed to the image of the first of those sons... Yahusha the Messiah:

> **Romans 8:28-30**
> [28] And we know that all things work together for good to them that love Yahuah, to them who are called <u>according to *Yahuah's* purpose</u>. [29] For whom Yahuah did foreknow, Yahuah also <u>predestined</u> *to be* **conformed to the image of Yahuah's** (first born) **Son** (Yahusha), that Yahusha might be <u>the firstborn among many brothers</u> (in the Family of Yahuah).

Yes, Yahusha is our brother not our "Elohim". There is but one Elohim, that is Yahuah and He is our Father. Yahusha is the firstborn of MANY more sons of Yahuah to come. The only difference between Yahusha and the rest of the sons of Yahuah is <u>birth right</u> and <u>authority</u>. There is no "trinity"; there is Yahuah and the rest of His Eternally Powerful Sons! So Yahuah has a purpose; that purpose is building a "family of gods", organizing them into a Spiritual Kingdom that will govern His Creation for eternity in His Righteousness.

The religious systems of this world, the largest which is the <u>Mystery Religion of Babylon</u> we call today "Christianity", has humanity <u>in complete ignorance of the very purpose of our life on Earth</u>! We sit in our churches in total ignorance of who we "could be" worshipping Hesus Horus Krishna (Jesus H. Christ) as God calling on Ba'al (the LORD) on the day of the sun (Sunday)! While we should be trained by these "churches" as **Lawyers in His Law** so that we can serve as Righteous Priests, Kings, and Judges in that Kingdom... we are taught to deny His Law and be <u>disobedient</u> to everything that is Yahuah's Kingdom.   When Yahusha declares in Revelation "come out of her, Mystery Babylon" he means it.   When he says if you stay in it you are "lukewarm" and he will spit you out of his mouth... he means it. There is no salvation in the Sunday/Trinity/Jesus/Christmas/Easter religion of Babylon.   **It is idolatry.**

We are on this Earth to be trained by this life to serve in the coming Kingdom of Yahuah as "gods" in Yahuah's image.   We are to be born in the image of Yahuah, the Father, after the example set by the first born in that family, Yahusha. We are **predestined** to be conformed to the image of Yahusha, who is the firstborn son of many sons to come through regeneration or the "transposition of our bodies" from this physical realm to the realm of the Spirit which we call today *resurrection.*

This life is literally a "predestined" obstacle course or training ground designed so that all things (good and evil) work in harmony for YOUR training to serve Yahuah in His Kingdom under the High Priest and King of Kings Yahusha.   We are to serve in the order of Melchizedek as "Zadok Priests" and we are <u>to serve</u> as Kings under the authority of the King of Kings.

> **Daniel 7**
> [13] "I kept looking in the night visions, and behold, with the clouds of heaven One (Yahusha) like **a Son of Man** was coming, and he (Yahusha) came up to the Ancient of Days (Yahuah, they are not the same being) and was presented before Him. [14] "And to him (Yahusha) was given (by Yahuah as an inheritance) dominion, Glory and a kingdom, That all the peoples, nations and *men of every* language

might **serve** him (not worship Yahusha, we serve Yahusha in the Kingdom). His (Yahusha's) dominion is an everlasting dominion which will not pass away; And Yahuah's kingdom is one which will not be destroyed.

Simply put… we were created to RULE this creation. But first, we must be properly trained in His Kingdom. That is "why" you are here. "Why" you exist. If you fail in this training you will **cease to exist** and not participate in that Kingdom. If you persist in sitting in your Sunday worshipping, trinity believing, Law abolishing, religious Babylonian Lie you will fail in your purpose in this life. This life will be your reward and you will never serve in a Kingdom you ***were not trained for***.

Yahuah's Purpose

Below I am going to paint a "picture" and summarize very simply the "purpose" of Yahuah:

> Yahuah created the Universe as an inheritance for His sons. His sons are being introduced to this creation and trained to serve in Yahuah's government/Kingdom through a life on Earth. It is this life on Earth where the sons are introduced to their Father, and by following the Way established by the first born son they all obtain eternal life. Upon resurrection, all sons inherit the Universe from their Father as co-heirs with their elder brother and first born son Yahusha who is the Messiah/Anointed King. These sons are organized into a literal Kingdom or government and further trained to govern and rule during a 1,000 year span on Earth. The first born son, Yahusha, reigns as King of Kings and High Priest. Over the 1,000 year Sabbath Millennium Yahusha teaches the other sons to properly judge and to govern by the Torah which is the constitution of this government. After the 1,000 year training period is over, this government or Kingdom grows exponentially until it effectively governs the entire Universe. This "Kingdom" or "Government" which reigns eternally over creation is... "Heaven" also called **the Kingdom of Yahuah** or Kingdom of Heaven. This Kingdom is our destiny, this Universe is our inheritance.
>
> Is the simplistic overview above true? Let us take a quick tour of scripture and see.

Matthew 10

⁷ And as you go, preach, saying, '***the Kingdom of Yahuah is at hand***.'

Let's examine exactly "What" that stated purpose is! To understand that purpose is to know why you are here. What is your purpose? What was Yahuah's purpose in creating the Universe? Why does Yahuah suffer evil and evildoers? Every question is answered with the understanding of Yahuah's purpose.

Next, I am going to expand on the summary I gave and demonstrate through scripture the reality of it. We will see on the following pages, that Yahuah created "all things" or **the Universe** to be given as an inheritance to His sons.

The Universe is Our Inheritance

The inheritance goes to the first born son Yahusha. Then through Yahusha, as sons ourselves and brothers to Yahusha (he is NOT our Elohim), we are co-heirs to the Universe:

> **Romans 8:16-17**
> "The Spirit Himself bears witness with our spirit that we are children of Yahuah, and if children, then heirs -- heirs of Yahuah and joint heirs with the Messiah, if indeed we suffer with him (Yahusha), that we may also be glorified together."

We all know that Yahusha (post resurrection) <u>after completing his training on Earth</u> was seated at Yahuah's right hand and given all authority over Yahuah's creation as an inheritance. We, the rest of the sons of Yahuah, are co-heirs with our first born brother; but only those who, like Yahusha, complete their training on earth.

This Universe, our inheritance, is currently being held captive to sin and death… waiting in eager expectation for us, the sons of Yahuah, to be introduced to His Creation. At which time, when we are introduced (resurrected like Yahusha), **we** will liberate this creation and free it from bondage and govern it righteously for eternity.

> **Romans 8:19**
> "Creation eagerly awaits the revelation of the sons of Yahuah" … vs. 21 "when creation will be set free from bondage and come into the glorious freedom of the sons of Yahuah"

What Sha'ul is stating is very true. "Come into the glorious freedom of the sons of Yahuah" is just another way of saying that creation will be liberated and governed by the sons of Yahuah who are organized into a Kingdom.

We are introduced to His creation through a life on Earth but our ultimate revelation occurs when those chosen few sons are resurrected.

This Life is Training in His Law

During our life on Earth... we are trained for service in **the Kingdom of Yahuah** by teachers and mentors (training aids organized into covenants that serve as physical teachers/examples/rehearsals of spiritual truths). This training process we are put through on earth comes in the form of predestined "test after test" of trials, tribulations, adversity, and affliction whereby we <u>apply His Laws</u> to our lives and grow. It is through this process of tests and trials that we learn the meaning of His Righteous Laws and become trained to govern.

> **Romans 5**
> 3 And not only that, but we also glory in tribulations, knowing that tribulation produces perseverance; 4 and perseverance, character; and character, hope.

We begin our journey as "children" of Yahuah no different than a servant. At the appointed time after being trained and tutored through covenants and applying physical to spiritual parallels we graduate to full sonship and are no longer "children". Our inheritance is granted <u>AFTER</u> our training when we have grown beyond that of a childish selfish slave into an obedient son trained in His Righteousness which is defined by His Laws.

> **Isaiah 30:20**
> 20 And though Yahuah give you the bread of adversity, and the water of affliction, yet shall not thy teachers be removed into a corner any more, but thine eyes shall (be

spiritually opened to) **see thy teachers** (understand *physical to spiritual parallels*):

Galatians 4:1-7
1 Now I say, That the heir, as long as he is a child, is no different from a slave, though he be master of all (we are destined to be masters of the Universe); 2 But as "children" we are under tutors and guardians (covenants, rehearsals, the Law) until the time appointed of the father (that we have mastered spiritual truth through physical examples). 6 And because you are (now) sons (after the appointed time of training), Yahuah has (then after training) sent forth the Spirit of his Son into your hearts, crying, Abba, Father. 7 At which time you are no longer a child (you are trained in His Kingdom), but a son; and if a son, then (only once you have become a son and not a child) an heir of Yahuah (to His Creation) through the Messiah (the first born son in the Family of Yahuah).

We are being trained as priests and kings

*The Kingdom **of Yahuah*** or Kingdom of Heaven or "Heaven" is a divine government made up of the family of Yahuah. Within this family government, we are trained as priests and kings during the Millennial Reign.

Revelation 5:10
10 And hast made us unto our Elohim kings and priests: and we shall reign on the earth.

That initial reign on Earth is for a 1,000 years.   During this time, the sons of Yahuah are trained and organized into a kingdom or *Divine Government* of priests and kings and trained to rule.

> **2 Timothy 2:12**
> 12 If we suffer, we shall also reign with Yahusha.

> **Revelation 20:6**
> 6 Blessed and holy is he that hath part in the first resurrection: on such the second death hath no power, but they shall be priests of Yahuah and of the Messiah, and shall reign (be kings) with him a thousand years.

We are in "Torah Training"

During these 1,000 years, we are trained ***in the Torah***, which is the constitution of the divine government being assembled.   We see below that clearly, in the coming kingdom, the Torah is the standard of government.

We also see that the Messiah Yahusha is the ultimate teacher of the Torah:

> **Isaiah 2:2-4**
> And it shall come to pass in the last days, that the mountain of Yahuah's house shall be established in the top of the mountains, and shall be exalted above the hills; and all nations shall flow unto it. 3 And many people shall go and say, Come ye, and let us go up to the mountain of Yahuah, to the house of the Elohim of Jacob; and Yahusha will teach us of his ways, and we will walk in his paths: for out of Zion shall go forth the Torah and the word of

Yahuah from Jerusalem. 4 And Yahusha shall judge among the nations, and shall rebuke many people:

The government that is being established, is founded on the Messiah Yahusha. That government will have no end *(it is eternal)* and will expand without end until all of creation, *the Universe*, is properly governed by this divine government made up of the sons of Yahuah. We learn that this child will be the first resurrected eternal and, as such, be the "father of everlasting life" just as Abraham is called "the father of faith". Being the first human perfected in this life, Yahusha will be resurrected and become the perfect image of Yahuah i.e. His literal son. As High Priest, Yahusha will be a wonderful counselor; and as King he will bring peace to the sons of Yahuah and Yahuah's creation.

> **Isaiah 9:6-7**
> "For to us a child is born, to us a son is given, and **the government** shall be on his shoulders and he will be called Wonderful Counselor, (*the perfect image of*) Mighty Elohim, (*fore*) Father of Everlasting (*life*), and Prince of Peace." **There will be no end to the increase of His government** or of peace, on the Throne of David and over His Kingdom, to establish it and to uphold it with justice and righteousness from **then on and forevermore**.

So there is no end to the increase of this government and it is eternal. First, the kingdoms on Earth are turned over to the Messiah:

> **Revelation 11:15**
> 15 And the seventh angel sounded; and there were great voices in heaven, saying, the kingdoms of this world are

become the kingdoms of Yahuah and of His Messiah; and Yahusha shall reign forever and ever.

The Kingdom will rule the Universe for eternity

After we are trained to govern within the divine government called ***the Kingdom of Yahuah***... we rule for eternity over all of creation... there is no "need for the light of the sun" because this government will transcend this solar system and encompass this entire Universe.

Revelation 22:5
5 And there shall be no night there; and they need no candle, neither light of the sun; for Yahuah gives them light: and they shall reign forever and ever.

The Purpose - Summary

With all that being laid out in scripture let me again state the summarized "Purpose of Yahuah" for simplicity:

> *Yahuah created the Universe as an inheritance for His sons. His sons are being introduced to this creation and trained to serve in Yahuah's government through a life on Earth. It is this life on Earth where the sons are introduced to their Father, and by following the Way established by the first born son obtain eternal life. Upon resurrection, all sons inherit the Universe from their Father as co-heirs with their elder brother and first born son Yahusha who is the Messiah. These sons are organized into a literal Kingdom or government and further trained to govern and rule during a 1,000-year span on Earth. The first born son, Yahusha, reigns as King of Kings and High Priest. He teaches the other sons to properly judge and govern by the Torah (the constitution of this government) over the 1,000 year Sabbath Millennium. After the 1,000-year training period is over, this government or Kingdom grows exponentially until it effectively governs the entire Universe. This "Kingdom" or "Government" which reigns eternally over creation is... "Heaven" also called the Kingdom of Yahuah and Kingdom of Heaven. This Kingdom is our destiny; this Universe is our inheritance.*

It is with this purpose of Yahuah in mind that we must approach the Bible and all things in it. This life is our training; the Bible is our text book.

Hope - The Fall of Creation by Design

In order to establish His Kingdom, Yahuah had to first create a "need" by causing the fall of creation. Adam's fall was by design; it didn't come as a surprise to Yahuah. It was necessary to fulfill His purpose in our training.

> **Isaiah 45:7**
> I form the light, and create darkness: I make peace, and create evil: I Yahuah do all these *things*.

Once the need was created and a system of training put into place (good vs. evil); then Yahuah could introduce His sons to His creation through a life on Earth where they experience the fallen nature of creation first hand and navigate this fallen state to find their true identity as sons of Yahuah. During this life, they would be trained through the process of "trial/error" in His Word. Man would learning, first hand, that His way is always the best way, and our way (will) is not.

Let's look at what the Apostle Sha'ul has to say as he very eloquently discusses this entire process in Romans. We see Sha'ul teaches the purpose of Yahuah, His Ordained Holy Days, and more. We see that Sha'ul had a deep understanding of the purpose of creation, the need for **the Kingdom of Yahuah**, and the meaning of the Feast Cycle as rehearsals.

Below is Romans 8:18-30:

> **Romans 8** - *Present Suffering and Future Glory*
> [18] I consider that our present sufferings are not worth comparing with the glory that will be revealed in us. [19] For the creation waits in eager expectation for the children of Yahuah to be revealed. [20] <u>For the creation was subjected to frustration, not by its own choice, but by the will of the one (Yahuah) who subjected it (creation to the fall)</u>, ***in hope*** [21] that the creation itself will be liberated from its bondage to decay and brought into the freedom and glory of the children of Yahuah (that was the purpose of the fall! That His sons could be trained by it and come to rule over it and liberate it). [22] We know that the whole creation has been groaning as in the pains of childbirth right up to the present time. [23] Not only so, but we ourselves, who have the first fruits of the Spirit, groan inwardly as we wait eagerly for our adoption to son ship, the redemption of our bodies. [24] For in this hope we were saved. But hope that is seen is no hope at all. Who hopes for what they already have? [25] But if we hope for what we do not yet have, we wait for it patiently. [26] In the same way, the Spirit helps us in our weakness. We do not know what we ought to pray for, but the Spirit himself intercedes for us through wordless groans. [27] And he who searches our hearts knows the mind of the Spirit, because the Spirit intercedes for Yahuah's people in accordance with the will of Yahuah. [28] And we know that in all things Yahuah works for the good of those who love him, who have been called according to his purpose. [29] For those Yahuah foreknew he also predestined to be conformed to the image of his Son, that

he might be the firstborn among many brothers and sisters. ³⁰ And those he predestined, he also called; those he called, he also justified; those he justified, he also glorified.

Many of us "think" we know what Sha'ul just said, but do we "really"?   I put (my comments in parenthesis) for clarification **in context** of *the Word of Yahuah* and all of Sha'ul's writings to help us understand what exactly Sha'ul is saying here:

> **Romans 8**
> ¹⁹ For the creation waits in eager expectation for the children of Yahuah to be revealed (because it is the sons of Yahuah that will govern it in righteousness). ²⁰ For the creation was subjected to futility (when Adam fell), not willingly, but because of Yahuah who subjected it (the fall of creation was part of Yahuah's plan) in hope (of liberating it through His future sons); ²¹ because the creation itself also **will be** delivered (Sha'ul uses future tense speaking of creation being delivered.   He is speaking of the future fulfillment of the Fall Feasts that are a rehearsal of the Second Coming when Yahusha atones for and delivers creation on the Day of Atonement. Sha'ul says "also" referring to the fact that the sons of Yahuah *were* delivered by Yahusha in the past fulfillment of the Spring Feasts on Passover) from the bondage of corruption *into the glorious liberty of the children of Yahuah.* (Sha'ul understands the "purpose" in all of this is that creation is turned over to be governed by the children of Yahuah) ²² For we know that the whole creation groans and labors (Sha'ul is confirming here the Sabbath

Covenant that for 6,000 years creation labors from the effects of sin per the Sabbath Covenant) **with birth pangs together until now** (the 7th Millennium, the Sabbath is yet to come Hebrews Chapter 4). [23] **Not only** *that,* **but we also who have** *the First fruits* (Sha'ul is confirming the Feasts of Yahuah here... the Passover Lamb/Feast of First Fruits/Spring Feasts) **of the Spirit** (Given on the Feast of Weeks or Shav'uot), **even we ourselves groan within ourselves** (along with creation because we have not yet been resurrected either), **eagerly waiting for the adoption** (into the Family of Yahuah through resurrection), **the redemption of our body** (the resurrection on the Feast of Trumpets as Sha'ul teaches the Fall Feasts). [24] **For we** *were saved* (Sha'ul stresses the past tense here because we were saved during the Spring Feasts by the Passover Lamb) **in this hope** (that Yahusha will return again and fulfill the Fall Feasts, resurrecting our bodies so that WE can then liberate creation), **but hope that is seen is not hope; for why does one still hope for what he sees** (Sha'ul is stressing that we must still have hope for what we have not yet witnessed in the fulfillment of the Fall Feasts, so hope endures)? [25] **But if we hope for what we do not see, we eagerly wait for** *it* (the Fall Feasts) **with perseverance** (Sha'ul is encouraging us to endure in hope of the future fulfillment of the Fall Feasts because those who persevere until the end shall be saved).

Sha'ul then goes on to clearly define Yahuah's purpose in creating his sons:

> ²⁸ And we know that in all things Yahuah works for the good of those who love him, **_who have been called according to his purpose_**. ²⁹ For those Yahuah foreknew he also predestined to be conformed to the image of his Son, **_that he might be the firstborn among many brothers and sisters_**. ³⁰ And those he predestined, he also called; those he called, he also justified; those he justified, he also glorified.

With Sha'ul's introduction to the entire "purpose" of Yahuah and the future destiny of the sons of Yahuah to liberate and govern His creation, let us continue our journey to understand **the Kingdom of Yahuah.** Let's look at **the Mystery of the Ages** which is the revelation that Yahuah is begetting a family of elohim in His literal image.

The Mystery of the Ages

The Mystery of Yahuah, hidden from the foundation of the Universe, is that Yahuah's predestined plan was to procreate a family of "godlike ones" called Elohim. This family is likened unto a "body" which will be **the Spiritual Temple of Yahuah** in and through which Yahuah dwells. The head of this body is the first born son Yahusha and the body is the assembly of Chosen Sons of Yahuah known as **Remnant Israel**.   It is through this family of "godlike ones" or elohim that the Universe will be governed in righteousness for eternity by **the Kingdom of Yahuah**.

Below are the scriptures to support this revelation with my commentary in parenthesis.

> **Hebrews 2:10-18**
> [10] In bringing many sons and daughters to glory, it was fitting that Yahuah, **for whom and through whom everything exists**; (Yahuah) should make the pioneer of their salvation (Yahusha) perfect through what he suffered (a life and death on Earth). [11] Both the one who makes people holy (Yahuah) and those who are made holy (Yahusha and all his brother/sisters) **are of the same family** (we are literally "elohim" and offspring of Yahuah). So Yahusha is not ashamed to call them (Remnant Israel) brothers and sisters (Yahusha is our elder brother, not our Elohim).
> [12] He says, "I (Yahusha) will declare Your Name (Yahusha declares the Shema or "Seal" of *the Kingdom of Yahuah*) to my brothers and sisters; in the assembly I will sing Your

praises (we don't sing praises to "Jesus" we worship Yahuah alone)." **13** And again, "I (Yahusha) will put my trust in Him (Yahuah)." And again he says, "Here am I, and the (rest of the) children Yahuah has given me (to rule)." **14** Since the (future) children have flesh and blood (are trained by a life on Earth), he (Yahusha) too shared in their humanity (as a human trained by a life on Earth) so that by his death he, Yahusha, might break the power of him who holds the power of death that is, the devil (the blood of Yahusha covers the decrees in the Law overcoming *the Law of Sin and Death*. With the decrees in the Law covered; the Law then becomes *the Law of the Spirit of Life*)— **15** and free those who all their lives were held in slavery by their fear of death (Yahusha freed us from the Law of Sin and Death by covering the decrees in the Law that demand our death. We are not held in slavery to the Law but fear of death for disobeying it). **16** For surely it is not angels Yahusha helps, but Abraham's descendants (the bloodline of the sons of Yahuah remains defined by the Abrahamic Covenant). **17** For this reason he (Yahusha) had to be made like them (he was made human not a demi-god), **fully human in every way** (can't get any clearer than that) in order that he might become a merciful and faithful high priest (Wonderful Counselor) in service to Yahuah (he is Yahuah's High Priest, not Yahuah in the flesh), and that he might make atonement for the sins of the people (because the Law that governs sacrifices and atonement has been transposed to Heaven to serve Melchizedek). **18** Because he himself suffered when he was tempted, he is able to help those (brothers and sisters in the Family of Yahuah) who are being tempted.

Above Sha'ul specifically identifies that family as being of the bloodline of Abraham/Isaac/Jacob re-affirming that the **Abrahamic Covenant** remains in effect.   Sha'ul also says we are being held captive to the threat of death i.e. "sin therefore you die by decree" which is known as *the Law of Sin and Death*.   We are not held captive by *the Holy Law of Yahuah*.   Let me explain.

We are Held in Bondage to the Fear of Death

Sha'ul is explaining above that Yahuah's purpose was to purchase the salvation of His entire family by making the first born son in that family a "perfect High Priest" who would make the final sacrifice of **the Passover Lamb** to cover our transgression of His Law.   Sha'ul is teaching the reality that Yahusha's blood covers **the decrees** within the Law that demand our death.   It is that fear of death, because of the active decrees, that held us captive. Below Sha'ul expounds on this truth:

> **Colossians 2:14**
> "Having canceled out the **certificate of debt** (levied against humanity) **consisting of (death) decrees** (penalties in the Law for transgressing His Commands and His Ordinances) against us and which (these death <u>decrees</u> which amounted to a Death Certificate against us keeping us in bondage to the fear of death) was hostile to us (because we did not keep His Commandments); and Yahusha has taken it (the Death Certificate i.e. <u>the decrees</u> in the Law not the entire Law) out of the way (making the final sacrifice of the Passover Lamb whose blood covers our transgression), having nailed it (the Death Certificate which are ... <u>THE DECREES AGAINST US</u> in the Law for falling short of His Commandments and His Ordinances... <u>NOT</u> the entire Law) to the stake.

> You see, Yahuah nailed what Sha'ul calls the **Certificate of Debt** which were **His Decrees** against us found in the "terms and conditions" of the Mosaic Covenant to the stake and said "*PAID IN FULL*" by the Blood of the Passover Lamb, Yahusha.

Yahusha's blood paid the debt consisting of death decrees we owed for violating **His Commands** and **His Laws**. He didn't nail **the Torah** OR **His Commands** OR **His Laws** to the stake. He nailed **His Death Decrees** to the stake for those who keep Passover in light of Yahusha's sacrifice.

Decrees, commands, and laws are not the same things...

> **Deuteronomy 5**
> 30 "Go, tell them to return to their tents. 31 But you stay here with me so that I may give you all **the commands**, **decrees** and **laws** you are to teach them to follow in the land I am giving them to possess."

I just wanted to clear that up before I continue. We have to understand what was "nailed to the stake" or we will never understand Sha'ul's writings. It was ONLY **His Decrees** that were opposed to us that were nailed to the stake for those who put their faith in the Passover Lamb (not the Easter pig).

I'll cover this in more detail in my books *the Yahushaic Covenant* and *the Law of Yahuah*.

Let me do a little defining of terms quickly as well:

> ***the Law of Sin and Death*** is *the Law of Yahuah* with <u>active death decrees</u>. Since all have sinned everyone is held to account for their own transgressions by His Decrees and death is the result.
>
> **the Law of the Spirit of Life** is *the Law of Yahuah* with the death decrees found in the Law covered by the blood of the Passover Lamb. With the death decrees covered, we are found in perfect obedience to *the Law of Yahuah* and the promise for obedience to His Law is realized; which is life eternal.

Now let's continue on topic with the revelation of the Family of Yahuah. Next, Sha'ul continues describing this amazing **Mystery of the Family of Yahuah**. This "family" is known as "Elohim" which means "gods". We now are human, Yahuah is not human He is "<u>E</u>lohim". Upon resurrection or the transposition of our bodies from physical to Spiritual we too will be "<u>e</u>lohim", begotten in Yahuah's full image as sons.

We see that pro-creating a family of "gods" was the very "purpose of Yahuah" in creation.

Ephesians 1
¹ Sha'ul, an apostle of Messiah Yahusha by the will of Yahuah, to the saints which are at Ephesus, and to the faithful in (covenant with) Messiah Yahusha: ² Grace be to you, and peace, from Yahuah our Father (of Elohim), and from the King Messiah Yahusha. ³ Blessed be the Elohim

(Sha'ul declares the Shema or "Seal" of *the Kingdom of Yahuah*) and Father of our King Messiah Yahusha, who (Yahuah) hath blessed us (His sons, Elohim) with all spiritual blessings in heavenly places (*the Kingdom of Yahuah*) in (covenant with) Yahusha (we are co-heirs): ⁴ According (to Yahuah's purpose) as He (Yahuah) hath chosen (predestined) us in Him(self), (we are in covenant with Yahuah through *the Yahushaic Covenant* which is a marriage covenant where "the two shall become one". It is in that way that Yahusha and all his brothers/sisters are ONE with Yahuah) before the foundation of the world (it was Yahuah's purpose from the beginning before creation to pro-create a family), that we should be holy and without blame before Him (Yahuah) in love (through a marriage covenant):⁵ Having predestinated us unto the adoption of children (sons of Yahuah) by (the life sacrifice of) Messiah Yahusha to Himself (Yahuah), according to the good pleasure of his (Yahuah's) will (to pro-create a family...   *His Purpose*),

⁶ To the praise of the glory of His (Yahuah's) grace, wherein Yahuah hath made us (through Yahusha whose blood covers <u>the decrees</u>) accepted in the beloved (family of Elohim). ⁷ In whom (Messiah Yahusha) we have redemption (from the Law of Sin and Death) through his blood (Yahusha is the Passover Lamb), (we have) the forgiveness of sins (decrees in the Law for violating His Commands are covered by the blood), according to the riches of His (Yahuah's) grace (==it is Yahuah who forgives sin and accepts Yahusha's sacrifice to satisfy== <u>the decrees</u> that

demand our death for breaking His Law, that is the definition of Grace);

⁸ Wherein (covenant with Yahusha) He (Yahuah) hath abounded toward us (unlimited Grace) in all wisdom and prudence; ⁹ Having made known unto us (**elohim**) <u>the mystery</u> of His will (to beget a family), according to His (Yahuah's) good pleasure which He **hath purposed** (predestined to create) in (the full image of) Himself (He is the Father of the family of Yahuah called elohim, Yahuah is the One True Living Elohim): ¹⁰ That in the dispensation of the fullness of times (as foretold by His prophets) He (Yahuah) might gather together (again) in one (family through the covenant of marriage, the two shall become one) all things in (covenant with Yahusha the) Messiah, both which are in heaven (***the Kingdom of Yahuah***), and which are on earth; even in Him(self, Yahuah will reconcile creation through the sacrifice of His Son): ¹¹ In whom (the first born Son, Messiah Yahusha) also we (too) **have obtained an inheritance** (as sons of Yahuah, we inherit the Universe), **being predestinated according to the purpose of Yahuah** who worketh all things after the counsel of His own will: ¹² That we (sons of Yahuah) should be to the praise of His glory, who first trusted in Messiah Yahusha (and express our faith in <u>the Passover Lamb</u> not the Easter Pig).

¹³ In whom (Yahusha) you also trusted (was the Messiah), after that you heard the word of truth, the gospel of your salvation (purchased through the blood sacrifice of Yahusha to consummate the covenant of marriage): in

whom (Yahusha) also after that you believed, you were sealed with that holy Spirit of promise (the Spirit of Yahuah is the "blood of the family of Yahuah" a Spiritual Parallel of a human bloodline or family).

[14] Which is the earnest (guarantee) of our (future) inheritance (as sons of Yahuah) until the redemption (transposition of our bodies from the Physical Realm to the Spiritual Realm) of the purchased possession unto the praise of His glory.

….

[17] That **the Elohim** (Sha'ul again declares the Shema) of our King Messiah Yahusha (Yahuah is Yahusha's Elohim too), the Father of glory, may give unto you the spirit of wisdom and revelation in the knowledge of Him(self): [18] The eyes of your understanding being enlightened (to His Purpose to procreate a Family); that you may know what is the hope of His (Yahuah) calling (**you as a son**), and what the **riches of the glory of His inheritance** in the saints (we inherit the Universe),

[19] And what is the exceeding greatness of Yahuah's power toward us (as sons) who believe, according to the working of His (Yahuah's) mighty power, [20] Which He (Yahuah) demonstrated in the Messiah, when Yahuah raised Yahusha from the dead (confirming Yahusha's sonship), and Yahuah set Yahusha at Yahuah's own right hand (of the throne of Creation.   Yahusha is Yahuah's proxy King) in ***the Kingdom of Yahuah***, [21] Far above all principality, and power, and might, and dominion, and every name that

is named, not only in this world, but also in that which is to come:

²² And (Yahuah) hath put all things under his (Yahusha's) feet, and Yahuah gave Yahusha (the first born Son) to be the head (of His Family) over all things to the assembly (of His sons), ²³ Which is His (Yahuah's Temple or) body, the fullness of Him (Yahuah) that fills all in all.

Sha'ul is describing **the Mystery of the Ages**, which is the revelation of the eternal family of Yahuah predestined and purchased through the blood of the Lamb. That Yahuah's family is His Glory. The head of the body (Yahuah's Spiritual Temple) is the Messiah, the first born Son, and the rest of His sons are the body. This body of sons of Yahuah (head and all) will liberate creation and rule over it within a divine system of government.

Chapter 3

Realm governed by the Kingdom of Yahuah

Progressive Revelation of the Realm

The realm governed by **the Kingdom of Yahuah** is all of His Creation i.e. the Universe. This *Spiritual Truth* was progressively disclosed over time through all 7 Covenants:

Edenic Covenant

The "realm" was very small, defined as the Garden of Eden.

> **Genesis 2**
> [15] Yahuah Elohim took the man and put him <u>in the Garden of Eden</u> to work it and take care of it (govern the Garden of Eden). [16] And Yahuah our Elohim commanded the man (**the Law of Yahuah** introduced), "You are free to eat from any tree in the garden; [17] but you must not eat from the tree of the knowledge of good and evil (command), for when you eat from it you will certainly die (death decree)." (the Law of Sin and Death introduced)

Adamic/Noahic Covenants

After failing to properly govern the Garden of Eden by the "Commandments of Yahuah", the realm at that time was scaled down to a <u>family unit</u>. Adam and Eve were "relieved" of their authority to govern any specific "realm" outside of learning to govern their own lives. Adam, however, did display the kind of "love" required to govern. He displayed that love toward his wife Eve. Adam, knowing that he would die for disobeying

Yahuah, chose to "identify" with Eve in eating the "apple" literally giving his life for Eve.

We learn that Adam's dominion, as a result, was limited to that which he demonstrated love enough to die for... his own family! Foreshadowing the love Yahusha must demonstrate by dying for his brothers/sisters:

> **Genesis 3**
> [16] To the woman he said, "I will make your pains in childbearing very severe; with painful labor you will give birth to children. Your desire will be to rule over your husband, **but   he will (be required to) rule over you**."

So Adams "rule" was limited then to that of himself and his family because Adam failed to govern the Garden by the Righteous Law of Yahuah.   Yahuah revealed that those who don't "keep *the Law of Yahuah*" will not receive eternal life but "since from the ground you were taken; for dust you are and to dust you will return".   Those disobedient to *the Law of Yahuah* die... they do not govern.   That which Adam was intended to "take care of" was instead cursed because of his failure to properly govern it. Adam now became a "slave" to the very realm he was intended to rule over and that realm cursed as a result.

> **Genesis 3**
> [17] To Adam he (Yahuah) said, "Because you listened to your wife and ate fruit from the tree about which I commanded you, 'You must not eat from it,' "**Cursed is the ground because of you**; through painful toil you will eat food from it all the days of your life. [18] It will produce thorns and thistles for you and you will eat the plants of

the field. ¹⁹ By the sweat of your brow you will eat your food until you return to the ground, since from it you were taken; for dust you are and to dust you will return."

In effect, man was given a taste of the consequences of utterly failing to govern by **the Law of Yahuah** (even as limited as man's knowledge of the Law was at that time in the process of Progressive Revelation).   <u>Man would have to "earn" his right to rule by first serving that which he is to govern.</u>   **the Sabbath Covenant** was now in full effect, for 6,000 years man would have to "work" before he would be given rest and restored to his position of authority.   Man would be trained to learn what it means to "govern properly" and that you first must SERVE and (if necessary) DIE for that which you govern.

This was an early shadow picture of the coming Messiah/King.   Like all the rest of the sons of Yahuah, Yahusha too would have to come first as *"the Suffering Servant"* during the 6,000-year period and serve before he could reign.

> **Galatians 4:1-7**
> 1 Now I say, That the heir, as long as he is a child, is no different from a servant, though he be master of all

Yahusha would be required **to serve** Yahuah's creation and future sons and earn his position as King over them before he could govern.   Yahusha would have to **prove he was worthy** to rule them **by being willing to die** for them first (just like Adam was willing to die for Eve).   Only upon Yahusha's death, as he identified with the sins of the world, was Yahusha resurrected and made proxy King at the right hand of Yahuah.

==the Kingdom==

There is no greater love than a man being willing to die for another man. True authority is based on that kind of love! A righteous ruler must love his "realm" enough to die for it. Yahusha had to demonstrate his ability to keep **the Law of Yahuah** before he could be crowned King. It would not be until the fulfillment of **the Sabbath Covenant** when it was time for the curse of Adam to be lifted that Yahusha would return as "the Conquering King" and establish **the Kingdom of Yahuah**.

Abrahamic Covenant

In **the Abrahamic Covenant**, the "realm" was extended beyond just the immediate family to a genetic bloodline that would run through Abraham/Isaac/Jacob and extend to Jacob's 12 sons. These 12 sons would evolve into 12 Tribes and would be known by the name Israel.

We see below that **the Abrahamic Covenant** has not been "abolished". Far from it; it is an everlasting covenant and it is from within this bloodline that a small remnant would be chosen to be sons of Yahuah called **Remnant Israel**. I will cover that in more detail when I discuss **the Citizens of the Kingdom of Yahuah**. We see the Land of Canaan promised to the descendants of Abraham; it wouldn't be until later in **the Mosaic Covenant** that this promise is realized.

Genesis 17

[3] Abram fell facedown, and Yahuah said to him, [4] "As for me, this is my covenant with you: You will be the father of many nations. [5] No longer will you be called Abram; your name will be Abraham, for I have made you a father of many nations. [6] I

will make you very fruitful; I will make nations of you, and kings will come from you. **⁷ I will establish my covenant as an everlasting covenant between me and you and your descendants after you for the generations to come, to be your Elohim and the Elohim of your descendants after you**. ⁸ The whole land of Canaan, where you now reside as a foreigner, I will give as an everlasting possession (Land of Canaan is a physical shadow of the Universe i.e. *physical to spiritual parallel*) to you and your descendants after you; and I will be their Elohim."

⁹ Then Yahuah said to Abraham, "As for you, you must keep my covenant, you and your descendants after you for the generations to come. ¹⁰ This is my covenant with you and your descendants after you, the covenant you are to keep: Every male among you shall be circumcised. ¹¹ You are to undergo circumcision, and it will be the sign of the covenant between me and you (physical circumcision is a shadow of circumcision of the heart; *physical to spiritual parallel*).

> **Note:**
>
> *Physical circumcision was the commitment to keep the letter of the Law of Yahuah and all the physical rituals/rehearsals etc. Spiritual circumcision is having a "heart for His Law" and seeking the spiritual intent of the Law and the spiritual truths of the physical moedim/rehearsals and rituals.*

Mosaic Covenant

In **the Mosaic Covenant**, the "realm" that the 12 Tribes of Israel would govern was given clearly defined borders known as the Land of Canaan or the Promised Land.

What is interesting to note here, is that Moses (who represented the transposition from oral tradition to the written law) was not allowed to lead the children of Israel into the Promised Land of Canaan.   As a "Physical Shadow" of the later Spiritual Truth to follow, it was "Yahusha sun of Nun" that took the mantle of Moses and leads the children of Israel into the Promised Land of Canaan.   Foreshadowing the coming Messiah with the same name, Yahusha, who would transpose the "Written Law" in **the Mosaic Covenant** to the Spiritual Fullness of "Written on our Hearts" and lead us into the Spiritual Kingdom of Yahuah (**physical to spiritual parallel**s).

> **Joshua 1:1-6**
> 1 After the death of Moses the servant of Yahuah, Yahuah said to Yahusha son of Nun, Moses' aide: [2] "Moses my servant is dead. Now then, you and all these people, get ready to cross the Jordan River into the land I am about to give to them—to the Israelites. [3] I will give you every place where you set your foot, as I promised Moses. [4] **Your territory will extend from the desert to Lebanon, and from the great river, the Euphrates—all the Hittite country—to the Mediterranean Sea in the west**. [5] No one will be able to stand against you all the days of your life. As I was with Moses, so I will be with you; I will never leave you nor forsake you. [6] Be strong and courageous, because

you will lead these people **to inherit the land I swore to their ancestors to give them**.

Yahuah also introduces the concept of "inheritance to His sons" through progressive revelation in verse 6 above.

It is also worthy of note that it was not until AFTER Yahuah fully disclosed His Law in writing (the governing constitution) that Yahuah then allowed His chosen to enter the Promised Land. The Written Law was the governing constitution of the physical Promised Land (*physical to spiritual parallel*).

The Davidic Covenant

The Davidic Covenant builds on all previous covenants as Yahuah:

- Established a physical righteous King to serve as an example of the coming Spiritual King (***Physical to spiritual parallels***).

- It was established that the Throne of David would be the throne and bloodline through which the Messiah and King would come to govern His Kingdom for eternity.

- Yahuah established His Throne, Capital City, Temple, and Altar in detail physically as ***Physical to spiritual parallels***.

Yahushaic Covenant

In ***the Yahushaic Covenant***, the shadow picture of the Promised Land of Canaan known as the land of Israel was "fulfilled" Spiritually in two stages:

1. First **the Sabbath Covenant** would be fulfilled and creation would enter a period of "rest" for a 1,000 years. The "realm" of **the Kingdom of Yahuah** would be limited to planet Earth in order to properly train the sons of Yahuah to govern within that Kingdom.

   ### Revelation 5:10
   10 And hast made us unto our Elohim kings and priests: and we shall reign on the earth.

   ### Revelation 20:6
   6 Blessed and holy is he that hath part in the first resurrection: on such the second death hath no power, but they shall be priests of Yahuah (Elohim) and of the Messiah (King), and shall reign with him (the King Yahusha) a thousand years.

2. Once the 1,000-year training period for His sons to learn their place in His government and rest for creation was complete, the final "realm" of **the Kingdom of Yahuah** would be expanded to all of Yahuah's Creation (the Universe).

   ### Revelation 22:5
   5 And there (the final fulfillment of the Realm) shall be no night there; and they need no candle, neither light of the sun; for Yahuah gives them light: and they shall reign forever and ever.

The Yahushaic Covenant did not "replace" the other covenants in defining the "realm". **The Yahushaic Covenant** "fulfilled" them in their fullest Spiritual Reality.

Our (the sons of Yahuah) primary responsibility to Yahuah has always been to serve Him as Priest/Kings of our <u>home</u> first. Then, once we have our house in order, our authority extends out to the community, province, and beyond until the Universe is properly governed in righteousness.   I will cover **the Yahushaic Covenant** in full detail in my next book.

We have seen the "realm" of **the Kingdom of Yahuah** progressively disclosed through the covenants in the Bible.   Each covenant valid and active in **the Yahushaic Covenant** as the 7th and final covenant Yahuah made with man is the renewing of all previous 6 and bringing them to their "fulfillment" Spiritually.

Chapter 4

The Sovereign King of the Kingdom of Yahuah

Introduction

The Kingdom **of Yahuah** has a sovereign King. This can get confusing because Yahusha was seated at the right hand of the throne that Yahuah sits on. You see, **the Kingdom of Yahuah** is not Creation. <u>the Kingdom of Yahuah is a government that rules creation</u>.

Yahuah sits on the **Throne of Creation** as <u>the Creator</u> over all Creation and Yahusha was installed by Yahuah as His **proxy** King to govern it within **the Kingdom of Yahuah**. Let us give Glory where Glory is due...

> **Isaiah 44**
> 6 "This is what Yahuah says — <u>*Israel's King (Yahusha had not yet been installed as Yahuah's proxy King) and Redeemer*</u>, Yahuah Almighty: I am the first and I am the last; <u>*apart from me there is no Elohim*</u>.
>
> **Isaiah 44**
> 24 "This is what Yahuah says— your Redeemer (Yahuah is the redeemer/savior, Yahusha is the acceptable sacrifice i.e. Lamb of Yahuah), who formed you in the womb: I am Yahuah, <u>*the Maker of all things*</u>, who stretches out the heavens, who spreads out the earth <u>*by myself*</u>.
>
> **Isaiah 42**
> 5 This is what Yahuah says— **He** who created the heavens and stretched them out, who spread out the earth and all that comes out of it, who gives breath to its people, and life to those who walk on it!

Isaiah 45

⁵ I am Yahuah, **and there is no other**; apart from me there is no Elohim. ⁷ I form the light and create darkness, I bring prosperity and create disaster; I**, Yahuah, do all these things**. ¹² It is I **who made the earth and created mankind upon it**. My own hands stretched out the heavens; I marshaled their starry hosts. ¹⁸ For this is what Yahuah says— **He** who created the heavens, **He** (alone) is Elohim; **He** who fashioned and made the earth, H**e** founded it; **He** did not create it to be empty, but formed it to be inhabited— **He** says: "I **am Yahuah, and there is no other** (Elohim)."

Isaiah 46

⁵ "**To whom will you compare me or count me equal**? To whom will you liken me that we may be compared? ⁸ "Remember this, fix it in mind, take it to heart, you rebels. ⁹ Remember the former things, those of long ago; I am Elohim, **and there is no other**; I am Elohim, and there is none like me. ¹⁰ I make known the end from the beginning, from ancient times, what is still to come. I say: My purpose will stand, and I will do all that I please.

Yahuah makes it crystal clear that it was He alone who is the Creator and He alone sits on *the Throne of Creation*. Yes, Yahuah is *the Creator* and He did it all alone.   Despite all the rhetoric from the Christian Church about "the Trinity" and "divine emanation" and so forth… Yahuah cleared it up.   He did it by Himself.   There was no one with Him.

There are two thrones, **the Throne of Creation** and the throne that rules over **the Kingdom of Yahuah**. Yahuah sits on **the Throne of Creation**, Yahusha sits at Yahuah's right hand and Yahusha's power/authority is given him by Yahuah as Yahuah's proxy King over **the Kingdom of Yahuah**:

> Matthew 26:64
> Yahusha said to him, "You have said so. But I tell you, from now on you will see the Son of Man seated at the right hand of (the) Power (of Yahuah) and coming on the clouds of heaven."
>
> **Ephesians 1:20**
> that Yahuah worked in Yahusha when Yahuah raised Yahusha from the dead and seated Yahusha at His right hand in the heavenly places (Kingdom of Yahuah).
>
> **Colossians 3:1**
> If then you have been raised with Yahusha, seek the (Spiritual) things that are above (in *the Kingdom of Yahuah*), where Yahusha is, seated at the right hand of Yahuah.
>
> **Hebrews 8:1**
> Now the point in what we are saying is this: we have such a high priest, one who is seated at the right hand of the Throne of Majesty (Throne of Creation) in (the Kingdom of) heaven.

Yahusha, the Ruling High Priest (*Melchizedek*)

The King installed at the right hand of Yahuah to rule His Creation within **the Kingdom of Yahuah** is His firstborn son into that Spiritual Kingdom.   Yahusha is that son.   As firstborn son, Yahusha received the inheritance of His Father to govern the Universe.

> ### Isaiah 9:6-7
> "For to us a child is born, to us a son is given, and the government (over Creation) shall be on his shoulders and he will be called Wonderful Counselor, (the perfect image of) Mighty Elohim, (fore) Father of Everlasting (life), and Prince of Peace."   There will be no end to the increase of His government (*the Kingdom of Yahuah*) or of peace, on the Throne of David and over His Kingdom, to establish it and to uphold it with justice and righteousness (the Law) from then on and forevermore.
>
> ### Hebrews 1
> 1 In the past (6 covenants) Yahuah spoke to our ancestors through the prophets at many times and in various ways, ² but in these last days (in **the Yahushaic Covenant**) Yahuah has spoken to us by his Son (Moses called Yahusha the <u>greatest</u> prophet of all who would properly teach the Law),
>
>> ### *Deuteronomy 18:15, 18-19*
>> *"Yahuah will raise up a Prophet like me from your midst, from your brethren. Him you shall hear.... And Yahuah said to me: I will raise up for them a Prophet like you from among their*

brethren, and will put My words in His mouth, and He shall speak to them all that I command Him. And it shall be that whoever will not hear My words, which He speaks in My name, I will require it of him"

Continuing with Hebrews 1...
whom Yahuah <u>appointed heir of all things (Yahusha did not create anything, he was appointed his position)</u>, **and for whom also Yahuah made the universe.** ³ The Son is the radiance (perfect image or reflection) of <u>Yahuah's glory</u> and the exact <u>representation</u> of Yahuah's being (just like all sons are the exact representation of their father physical to spiritual parallel. Yahusha was transposed into the full image of Yahuah as His <u>literal son</u> through resurrection), upholding all things by Yahuah's powerful word (governs the Universe by **the Law of Yahuah**). <u>**After**</u> he had provided purification for sins, he sat down at the right hand of the Majesty (Throne of Creation) in **the Kingdom of Yahuah**. ⁴ So he (was not born but) **became** (after his transposition and birth as a elohim in the exact representation of Yahuah's being) as much superior to the angels as the name he **has inherited** is superior to theirs.

The King's Training

Like all of the sons of Yahuah who are being trained to govern under Yahusha, Yahusha had to be "trained" through a life on Earth.

> **Hebrews 2:14-18**
> **14** Since the (future) children (of Yahuah) have flesh and blood (by which they are trained by a life on Earth), he (Yahusha) too shared in their humanity (was trained by a life on Earth) so that by his death he, Yahusha, might break the power of him who holds the power of death—that is, the devil— **15** and free those who all their lives were held in slavery by their fear of death (not slavery to the Law). **16** For surely it is not angels Yahusha helps, but Abraham's descendants (the bloodline of the sons of Yahuah remains defined by the Abrahamic Covenant). **17** For this reason he (Yahusha) had to be made like them, **fully human in every way** (he was not half man half elohim), in order that he might become a merciful and faithful high priest in service to Yahuah (he is Yahuah's High Priest, not Yahuah in the flesh), and that he might make atonement for the sins of the people. **18** Because he himself suffered when he was tempted (trained in this life), he is able (qualified through training) to help those (brothers and sisters in the Family of Yahuah) who are being tempted (in their training).

So we see that before Yahusha would obtain his inheritance **he had to be trained**.   Yahusha's unique role of Melchizedek (*Ruling Zadok Priest*) required Yahusha to be trained both in the Law *to govern* but also in the Law of the Priesthood to make atonement.

I cover this in great detail in the 4th book in this series ***Melchizedek and the Passover Lamb*** and will fully develop Yahusha's role in my book ***the Yahushaic Covenant***.

Most people "assume" (*mainly because they are taught so in Christianity*) that Yahusha was born perfect (*teaching he was literally Yahuah in the flesh*). This is not the case, if it were Yahusha would have had no reason to be put through a life on Earth like the rest of us and certainly could not have died. In fact, scripture teaches us that Yahusha was <u>not born perfect</u>:

Luke 2:40, 52

⁴⁰ And the Child (Yahusha) grew and **became strong in spirit** (learn through *physical to spiritual parallels*), (and became) **filled with wisdom; and the grace** (favor) **of Yahuah was upon him.** ... ⁵² And Yahusha **increased in wisdom and stature and in favor with Yahuah** and men.

Yahusha GREW in wisdom, strength, stature, etc. just like John the Baptist who was Yahusha's teacher, (see Luke 1:80). This shows that **Yahusha was not born "perfect" but <u>BECAME</u> perfected** like all other righteous men of Israel (Yet Yahusha <u>was</u> the most Anointed One).

Hebrews 1:4

⁴ **having <u>become</u> so much better than the angels, as Yahusha has <u>by inheritance</u> obtained** (after life training) **a more excellent name than they** (Yahusha wasn't born with it; he had to earn the position of King).

Hebrews 5:8-9

⁸ though Yahusha was a Son, yet **he <u>learned</u> obedience** (Yahusha wasn't always perfectly obedient that had to be learned) by the things which he suffered. ⁹ And <u>having been perfected</u> (Yahusha wasn't born perfect, he was trained to perfection), Yahusha **became** the author (forefather) of eternal salvation (the forerunner to obtain it) to all who obey him (enter into covenant with him and follow his example),

Hebrews 7:28

²⁸ For the law appoints as high priests **men** who have weakness (Yahusha included, as he was a man in need of being perfected), but the word of the oath, which came after the law, appoints the Son **who <u>has been perfected</u>** (Yahusha was the first to achieve perfection and attain eternal life) forever.

The King's Qualification

Yahusha, like all the sons of Yahuah, must have proven himself <u>worthy to rule</u>.   He must demonstrate while on this Earth:

- He was willing to serve Yahuah's creation and the sons of Yahuah before ruling over them.

- He loved Yahuah, His Creation, and His family with the kind of love required to rule by giving his life for them first.

- He had to study Yahuah's Righteousness defined by the Law and live it.

- He had to demonstrate that he possessed the Seal of Yahuah's Kingdom.
- He had to faithfully carry "the standard" or display the Sign of Yahuah's Kingdom.
- He had to be obedient to the ritual that Yahuah defined in His Law; whereby he could obtain Yahuah's Grace and Forgiveness.
- He had to demonstrate he could be trusted with great wealth and remain humble.
- He had to be TRANSPOSED into **the Kingdom of Yahuah** demonstrating *with power* Yahuah's choice of Yahusha as a son.

Yahusha demonstrated he was willing to serve Yahuah's creation and the sons of Yahuah before ruling over them. At this point in this book, I have not yet defined all the qualifications every son of Yahuah must have to enter His Kingdom. However, below I will quickly demonstrate that Yahusha was a son by the evidence in his life. I will fully define them in later chapters of this book.

Yahusha was the Second Adam

Adam identified with his wife Eve in her sin and as a result died for her. **Adam** then had to serve after failing to properly rule the Earth. **Adam** was given dominion over his wife. **Adam** had to go through a life on Earth and serve Yahuah's creation that he was intended to govern. **Adam** was literally the son of Yahuah having no parents.

Yahusha, the bridegroom, had to identify with the transgressions of his "bride" as **the Passover Lamb** and die for her. **Yahusha**

had to serve her in this life before ruling over her in the next life. **Yahusha** had to go through a life on Earth and serve Yahuah's creation that he would later govern. **Yahusha** was resurrected, becoming the actual son of Yahuah, into **the Kingdom of Yahuah**.

Yahusha was the Messiah ben Joseph

Yahusha had to fulfill the requirements of the Messiah as foretold by the prophets of Yahuah. The prophets describe a suffering servant known in prophetic circles as *"the Messiah ben Joseph"*. Joseph was a prototype or forerunner of the suffering Messiah (***physical to spiritual parallel***). Joseph was betrayed by his brothers, thrown in the pit left to die, rose from the pit to be at the right hand of Pharaoh.

Joseph then extended forgiveness to his brothers and saved their lives in the 7-year Egyptian drought. The entire story of Joseph son of Jacob is a ***physical to spiritual parallel*** of the life of the coming Messiah.

Yahusha too would be betrayed by his brothers (the Jews), go down into the pit (death), rise again to the right hand of Yahuah and deliver the sons of Yahuah from death.

Upon Yahusha's death which he suffered in love for his brothers; he was found worthy as a servant and given the crown to rule. Let's take a look at a few prophecies that speak of Yahusha's role as the suffering servant. Again, this book is only to serve as *Cliff Notes* to **the Kingdom of Yahuah**. This is not intended to be an in depth study of the suffering servant.

Just an introduction... let's look at Isaiah 53.

Isaiah 53:1-12

1 Who has believed our message and to whom has the arm of Yahuah been revealed? ² He (Yahusha) grew up before Him (Yahuah) like a tender shoot, and like a root out of dry ground (Yahusha had to grow in wisdom and favor and was trained to perfect obedience). He had no beauty or majesty to attract us to him, nothing in his appearance that we should desire him. ³ He was despised and rejected by mankind, a man (not a God) of suffering, and familiar with pain. Like one from whom people hide their faces he was despised, and we held him in low esteem. ⁴ Surely he took up *our pain* and bore *our suffering*, yet we considered him punished by Yahuah, stricken by Him, and afflicted. ⁵ But he was pierced for *our transgressions*, he was crushed for *our iniquities*; the punishment that brought us peace was on him, and by his wounds we are healed. ⁶ We all, like sheep, have gone astray, each of us has turned to our own way; and Yahuah has laid on him (as THE Passover Lamb) the iniquity (breaking the Law) of us all. ⁷ He was oppressed and afflicted, yet he did not open his mouth; he was led like a (Passover) lamb to the slaughter, and as a sheep before its shearers is silent, so he did not open his mouth. ⁸ By oppression and judgment he was taken away. Yet who of his generation protested? For he was cut off from the land of the living; for the transgression (of the Law) of My people he was punished. ⁹ He was assigned a grave with the wicked, and with the rich in his death, though he had done no violence, nor was any deceit in his mouth.

(Yahusha was tried and found innocent for insurrection which is violence as well as blasphemy which is deceit) ¹⁰ Yet it was <u>Yahuah's will</u> to crush him and cause him to suffer,(Yahusha had to be trained and proven worthy to rule Yahuah's Creation) and though Yahuah makes **his life** (Yahusha's entire life <u>not his death</u>) an offering for sin, he will see his offspring and prolong his days (promise of eternal life), and the **will of Yahuah** (to procreate a family to govern Creation, Yahusha being the first born son) will prosper in his hand (Yahusha will set the Way for all future sons to follow). ¹¹ **<u>After he has suffered</u>** (to pave the Way through the Narrow Passover Gate only), he will see the light of life and be satisfied (resurrected to eternal life); by his knowledge (of the Law) My righteous (Torah Observant) servant will justify many (by covering the death decrees in the Law as Passover Lamb), and he will bear their iniquities (inability to keep His Law). ¹² Therefore (by his knowledge of the Law and obedience unto death) I will give him a portion among the great (seat Yahusha at the right hand of Yahuah as King in **the Kingdom of Yahuah**), and he will divide the spoils with the strong, because he poured out his life (for Yahuah's purposes and his brothers) ***<u>unto death</u>***, (the greatest expression of true love) and was numbered with the transgressors. For he bore the sin of many (as Passover Lamb), and made intercession for the transgressors (as High Priest).

Yahusha displayed, what at that time was, the greatest expression of a "servant"; just before Passover Yahusha washed the feet of his disciples. Yahusha set the example that **<u>we too must be servants</u>** before we can be found worthy to govern with him.

Washing the feet of his disciples was a ***physical to spiritual parallel***.

> John 13:1-17
> 1 It was just before the Passover Festival. Yahusha knew that the hour had come for him to leave this world and go to the Father. Having loved his own who were in the world, he loved them to the end (Yahusha demonstrated the love required to rule). ² The evening meal (yes, Yahusha kept Passover not Easter) was in progress, and the devil had already prompted Judas, the son of Simon Iscariot, to betray Yahusha. ³ Yahusha knew that the Father had put all things under his power, and that he had come from (the predestined Will of) Yahuah and was returning (as a trained son) to Yahuah; ⁴ so he got up from the meal, took off his outer clothing (and Mikveh'd himself), and wrapped a towel around his waist. ⁵ After that, he poured water into a basin and began to wash his disciples' feet, drying them with the towel that was wrapped around him. ⁶ He came to Simon Peter, who said to him, "Master, are you going to wash my feet?" ⁷ Yahusha replied (speaking of the ***Physical to spiritual parallel*** of what he was doing), "You do not realize now what I am doing, but later (when you have the Spirit of Yahuah) you will understand." ⁸ "No," said Peter, "you shall never wash my feet." Yahusha answered, "Unless I wash you, you have no part with me." (Yahusha knew he must demonstrate the heart of a servant to be King, and all those who rule with him must do the same) ⁹ "Then, Master," Simon Peter replied (not understanding the spiritual parallel), "not just my feet but my hands and my head as well!" ¹⁰ Yahusha answered,

"Those who have had a bath (already been Mikveh'd) need only to wash their feet; their whole body is clean. And you are clean (his disciples had been Mikveh'd making them spiritually white as snow in the eyes of Yahuah), though not every one of you." [11] For he knew who was going to betray him, and that was why he said not everyone was (spiritually) clean. [12] When he had finished washing their feet, he put on his clothes and returned to his place. "Do you understand (the spiritual significance) what I have done (physically) for you?" he asked them. [13] "You call me 'Teacher' and 'Master,' and rightly so, for that is what I am. [14] Now that I, your Master and Teacher (not their God), have washed your feet, you also should wash one another's feet (*physical to spiritual parallel* of having the heart of a servant). [15] I have set you an (physical) example that you should do as I have done for you (we too must live a life of service to our brothers). [16] Very truly I tell you, no servant (all the sons of Yahuah) is greater than his master (Yahusha), nor is a messenger (Yahusha) greater than the one (Yahuah) who sent him (Yahusha is saying that Yahuah's Will is that His sons must first serve to be qualified to rule). [17] Now that you know these things, you will be blessed if you do them.

Messiah ben David

Only after fulfilling the prophecies of the suffering servant, could Yahusha then return and fulfill the prophecies of conquering king known as "Messiah ben David". King David was a forerunner or prototype (*physical to spiritual parallel*) of the eternal Righteous King. Like David, Yahusha would return, vanquish the enemies of Yahuah, set up the Kingdom of Yahuah, and be a righteous ruler after Yahuah's own heart.

At this time, 6000 years into the Plan of Yahuah defined by **the Sabbath Covenant,** Yahusha has fulfilled the prophecies of the suffering servant or **Messiah ben Joseph** but has yet (it is not time) to fulfill the prophecies of the conquering king.   That time is now imminent.

Speaking to his disciples on the importance and meaning of being a servant, Yahusha instructed his disciples:

> **Luke 22**
> ²⁴ A dispute also arose among them as to which of them was considered to be greatest. ²⁵ Yahusha said to them, "the kings of the Gentiles <u>lord it over them</u>; and those who exercise authority over them call themselves benefactors. ²⁶ <u>**But you are not to be like that. Instead, the greatest among you should be like the youngest**</u>, and <u>the one who rules like the one who serves</u>. ²⁷ <u>**For who is greater, the one who is at the table or the one who serves?**</u> Is it not the one who is at the table? <u>**But I am among you as one who serves.**</u> ²⁸ You are those who have stood by me in my trials. ²⁹ And I confer on you a kingdom (through inheritance), just as my Father conferred one on me (as the first born son), ³⁰ so that you may eat and drink at my table in my kingdom and sit on thrones, judging the twelve tribes of Israel.

The Apostle Sha'ul discussed this same topic expressing that the "heir", although destined to be master of all, <u>must first be a servant</u>.

Galatians 4:1-7

1 Now I say, That the heir (Yahusha and all the sons are heirs of Yahuah), as long as he is a child (not properly trained), is no different from a servant, **though he be master of all**

Yahusha demonstrated the love of a true King

Yahusha understood that in order to rule as King, he must not only be willing to serve those whom he would govern, but also demonstrate perfect love for them.   Yahusha explained that type of love:

John 15

[12] My command is this: Love each other as I have loved you. [13] Greater love has no one than this: to lay down one's life for one's friends.

The Apostle Sha'ul addresses this concept as well.   He stresses how RARE it is for one man to die for a Righteous man.   He then says that it is almost inconceivable for a man to die for a "good person".   But it is the highest expression of love for a man to die for a sinner:

Romans 5

[6] You see, at just the right time, when we were still powerless, Yahusha died for the ungodly. [7] Very rarely will anyone die for a righteous person, though for a good person someone might possibly dare to die. [8] But Yahuah demonstrates (John 3:16) his own love for us (by giving His first born son) in this: While we were still sinners, Yahusha died for us.

Yahusha had to demonstrate he could be trusted with great wealth

When we think of Yahusha, we envision he was a poor carpenter's son because that is what we are taught in Christianity. If you are reading this book, you should have already read the 4th book in this series **Melchizedek and the Passover Lamb**. In that book I reveal the true lineage of Yahusha. Yahusha was the product of an arranged marriage between Joseph and Miriam who were both considered Royalty in Israel at that time.

Joseph was a prince from the Royal Davidian Line and considered one of the young "Lions of Judah". Miriam was a princess; the grand-daughter of the Zadok High Priest Yahusha III on her mother's side and was the granddaughter of Prince Mattathias and Princess Alexandra II (Ester of Jerusalem) on her father's Eli's side. Miriam's father was Heli ben Mattat or Prince Alexander Helios III (Eli).

The reason Yahusha was living a simple life of a carpenter was because he and his mother Miriam were literally being held in protective custody of the Temple from King Herod's wrath where Yahseph, the father of Yahusha, had "sent them away" when he discovered Miriam was with child. Yahseph (Joseph) sent them to live with Elizabeth who herself was living in protective custody. The life they were living in protective custody had nothing to do with their wealth as they all were Jewish Royalty (that is why King Herod wanted them all dead, they all were a threat to Herod's Throne).

That brings me to the Prophet Daniel and the "Babylonian Wise Men" who delivered a King's Ransom to Yahusha at his home. The "Christian" tradition of the 3 wise men at the manger is totally unscriptural. Not only were there not just 3, but they didn't deliver that wealth to Yahusha in a manger.

Let's look a little closer at exactly what transpired to understand the inheritance Yahusha received from the Prophet Daniel:

- Daniel was a young Jewish man, was made a eunuch (castration)

- Daniel was given a Babylonian name of Belteshazzar

- Daniel served under Nebuchadnezzar, Belshazzar, Darius, and Cyrus

- Daniel was given charge over the Chaldeans (Semitic wise men/astronomers) of whom many where Jews

- Daniel was visited by the Angel of Yahuah, *Gabriel*, and given many revelations concerning future events and of the coming of the Messiah

Daniel rose to such prominence in the Babylonian Court that he amassed a fortune. He rose to the position of 3rd Ruler in all of Babylon and was the King of the Chaldeans:

Daniel 5:29-30
Then commanded Belshazzar, and they clothed Daniel with scarlet, and put a chain of gold about his neck, and made a proclamation concerning him, that he should be the third ruler in the kingdom. {30} In that night was Belshazzar the king of the Chaldeans slain.

Daniel was so prominent in Babylon; he was literally favored above all and was set over the King's entire realm!

Daniel 6:3
Then this Daniel was preferred above the presidents and princes, because an excellent spirit was in him; and the king thought to set him over the whole realm.

Daniel was a very wealthy "King" by the time of his death. Since Daniel was a eunuch he **_had no son_** to pass on his inheritance. Knowing his Messiah would one day be born in Bethlehem, Daniel gave instructions to his Jewish Chaldean astronomers (whom Daniel trained) to secure and save his inheritance until the sign of the "Coming of the King" in the heavens was revealed. The executors of Daniel's will (*the school of Chaldean Astronomers trained by Daniel*), 500 hundred years later, saw this "sign in the heavens" and began to prepare to deliver Daniel's treasure to the child born "King of the Jews" in Israel.

> The wealth of Babylon, was delivered to the King of the Nazarenes!

500 hundred years after the death of Daniel, Daniel's treasure finally reappears in Scripture with the Chaldean "wise men" at Yahseph's (Joseph) and Miriam's (Mary's) home **in Judea**. It doesn't show up in a manger in Bethlehem (*oh how tradition lies*)...

Matthew 2:11
And when they were come into the house (of Joseph and Mary) they saw the young child with Miriam his mother, and fell down, and worshipped him: and when they had opened their treasures, they presented unto him gifts; gold, and frankincense, and myrrh.

Yahusha was about 2 years old at this time. We don't know the extent of the estate of Prince Yahseph and Princess Miriam (Joseph and Mary). We don't know the extent of Daniel's Estate that was given to the Messiah as an inheritance since Daniel had no family. We can rightfully deduce, however, that Yahusha was FAR FROM POOR but a very wealthy prince of Israel.

The point here is that in lieu of Yahusha's great wealth, that rivaled that of a King... we know nothing about it and assume he was poor. Yahusha could have, as was the practice of the Jews at that time, PURCHASED his place in the Temple inner circle from Rome. Instead, Yahusha demonstrated a simple life of a poor servant proving his worthiness to rule in the face of great wealth.

Yahusha mastered Yahuah's Righteousness

As I pointed out in the 4th book in this series, *Melchizedek and the Passover Lamb*, Yahusha studied under his elder cousin (and High Priest of Israel) John the Baptist. John was the leader of the Nazarene's who were considered "Keepers of the Law".

Nazarenes were a sect among the Jews in Israel who followed John the Baptist at the time Yahusha lived. Under John's direction, the Nazarenes (knowing the prophecies of Daniel concerning the timing of the Messiah's coming) bathed in the Mikveh daily in expectation of the Messiah's arrival.

Yahusha and many of his disciples were first followers of John the Baptist and were all... Nazarenes. When John consecrated Yahusha as his successor, his followers then followed Yahusha "the Nazarene" and accepted him as the Messiah.

Nazarenes were spoken of as guardians of the Torah, Prophets, and Messiah. It is a mistranslation in our Bibles where it says "Jesus of Nazareth". Not only is his name not Jesus, not only did the town of Nazareth not exist then, but the terms "sect of the Nazarenes" and "Yahusha of Nazareth" are the same. They both employ the adjective *nasraya* or Notsri meaning branch, which is referring to the prophecy in Isaiah concerning the Branch and prophecy of Zachariah concerning the Branch. The English word "Nazarene" (Greek Nazaraios," Aramaic "Natsraya," or Hebrew "Notsri") comes from the Hebrew word netser (branch), which itself is derived from the verb natsar which means "to guard, watch, keep, or preserve." in context speaking of the Torah.

Yahusha was indeed a Notsri and keeper of the Torah. That is why he was called <mark>Yahusha the Nazarene</mark>.

For more see my book **The Nazarene**.

Yahusha studied under John and was a Nazarene or "keeper of the Law" who was trained by John "to guard, watch, keep, or preserve" the Torah.   When the time presented itself, Yahusha clearly proclaimed he did NOT abolish the Torah (Law and Prophets) but actually brought them to their fullest meaning and intent spiritually:

> **Matthew 5**
> [17] "<u>Do not think that I have come to abolish the Law or the Prophets; I have not come to abolish them but to fulfill them</u>. [18] For truly I tell you, until heaven and earth disappear, not the smallest letter, not the least stroke of a pen, will by any means disappear from the Law until everything is accomplished. [19] Therefore anyone who sets aside one of the least of these commands and teaches others accordingly will be called least in the kingdom of heaven, but whoever practices and teaches these commands will be called great in the kingdom of heaven. [20] For I tell you that unless your righteousness surpasses that of the Pharisees and the teachers of the law, you will certainly not enter the kingdom of heaven.

The Yahushaic Covenant is defined by the Law.

> **Hebrews 10:16**
> This is the covenant I will make with them after that time, says Yahuah. I will put my laws in their hearts, and I will write them on their minds.

the Law was transposed to serve Yahusha as High Priest/Righteous Judge/King.

Hebrews 7:12

"for when there is a transfer of the priestly office (of Levi to Melchizedek), out of necessity there is ALSO A TRANSFER of the LAW of the priesthood (by which the Priesthood has authority)"

To be in covenant with Yahusha is to keep the Law as he did:

John 15

[9] "As the Father has loved me, so have I loved you. Now remain in my love. [10] If you keep my commands, you will remain in my love, just as I have kept my Father's commands and remain in his love."

For more see my book The Law and The Pauline Doctrine.

Yahusha possessed the Seal of Yahuah's Kingdom

The literal "seal" or "mark" on the forehead of the children of Yahuah is known as the Shema. It is literally the name of Yahuah and the knowledge that He is ONE (not a Trinity). It is the GREATEST commandment in all of the Word of Yahuah. It is required for entry into **the Kingdom of Yahuah**. I will explain the Shema or the Seal in detail in Chapter 8 of this book.

Here I want to show that Yahusha properly proclaimed the Shema and demonstrated **the Seal of the Kingdom of Yahuah** and proclaimed that it is required to attain eternal life:

> **Mark 12** - *Seal on your forehead*
> ²⁸ One of the teachers of the law came and heard them debating. Noticing that Yahusha had given them a good answer, he asked him, "Of all the commandments, which is the most important?" ²⁹ "The most important one," answered Yahusha, "is this: 'Hear, O Israel: Yahuah our Elohim, Yahuah is one Elohim!"
>
> **John 17:3**
> Now this (the knowledge that Yahuah is the only true Elohim, the Shema) is eternal life: that they know you, the only true Elohim, and (be in covenant with) Yahusha the Messiah, whom you have sent.

Yahusha faithfully carries "the standard"

I will fully explain the Sign of **the Kingdom of Yahuah** in Chapter 9 of this book. **The Sign of the Kingdom of Yahuah is the keeping of the Sabbath.**

Yahusha kept the Sabbath and repeatedly taught on the Sabbath:

> **Mark 6:2**
> And when the Sabbath had come, He began to teach in the synagogue.

> **Luke 4:16**
> So he came to Nazareth, where he had been brought up. And as his custom was, he went into the synagogue on the Sabbath day, and stood up to read.

> **Luke 6:6**
> Now it happened on another Sabbath, also, that he entered the synagogue and taught.

> **Luke 13:10**
> Now he was teaching in one of the synagogues on the Sabbath.
>
> **Luke 4:31**
> Then he went down to Capernaum, a city of Galilee, and was teaching them on the Sabbaths.

In fact, Yahusha understood **the Sabbath Covenant** and that he would return to rule as King to fulfill the Sabbath Covenant in the 7th prophetic day or 7th Millennium known as the Millennial Reign:

Mark 2:27-28

And he said to them, "the Sabbath was made for man, and not man for the Sabbath. Therefore the Son of Man is also King of the Sabbath.

Yahusha was obedient to the ritual of Yahuah called "Mikveh"

In my book, **Melchizedek and the Passover Lamb**, I go into detail concerning the Mikveh (Baptism) of Yahusha by John. Mikveh, is the ritual cleansing of sin defined in the Law whereby Yahuah washes away our sin. It is a requirement of salvation.

The Mikveh of Yahusha was also the process by which he was anointed High Priest and Passover Lamb by John, the outgoing High Priest of Israel.

Matthew 3:13-15

> 13 Then Yahusha came from Galilee to the Jordan to be Mikveh'd by John. 14 But John tried to deter him, saying, "I need to be Mikveh'd by you, and do you come to me?" 15 Yahusha replied, "Let it be so now; it is proper for us to do this to fulfill all requirements in the Law." Then John consented.

After Yahusha was Mikveh'd by John he fled into the wilderness to seek Yahuah's confirmation. We see a vision of Yahusha after being in the desert for 40 days in Zachariah 3.

We see Yahuah confirm that Yahusha was in fact the Messiah and High Priest:

> **Zechariah 3** - *Garments for the High Priest, Yahusha*
> 1 Then he showed me Yahusha **the high priest** standing before the angel of Yahuah, and Satan standing at his right side to accuse him. 2 Yahuah (through His proxy the Angel before whom stood Yahusha and Satan) said to Satan, "Yahuah rebuke you, Satan! Yahuah, who has chosen Jerusalem, rebuke you! Is not this man **a burning stick snatched from the fire?**" 3 Now Yahusha was dressed in filthy clothes (metaphor of sin) as he stood before the angel. 4 The angel said to those who were standing before him, "Take off his filthy clothes." Then Yahuah said to Yahusha, "See (after taking off his filthy rags), I have taken away **your sin** (fifthly rags Isaiah 64:6, it is through Mikveh that sin is ritually washed away by Yahuah), and I will put fine garments (of the High Priest) on you." 5 Then I said, "Put a clean turban (of the High Priest) on his head." So they put a clean turban on his head and clothed him (in the garments of the High Priest), while the angel of Yahuah

stood by. 6 The angel of Yahuah gave this charge to Yahusha: 7 "This is what Yahuah Almighty says (again Yahuah speaking through His proxy Angel): 'If (Yahuah makes a conditional promise) you will walk in obedience to me and keep my requirements (the Torah), **then** (here is the promise if he keeps the Torah and obeys the Will of Yahuah) you will **govern** my house (i.e. King over creation) and have charge of my courts (Eternal Judge), and I will give you a place (right hand of Yahuah) among these standing here.   8 "'Listen, High Priest Yahusha, you and your associates seated (who came) before you (probably Adam, Enoch, Moses, Elijah, etc.), **who (those seated before him) are men symbolic of things to come (Physical to spiritual parallels)**: I am going to bring (you) my servant (from this point forward), **the Branch** (he is the Messiah). 9 See, the stone I have set in front of Yahusha! There are seven eyes on that one stone, and I will engrave an inscription on it,' says Yahuah Almighty, '**and I will remove the sin of this land in a single day** (the day Yahusha, in obedience, dies as Passover Lamb).

But, when did this vision occur in Yahusha's life? It occurred just after John the High Priest consecrated (through Mikveh) Yahusha as High Priest in succession. The ritual of Mikveh washed away his prior life and as Yahuah said, "He had taken away his sin" and removed the sin of the world (dirty rags) from him. Yahusha then fled into the desert like the scapegoat. After spending 40 days/nights in the desert sun *starving to death*, Yahusha literally looks like a "***burning stick snatched from the fire***" of the desert sun.

Now, after just being cleansed of sin through Mikveh (baptism), Yahusha is stripped of his "filthy rags" or sin of the world, and clothed in the garments of a High Priest. Yahusha was literally **by blood** the successor to John the Baptist who succeeded High Priest Yahusha III who restored the House of Zadok to the Office of High Priest in the Second Temple.

Yahuah then declares "**See (*as I promised you in the Torah concerning Mikveh*), I have taken away your sin, and put fine garments on you**". And then it goes on to describe the garments of the High Priest that were put on Yahusha.

Then Yahuah tells Yahusha to "**listen**" because Yahuah would bring about (in Yahusha) his servant, **the Branch *(obvious reference to the Messiah)***, in other words Yahuah would make **THIS** High Priest His Messiah! And if Yahusha "***will walk in obedience to me and keep my requirements* (the Torah)*, then you will govern my house and have charge of my courts, and I will give you a place among these standing here***". This is an "if... then..." statement. **If** Yahusha will keep the Torah, **then** Yahuah will engrave in stone that He (Yahuah) will *"**remove the sin of this land in a single day**"* because of Yahusha's piety.

The Apostle Sha'ul taught the exact same "conditional" role, that Yahuah heard Yahusha BECAUSE of his piety (obedience to the Law) not because Yahusha was the second member of a pagan Babylonian Trinity as we have been taught:

> **Hebrews 5:7**
> During the days of Yahusha's life on earth (as a human), he offered up prayers and petitions with fervent cries and tears to the one (Yahuah) who could save him from death,

and he was heard (by Yahuah as Yahuah promised in Zachariah 3) because of his reverent submission/piety (obedience to the Law).

So Yahusha, through reverent obedience **to the Torah** would become qualified as the Ruling Zadok through inheritance; he then could offer himself up as the first born son and proper sacrifice for sin. Doing away with the yearly "substitute" of a physical lamb (physical to spiritual parallel), and fulfilling the prophetic portrait of Abraham sacrificing Isaac (physical to spiritual parallel), but this time with no substitute! Yahuah actually sacrificed His first born.

Yahuah is My Strength – the Creation of the King!

Isaiah 12 - *Yahuah Is My Strength and My Song*
1 You will say in that day:
"I will give thanks to you, O Yahuah,
 for though you were angry with me,
your anger turned away,
 that you might comfort me.
2 "Behold, Yahuah is my salvation (Yahu'sha);
 I will trust, and will not be afraid;
for Yahuah Elohim is my strength and my song,
 and he has become my salvation (fulfilling His word to send a Messiah)."
3 With joy you will draw water from the wells of salvation.
4 And you will say in that day:
"Give thanks to Yahuah,
 call upon (or cry out to 'shua') his name (Yah'shua),
make known his deeds among the peoples,
 proclaim that his name is exalted.
5 "Sing praises to yahuah, for he has done gloriously;
 let this be made known in all the earth (he sets a sign among the nations).
6 Shout, and sing for joy, O inhabitant of Zion (Remnant Israel in exile among the nations),
 for great in your midst is the Holy **One** of Israel (Yahuah is ONE, not a bi-entity or a Trinity, the Shema)."

So we see in this prophecy many interesting things, which I would like to discuss. Many times we just "read over" the scriptures, especially the prophetic word that came from Yahuah through the mouths of His prophets. We are not going to make that critical error today, we are going to do as David did, that endeared David to the heart of Yahuah, meditate on His Word (Psalms 1:2). As sons of Yahuah, we are to "meditate on His word day and night" so that is what we will do here.

> **Psalm 1:2**
> but his delight is in the law of Yahuah, and on his law he meditates day and night.

> Many times, we just read over the scriptures for the sake of laying claim to the personal fame of "I have read the entire Bible!"

While that is important, it is even more important to meditate on it, seek out the context of it, and understand it from the standpoint of intent.

This chapter of Isaiah (Yesha Yahu) provides a very good opportunity for me to demonstrate the process by which prophecy should be understood... which is in context of all scriptures! There are a few things that stand out in this prophecy that I would like to address:

- Dual prophecy – speaking of Yahusha personally, and then Remnant Israel and the greater exodus
- "Yahuah is my strength" declaring "in that the day" the Messiah was created by Yahuah
- "In that day you will say" – Ages... the end of this age
- "Yahuah is my salvation" proclaiming the name of the Messiah Yahu'sha

- "call upon his name" or "cry out to Yahuah" proclaiming another version of the Messiah's name Yah'shua
- "Yahuah is my song" referring to the Song of Moses and the Lamb sung by the Elect
- "with joy you will draw water from the wells of salvation" – the Water Ceremony and the Age of Aquarius the Water Bearer
- "people of Zion" referring the Remnant Israel, His people in captivity among the nations

This prophecy, as is the case with many, is a dual prophecy. It has an application for the Messiah personally, and then for the greater family of Yahuah at the end of the age of Pisces as we enter into the Age of Aquarius (the Kingdom Age). This teaching will be controversial as I address the humanity of the Messiah, the Mazzaroth (we call Zodiac), the Ages of mankind, the two ways of writing the Messiah's name, and more. All hidden within this one Chapter of Isaiah! Let me begin by illustrating the first somewhat hidden application; the Messiah.

"You (Yahusha) will say in that day (you are created) YAHUAH ELOHIM is my strength!"

When exactly did Yahuah become the God/Elohim and strength of Yahusha? Let us examine scriptures and clearly define that exact moment when Yahusha was created by Yahuah. While this is going to be controversial, it is only so because we have elevated the image of a man as God in error (Romans 1). Yahusha was the "image" of Yahuah... the human image. Now, Yahusha is the perfect Spiritual image of his Father. In fact, we all are instructed to conform during this life to the image of Yahusha by following his human example. In doing do, we too will be resurrected into the perfect Spiritual image of our Father. Yahusha is the "first born brother" of many more sons/daughters of Yahuah to come!

> **Romans 8:29**
> 28 And we know that Yahuah causes all things to work together for good to those who love Him, to those who are called according to His purpose. 29 For those whom He foreknew, He also predestined to become conformed to the image of His Son, so that Yahusha would be the firstborn among many brethren.

> An image is not, by definition, the subject; any more than a photograph of you is actually... you! One is an "image" and the other is the source, no matter how perfect that image is... it will never be the actual source... it is an image.

In no known Universe, or language, is an "image" the source, or it would not be called an "image"! That is the very definition of "image" ... it is a likeness of (reflection of) the source... but not the source.

I am going to prove, in this teaching, that Yahuah became Yahusha's God (Elohim), Strength, and Hope... when he was created human in his mother's womb; just like every other human being. I will also show, that Yahusha claimed to be nothing more than a human being 87 times before his resurrection, we just won't listen to him!   We are determined to remake Yahuah in our image, and reject the true human image of Yahusha, and we say he is the source instead of the reflection/image of Yahuah.

We have believed in error that Yahusha "pre-existed" and "was co-creator" and "was the Angel of Yahuah" in the original scriptures (OT), and in fact, was a demi-god born into this Earth half man half God.   Some, even go so far as commit blasphemy against Yahuah saying He lied and broke His promise to never come to Earth as a human being by saying "Yahusha IS Yahuah in the flesh".   That is the Spirit of the False Messiah speaking, not the Ruach of Yahuah!

This "idea" is a Babylonian doctrine where Ishtar was impregnated by the "rays of the Sun" a god named "the LORD/Ba'al" and "came back to Earth as her son" Tammuz.   This is the source of this belief that has led the Christian Church to commit the Abomination of Desolation.   It is called in scripture "the Spirit of the False Messiah" which is the denial that Yahusha was simply a human being.

> **1 John 4**
> 4 Beloved, do not believe every spirit, but test the spirits to see whether they are from Yahuah, because many false prophets have gone out into the world (claiming to be the incarnation of God). 2 By this you know the Spirit of Yahuah: every spirit that confesses that Messiah Yahusha has 'come in the flesh' (an idiom for human being) is from Yahuah; 3 and every spirit that does not confess Yahusha has come in the flesh (but says the Messiah is God in any way, or the Trinity) is not from Yahuah; this is the spirit of the antichrist (or False Messiah.   The False Messiah is an

image of a man worshipped above Yahuah as 'God') ...
12 No one has seen Yahuah at any time! (Because Yahusha was not 'Yahuah in the flesh' or a demi-God in any way).

We see above, a "promise" made by Yahuah, and a challenge to all of us to remember that He is not a human, and will NEVER come to Earth as a man.   Any attempt to idolize the Messiah by claiming He is "Yahuah in the flesh" or was a god in any way... is elevating the "image of a man who died" in our hearts as "God" above Yahuah, and is forbidden (see Romans 1).

Some translations of Numbers 23:19 say 'human being' and others say 'son of man'.   That is because they are the same thing, 'son of man' and 'came in the flesh' are Hebrew Idioms for 'human being' born to two human parents.

Yahusha was a human being, who repented before John at his Mikveh (baptism)

So we Yahuah will never come to Earth as a man and would never repent. That He is perfect and invisible. We also know Yahusha's favorite title for himself (no matter what we think he was) was 'son of man'. 87 times he outright declared he was a 'human being'! The son of his Earthly father Yahsep (yes, Miriam was a virgin, but Yahuah used Yahseph's seed in the miracle just like He did Isaac, Sampson, Jeremiah, and John the Immerser... all born miraculous births OUTSIDE of sexual intercourse... and Yahuah used the seed of their fathers! Yahuah would not violate the order of His Own Creation).

Yahusha, we know, went to John the Immerser to be baptized for repentance of sin (that was John's commission, to set the path straight for the Messiah), to fulfill all righteousness through the ritual of Mikveh. In other words, for the Messiah to begin his ministry as High Priest of Israel (being the great grandson of Yahusha III, the last Zadok High Priest), he had to have "his sin washed away" to fulfill all righteousness in him, so that as High Priest he could walk and know no sin. I know, we all have been misled to believe Yahusha was a "perfect god" from birth. Let's see what scripture says!

> **Hebrews 4:15**
> For we do not have a HIGH PRIEST who is unable to sympathize with our weaknesses, but a HIGH PRIEST who in every respect has been tempted (Yahuah cannot be

tempted *James 1:13*; therefor Yahusha cannot be "God in the flesh") as we are, yet, as HIGH PRIEST, without sin.

So Sha'ul was correct in stating that as High Priest, Yahusha was tempted and sinned not. It is through Mikveh that we are made whole in keeping the Law before Yahuah; and we fulfill the righteous requirements of the Law. Remember, Yahuah is not a man, nor the son of man, that he should repent. Yahusha was both, and went to John for repentance of sin as John fulfilled his commission to "set the path of the Messiah straight" as his father Zechariah the priest foretold in **Luke 1:77** *"To give knowledge of salvation unto his people by the remission of their sins."* This is why Yahusha went to John! He had to be Mikveh'd in order to "fulfill all righteousness" in him, set his path strait, through Mikveh, and anoint him High Priest of Israel and transfer the sins of the world onto the shoulders of Yahusha as the scapegoat. I explain all of this in great detail in my book ***Melchizedek and the Passover Lamb***. In that book I introduce us all the REAL Messiah of Israel!

John 1
John said, "I am the voice of one crying out in the wilderness, 'Make straight the way of the Messiah,' as the prophet Isaiah said."

In Zachariah Chapter 3, we see a prophetic picture of this very day, when Yahusha was Mikveh'd by John, then fled into the desert for 40 days and 40 nights. This is where the Eternal High Priest Yahusha, the King of Kings, and the Judge is anointed directly by Yahuah after "having his sin forgiven" through Mikveh. Zachariah Chapter 3 gives us a prophetic "front row seat" in the desert, and picks up after 40 days when Yahusha is laying there starving to death, having just rejected Satan's proposal, Satan now very mad about it, and the Angel of Yahuah finally comes to him. Satan immediately turns on Yahusha and begins to accuse him before the Angel of Yahuah:

Zechariah 3 - *Garments for the High Priest, Yahusha*

1 Then he showed me Yahusha the high priest standing before the angel of Yahuah, and Satan standing at his right side to accuse him. 2 Yahuah (through His proxy the Angel before whom stood Yahusha and Satan) said to Satan, "Yahuah rebuke you, Satan! Yahuah, who has chosen Jerusalem, rebuke you! Is not this man a burning stick snatched from the fire?" 3 Now Yahusha was dressed in filthy clothes (metaphor of sin) as he stood before the angel. 4 The angel said to those who were standing before him, "Take off his filthy clothes." Then Yahuah said to Yahusha, "See (after taking off his filthy rags), I have taken away your sin (filthy rags Isaiah 64:6, it is through Mikveh that sin is ritually washed away by Yahuah), and I will put fine garments (of the High Priest) on you."
5 Then I said, "Put a clean turban (of the High Priest) on his head." So they put a clean turban on his head and clothed him (in the garments of the High Priest), while the angel of Yahuah stood by.   6 The angel of Yahuah gave this charge to Yahusha:

7 "This is what Yahuah Almighty says (again Yahuah speaking through His proxy Angel): 'If (Yahuah makes a conditional promise) you will walk in obedience to me and keep my requirements (The Torah), then (here is the promise if he keeps The Torah and obeys the Will of

Yahuah as High Priest) you will govern my house (i.e. King over creation) and have charge of my courts (Eternal Judge), and I will give you a place (right hand of Yahuah) among these standing here.   8 "'Listen, High Priest Yahusha, you and your associates seated (who came) before you (probably Adam, Enoch, Moses, Elijah, etc.), who (those seated before him) are men symbolic of things to come (Physical to spiritual parallels): I am going to bring (you) my servant (from this point forward), the Branch (he is The Messiah).

9 See, the stone I have set in front of Yahusha! There are seven eyes on that one stone, and I will engrave an inscription on it,' says Yahuah Almighty, 'and I will remove the sin of this land in a single day (the day Yahusha, in obedience, dies as Passover Lamb).

What is important here, is that there is NO REQUIREMENT for Yahusha to be "God" or to live his entire life with no sin.   In fact, it is openly stated here, that Yahusha's sin was forgiven through Mikveh when anointed High Priest by John (the outgoing High Priest).   The ONLY requirement, directly from Yahuah's mouth, is that Yahusha walk the path of HIGH PRIEST with no sin; exactly as Sha'ul declared!   If Yahusha could do that, then Yahuah would accept his life as a sin offering, and forgive the rest of the sons of Yahuah their sin.   That is why John and Yahusha said he willingly gave his life for his brothers (he is our brother not our God), there is no greater love than that!

Yahuah had made Yahusha a promise and Yahusha was following through with his end of the agreement.

1 John 3:16
By this we know love, that he laid down his life for us, and we ought to lay down our lives for the brothers.

John 15:13
Greater love has no one than this, that someone lay down his life for his friends.

Yahuah had made Yahusha a conditional promise... if he would walk sin free as High Priest in obedience to the Torah, then willingly lay down his own life out of love for his brothers... Yahuah would forgive each of us. Yahusha's life was willingly given in an act of ultimate love, it was not a human sacrifice!

You see, Yahuah is invisible and the everlasting Almighty Elohim. Yahusha was his human image/proxy and then became the first born of eternal creation, being the first fruits of the resurrection.

Colossians 1:15
The Son is the (human) image (or proxy) of the invisible Yahuah, the firstborn over all creation.

The Bible is explicitly clear that Yahusha was born 100% fully human in every way. In fact, Yahusha HAD TO BE HUMAN to make atonement, a "God" cannot atone for something a human (Adam) brought into this world.

If Yahusha was Yahuah in the flesh or a demi-god in any way... we are dead in our sins:

Hebrews 2:10-18
10 In bringing many sons and daughters to glory (not just His first born son), it was fitting that Yahuah, for whom and through whom everything exists, (Yahuah) should make the pioneer of their salvation (Yahusha) perfect through what he suffered. 11 Both the one who makes people holy (Yahuah) and those who are made holy (Yahusha and all his brother/sisters) are of the same family. So Yahusha is not ashamed to call them brothers and sisters (he is not our God, he is our elder brother, High Priest, and King). 12 He says, "I will declare your name (Yahuah) to my brothers and sisters; in the assembly I will sing your praises." 13 And again, "I (Yahusha) will put my trust in him (Yahuah)." And again he says, "Here am I (your son), and the (rest of the) children Yahuah has given me (to rule over)."   14 Since the children have flesh and blood, he too shared in their humanity (he was human too) so that by his death (the death of a man not God) he might break the power of him who holds the power of death (defeat the Law of Sin and Death)—that is, the devil— 15 and free (all who now live by the Law of the Spirit of Life) those who all their lives were held in slavery by their fear of death (we were held in slavery to the death decrees not the Law). 16 For surely it is not angels Yahusha helps, but Abraham's descendants (alone). 17 For this reason he (Yahusha) had to be made like them (he was made human just like I was), **fully human in every way** (doesn't get any clearer than that), in order that he might

become a merciful and faithful high priest (all High Priests are chosen from among men... **Hebrews 5:1**) in service to Yahuah, and that he (being a human High Priest) might make atonement for the sins of the people. 18 Because he himself (as a man not a god) suffered when he was tempted (proof he was not Yahuah, Yahuah cannot be tempted by evil), he (as a man, a human High Priest) is able to help those who are being tempted.

Yahusha was not born a "perfect" demi-god, but "perfected" through a life of tribulations as a human being (son of man). He was not born "obedient", but rather disobedient; and had to learn obedience like every other human being. He was not "Yahuah in the flesh", in fact he did not even know Yahuah, but had to grow in the knowledge of his Heavenly Father like every other human being! Yahusha became, after resurrection, not before... better than the angles. Before that, he was but human.

Hebrews 5:8-9
8 though He was a Son, yet He learned obedience (to Yahuah) by the things which He suffered. 9 And having been <u>perfected</u>, He became the author of eternal salvation to all who obey Him (Yahuah)

Luke 2:40, 52
40 And the child (Yahusha) grew and became strong in spirit, (and became) filled with wisdom; and the grace (favor) of Yahuah was upon him (the Ruach). ... 52 And Yahusha increased in wisdom and (increased in) stature, and (increased) in favor with Yahuah and men.

Hebrews 1:4
4 having become so much better than the angels, as Yahusha has by inheritance (not because he was a god) obtained a more excellent name than they.

In fact, the concept that Yahusha was somehow a God or Yahuah in the flesh, was not something he could even comprehend!

Philippians 2
5 Let this mind be in you (that Yahuah alone is the ONLY true Elohim *John 17:3*) which was also in Yahusha the Messiah, 6 who, being in the form (human image) of Yahuah, 6 who, although Yahusha existed in the (human) form (or image) of Yahuah, did not regard equality with Yahuah a thing to be grasped, 7 but made himself of no reputation, taking the form of a bondservant, and coming in the likeness of men (according to the flesh i.e. born human *Romans 1:1-6*). 8 And being found in appearance as a man (not a god or demi-god), He humbled himself (before Yahuah) and became obedient (to the will of Yahuah) to the point of death (to save his brothers), even the death of the stake.   9 Therefore (after his death) Yahuah also has highly exalted Yahusha (they are not the same being nor are they equal) and (Yahuah) has given Yahusha (upon resurrection) the name which is above every name, 10 that at the name of Yahusha every knee should bow (in respect to authority not divine worship), of those in heaven, and of those on earth, and of those under the earth, 11 and that every tongue should confess (*Strongs #3670*, homologeo, enters into a marriage covenant) that Yahusha the Messiah is our King, to the

glory of Yahuah the Father (we bow in reverent respect to Yahusha as King and through Yahusha glory i.e. worship is reflected to Yahuah the only true Elohim).--------

It should be quite obvious that the son is not the Father, he is not invisible, and he was created human (in every way) and THEN begotten eternal upon resurrection.   Prior to that, Yahusha was the "son of man" i.e. a human being.   In fact, Yahusha did not even exist prior to being formed in his mother's womb!   As I will clearly show.   Many of you reading this will simply ignore the obvious... and continue in your belief that Yahusha was somehow, some way a god because "a mere man could never accomplish" and fulfill the Plan of Salvation.   I put forward, that if he was a "god" how does that make his life/death meaningful in any way? A "god" would simply be unaffected by his suffering or "fake death" as a god cannot die.   This is the definition of   a god! Now, the reality that Yahusha was a human being, makes what he did exponentially more impressive!   WORTHY is the Lamb... what a demonstration of faith and love.

Isaiah 12 picture of Yahusha

Yahuah was Yahusha's "strength" ...   and Yahusha, as proxy, is the strength of Yahuah.   But "when" did Yahuah become Yahusha's strength and song/hope?   This is an important issue because as Yahusha said 87 times, he was a human being.   But many of still cling on to the pagan philosophy of god-men, and believe Yahusha to be a demi-god... not a human being; even though that is what he said over and over again.

Note: See my teaching on Incarnation a Pagan Philosophy.

But is there scripture that clarifies the prophecy in Isaiah 12 that Yahuah was Yahusha's strength beginning in the womb of his mother?   If so, can we determine exactly when Yahuah became Yahusha's "strength".   Was it at creation that Yahuah created Yahusha?   Has Yahuah always been Yahusha's strength because they are the same being?   Or, as Yahusha said 87 times, Yahuah become Yahusha's "strength" when He created Yahshua as a human being beginning in his mother's womb? **The son of man.**

Yahusha "came into being in his mother's womb"!

The answer to this age old question, as we battle back and forth trying to turn Yahuah into a man (making Him out to be a liar) and Yahusha into a demi-god against his will (remember he said he was a human being 87 times) is found it Psalms.   We find out that Yahuah became Yahusha's strength as stated in Isaiah 12 when he was created and set apart by the Holy (Set Apart) Spirit, which was upon him at his human birth.   This is "when" Yahusha was created by Yahuah and only from that point forward was Yahuah the strength of Yahusha!   Let's take a look.

The Psalm in question is Psalm 22, a clear prophecy of the coming Righteous King, who would sit on the throne of David.   King David speaks in first person for his heir to come, and declares that Yahusha's existence began when he was created human in his mother's womb.   Yahusha knew this prophecy of himself, and even quoted it on the stake when he died (fully begotten sons of Yahuah cannot die Luke 20:36)!   The fact that Yahusha died is 100% evidence that he was in no way a god!   He was, yes, the son of man a human being, hence he died.   He was not fully begotten by Yahuah's seed until he was resurrected.

Luke 20:36
for they cannot die anymore, because they are equal to angels and are sons of Yahuah, <u>being sons of the resurrection</u>.

Again we see references to both ways of writing the Messiah's name: Yahusha and Yahshua in this text (and many others).

Psalm 22
1 My God, my God, why have you forsaken me? Why are you so far from saving me, from the words of my groaning?   2 O my God, I cry (shua) by day, but you do not answer, and by night, but I find no rest. 3 Yet you are holy, enthroned on the praises of Israel. 4 In you our fathers trusted;   they trusted, and you delivered (yasha) them. 5 To you they cried (shua) and were rescued (yasha); in you they trusted and were not put to shame. 6 But I am a worm and not a man, scorned by mankind and despised by the people. 7 All who see me mock me; they make mouths at me; they wag their heads; 8 "He trusts in the Lord; let him deliver him; let him rescue him, for he delights in him!" 9 **<u>Yet you are he who took me from the womb; you made me trust you at my mother's breasts. 10 On you was I cast from my birth, and from my mother's womb you have been my God.</u>**

We see in Isaiah 12; it begins with "You will say in that day (the day of his crucifixion): I will give thanks to you, O Yahuah, for though you were angry with me, your anger turned away, that you might comfort me." This is the same perspective as we find in Psalms 22 as Yahusha felt forsaken by Yahuah.

For the sake of Isaiah 12, I want to focus on verses 9 and 10 of Psalms 22:

> 9 Yet you are He who took me from the womb (Yahuah set Yahusha apart by His Ruach as He did Sampson and John the Immerser and others when he was born, not before); you made (created) me trust you at my mother's breasts (this is when Yahusha was created). 10 On you was I cast from my birth (not before), and from my mother's womb you have been my Elohim (Yahuah was not Yahusha's Elohim before that... because he did not exist!).

You see, Yahuah was not lying when He declared He was all alone at creation, and did it all by Himself! Yahusha was not there, he wouldn't be created by Yahuah for another 4,000 years as the prophets foretold. Yahuah, speaking prophetically of the coming Messiah said the exact same thing:

Isaiah 44
> 24 "This is what Yahuah says— your Redeemer, who formed you in the womb (Psalms 22:9-10): I am Yahuah, *the Maker of all things*, who stretches out the heavens, who spreads out the earth *by myself*.

Isaiah 42
> 5 This is what Yahuah says— **He** who created the heavens and stretched them out, who spread out the earth and all that comes out of it, who gives breath to its people, and life to those who walk on it:

Isaiah 45

⁵ I am Yahuah, **and there is no other**; apart from me there is no God. ⁷ I form the light and create darkness, I bring prosperity and create disaster; I**, Yahuah, do all these things**. ¹² It is I **who made the earth and created mankind upon it**. My own hands stretched out the heavens; I marshaled their starry hosts. ¹⁸ For this is what Yahuah says— **He** who created the heavens, **He** (alone) is God; **He** who fashioned and made the earth, H**e** founded it; **He** did not create it to be empty, but formed it to be inhabited— **He** says: "I **am Yahuah, and there is no other (**God)."

Isaiah 46

⁵ "**To whom will you compare me or count me equal**? To whom will you liken me that we may be compared (not even Yahusha, there is no one)? ⁸ "Remember this, fix it in mind, take it to heart, you rebels. ⁹ Remember the former things, those of long ago; I am God, **and there is no other**; I am God, and there is none like me (not even Yahusha). ¹⁰ I make known the end from the beginning, from ancient times, what is still to come. I say: My purpose will stand, and I will do all that I please (Yahusha did the will of Yahuah not the other way around).

Isaiah 44

6 "This is what Yahuah says — Israel's King (Yahusha had not yet been installed as Yahuah's proxy King and wouldn't until the end of the Age of Pisces) and Redeemer, Yahuah Almighty: I am the Aleph and I am the Tav (unity and perfection); apart from me there is no God (don't call me

good, there is only One who is good and that is Yahuah Mark 10:18).

No matter how clear scripture is that Yahusha was born human "by the seed of David NOT Yahuah", then resurrected divine as the first born son of Yahuah by Yahuah's "seed" which is the Spirit or Ruach… we just simply will not accept this overwhelming scriptural truth. We see Sha'ul teach this crystal clear truth just before he warned us NOT to elevate the image of a man who died above Yahuah as God in our hearts (exactly what we have done, Yahusha was a human being who died, on Yahuah):

> **Romans 1**
> 1 Sha'ul, a servant1 of Christ Jesus, called to be an apostle, set apart for the gospel of Yahuah, 2 which Yahuah promised (to send a human messiah) beforehand through his prophets in the holy Scriptures, 3 concerning his (first born) Son (of the resurrection), who, Yahusha, was descended from David (the seed of man) 2 according to the flesh (an idiom for human being) 4 and Yahusha was then declared to be the Son of God (fully begotten divine) in power according to the Spirit of holiness (the seed of Yahuah) by his resurrection from the dead, Yahusha the Messiah our King…. 24 For although they knew Yahuah (was not a man **Numbers 23:19**), they did not honor Yahuah as (the only) Elohim or give thanks to Him (as creator), but they became futile in their thinking (that God had come to Earth as a man), and their foolish hearts were darkened. 22 Claiming to be wise, they became fools, 23 and exchanged the glory of the immortal Elohim, Yahuah, for images (Yahusha is the 'image' of the invisible Yahuah **Colossians 1:15**) resembling mortal man (Yahusha

declared he was a human being, the "son of man" 87 times)

We have been misled to believe that it could only take a God to come to Earth and die to save us, even though scripture clearly says that only a man can undue and atone for what a man brought into this world. Yahusha HAD TO BE HUMAN to atone for humanity. A "God" cannot make atonement for something a "God" did not do! If Yahusha was a god in anyway, we are dead in our sins! Only a human High Priest can make such atonement before Yahuah.

Hebrews 2

14 Since the children have flesh and blood (*and are held captive to the Law of Sin and Death*), he too shared in their humanity (*he was human too and captive to genetic death*) so that by his death (*the death of a human not God*) he, Yahusha, might break the power of him who holds the power of death—that is, the devil— 15 and free those who all their lives were held in slavery by their fear of death. 16 For surely it is not angels he helps, but Abraham's descendants. 17 For this reason (*to break the Law of Sin and Death*) he (*Yahusha*) had to be made like them fully human in every way, in order that he might become a merciful and faithful high priest (*who are chosen from among men*) in service to Yahuah, and that he (being a human High Priest) might make atonement for the sins of the people. 18 Because he himself (as a man, not a god) suffered when he was tempted (proof he was not Yahuah, Yahuah cannot be tempted by evil), he (as a man, a human High Priest) is able to help those who are being tempted

"From my mother's womb, you are my strength"

Let me get back to our teaching on Isaiah 12 and how Yahuah is our strength, we are discussing Psalms 22 and the fact that Yahusha was created by Yahuah from his mother's womb and not before that. Now, as if that is not crystal clear enough, there will be those who simply will not accept this clear declaration of when Yahusha was created by Yahuah. We love to cling to our own understanding even though it is a clear contradiction of explicit scripture.

> We will remake Yahuah in our own image (a man in the image of Yahusha) no matter what! We have been doing this since Tammuz in Babylon.

I will be called a "false teacher", and as I frequently am... shunned by many over this teaching when all I am doing is teaching exactly what the Bible declares about Yahusha. He as a human being, son of man, created in his mother's womb... as all men are. Let's take a deeper look into these two verses 9 & 10 in Psalms 22, as we "meditate" on His Word and seek out even deeper meaning. Some translations read:

> **Psalm 22:9-10**
> 9 But you took Me from My mother's womb, Yahuah! You made Me trust in You, even from My mother's breast. 10 I was cast upon You from My birth; from My mother's womb, **You are My Strength**.

The word-for-word Hebrew translation of Psalm 22:9-10, from
The Interlinear Hebrew-English Old Testament shows the word
'from' in these Scriptures circled below, it is Hebrew 'mem':

```
22:9 (22:10)  ki   athe  gch-i            m-btn      mbtich-i                    ol-
              that you   one-rushing-forth-of-me from-belly one-causing-to-trust-of-me on

              shdi       am-i
              breasts-of mother-of-me

22:10 (22:11) oli-k   eshlkthi     m-rchm     m-btn          am-i       al-i      athe
              on-you  I-was-flung  from-womb  from-belly-of  mother-of-me El-of-me you
```

⁹ But thou [art] he that took me out of the womb: thou didst make me hope [when I was] upon my mother's breasts.

¹⁰ I was cast upon thee from the womb: thou [art] my God from my mother's belly.

The Dictionary of Old Testament Words for English Readers, says
that the Hebrew letter circled above, *mem*, is *'prefixed to a
substantive, which denotes the preposition'*.   OK Sha'ul, we are
not Hebrew linguistic experts... put this in layman's terms
please.... Alright, let's look at **The Hebraic Tongue Restored, by
Fabre d'Olivet**, which tells us what these prepositions mean when
the Hebrew letter *'mem'* is prefixed.

> EXTRACTIVE OR PARTITIVE ARTICLE. __ The movement
> which this article expresses, with nouns or actions that it
> modifies, is that by which a noun or an action is taken for
> the means, for the instrument, by which they are divided in
> their essence, or drawn from the midst of several other
> nouns or similar actions. <u>**I render it ordinarily "by from,
> out of, by; with,   by means of, among, between, etc."**</u>

**The New World Dictionary of the American Language, Second
College Edition,** gives a complete definition of the word *'from'* in
Hebrew *'mem'* as **"*beginning at, starting with, out of*"**.
Therefore, the word translated *'from'* in Psalm 22:10, means
"beginning at, starting with".

144

Yahusha is prophetically pictured through King David to say that; *"Yahuah was His strength from the beginning, starting with the point Yahusha Messiah was conceived in His mother's womb"*.

> This can only mean one thing: that before Yahusha was in His mother's womb, Yahuah was not His strength, hope, or his "God", <u>because Yahusha did not yet exist</u>.

He had no need of strength, nor hope, nor a God. Yahuah was only Yahusha's strength, hope, and God, beginning at, starting with, His mother's womb.   That is the truth of scripture concerning when Yahusha's existence began.   There should be no debate, it is settled right there in the Word of Yahuah in explicit form.

The belief that Yahusha had his beginning in the womb as flesh is the Spirit of Yahuah.   The denial and belief in the incarnation and Trinity is the Spirit of the False Messiah.

Anyone who elevates the image of a man in their hearts as God above Yahuah, will be given over by Yahuah to believe a lie.   The Spirit of the False Messiah is anyone who denies that Yahusha was a mere man (came in the flesh) beginning with, started at the time he was conceived in his mother's womb.

1 John 4
1 Beloved, do not believe every spirit, but test the spirits to see whether they are from Yahuah, because many false prophets have gone out into the world (claiming to be the incarnation of God). 2 By this you know the Spirit of Yahuah: every spirit that confesses that Messiah Yahusha

has **_come in the flesh_** (a human being, son of man) is from Yahuah; 3 and every spirit that does not confess Yahusha has **_come in the flesh_** (but says Yahusha is a demi-god, or Yahuah in the flesh) is not from Yahuah; this is the spirit of the antichrist ...   12 No one has seen Yahuah at any time! (Because Yahusha was not Yahuah in the flesh or a demi-god).

What does "come in the flesh" and "according to the flesh" mean?

We see in 1 John 4 above that Yahusha had *"come in the flesh"*. We see this every time Yahusha's creation, or when he was born or manifested (all mean the same thing), is mentioned Scripture reveals that he came in the **_"flesh"_**. That knowledge is so key, that you cannot be saved if you deny it!   It is literally THE fundamental understanding of The Plan of Salvation.   So we better understand what the scripture is telling us.   We see again in 2 John that the denial that Yahusha *"came according to the flesh"* is a deceiving Spirit of the False Messiah:

> **2 John 1:7**
> For many deceivers are entered into the world, that do not confess that Yahusha the Messiah **_is come in the flesh_** (g4561 'sarki' – merely of human origin).   This is a deceiver and an antichrist.

The word _**flesh**_ means... natural/physical origin (not Spiritual), born of natural origin ONLY, mere human/natural birth only... APART FROM DIVINE INFLUENCE...

> g4561 '**sarki**'   - Thayer:
> 2a) the body of a man
> 2b) used of natural or physical origin, generation or relationship
> 2b1) born of natural generation
> 4) the flesh, denotes mere human nature, **the earthly nature of man apart from divine influence, and therefore prone to sin and opposed to God**

There is the proof!   Yahusha was not only NOT Yahuah in the flesh (that is impossible per the definition of 'flesh' is outside Divine Influence), but Yahusha was not born from any "divine influence" or "divine seed" of Yahuah at all!   He was totally human born apart from any divine influence, and therefore prone to sin and APPOSED TO GOD.   Just like every other human being.

> He was born 100% human, 0% Divine upon his human birth.   He would later be born again upon Mikveh, fill with the full measure of deity in his body when the Spirit descended upon him, and the begotten Divine through resurrection.

Exactly like each and every other son/daughter of Yahuah. Yahusha is **The Way** NOT the exception to **The Way**.   It just does not get any clearer that this...

Romans 1

2 which Yahuah promised beforehand through His prophets in the Holy Scriptures (he was foretold, predetermined, predestined... did not pre-exist), 3 regarding His Son, who was a descendant of David according to flesh (outside of any Divine influence), 4 and who through the Spirit of holiness (this is Yahuah's seed) was declared (Divine) with power to be the Son of Yahuah by His resurrection from the dead: Yahusha the Messiah

---

Born human... begotten Divine!   Yahusha is The Way... not the exception to The Way. We are all born human... and will be begotten Divine.

When looking at Isaiah Chapter 12 as a prophecy concerning the coming Messiah, In verse 2 we read "Behold, Yahuah is my salvation; I will trust, and not be afraid; for Yahuah Elohim is my strength (beginning when I was created human in my mother's womb Psalms 22) and my song and he has become my salvation (when He resurrected me from the grave Romans 1:4)".   Now let us look at this prophecy in Isaiah Chapter 12 from the second prophetic viewpoint; Remnant Israel at the end of the age of Pisces.

the Kingdom

In that day you will say "Behold! Yahusha"

Now I want to show how this prophecy in Isaiah 12 points to Yahusha at the end of this Age, as Remnant Israel enters the Kingdom Age of Aquarius. In my book Creation Cries Out! I fully define the ages of mankind as foretold in the Heavenly Scroll called the Mazzaroth in the Bible. We know it today as the Enoch Zodiac.

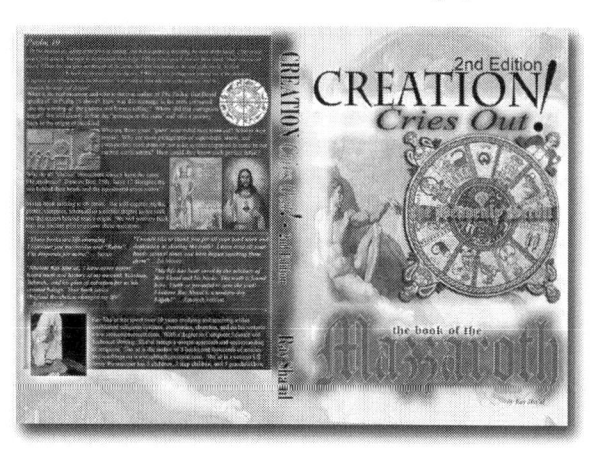

The Ages begin with Adam and Eve in the Age of Gemini and progress every 2000 years culminating in the Age of Aquarius the Water Bearer...

Every 2000 years a major event occurs during the transition of the Ages. These

Ages & Epochs of Mankind
The Heavenly Scroll of Enoch

Heavenly Scroll
The Heavenly Scroll is held by the living creature over the Age of Gemini/creation of man... and ends with the position of the next "living creature" over the Age of Aquarius/The Sabbath Kindgom!

149

events are heralded by what Yahusha called *"the sign of the son of man"* in the *"sky"*. The Hebrew word for *"sky"* in **Shamayim** which means *"visible place in the sky where the stars are located"* referring to the Mazzaroth. This *"sign in the Mazzaroth/Zodiac"* is described in great detail in Revelation Chapter 12. It is a sign in the constellation Virgo giving birth to a child/king (the King planet Jupiter).

In my book **Creation Cries Out! The Mazzaroth**, I explain how the transition from the Age of Taurus to the Age of Aries was marked by the *"sign of the son of man"* in the sky, that heralded the birth of Abraham. Then that same sign appeared in the sky 2000 years later at the transition of Aries to Pisces, and heralded the birth of Yahusha. Then I demonstrate that same sign appears in the sky again in 2017 on the Feast of Trumpets to herald the transition to the Age of Aquarius, the Kingdom Age.

The prophecy in Isaiah Chapter 12 is speaking in a dual nature both of the *"that day"* when Yahusha was born in his mother's womb on the cusp, and *"that day"* he returns on the cusp of the Age of Aquarius… the water bearer. So let us take a look at this prophecy a little closer.

We know that *"in that day"*, spoken of by Isaiah, when we will *"draw water from the wells of salvation"* is specifically talking about the Age of Aquarius the Water Bearer. Yahusha made this clear as well. Knowing the Plan of Salvation written in the Heavenly Scroll, Yahusha was well aware of the Sabbath Covenant and meaning of 2000 year ages. He knew he would not return until the end of the Age of Pisces 2000 years later.

Matthew 28:20
teaching them to observe all that I have commanded you. And behold, I am with you always, to the end of the Age (of Pisces)."

Isaiah tells us that *"in that day you will say behold! Yahuah is my salvation"* and *"you draw water from the wells of salvation"* and *"proclaim unto all the Earth that the Holy One of Israel has delivered Zion out of the nations"*. This is speaking of the end of this age (*Pisces*) and the beginning of the Age of Aquarius, when the Messiah returns as the Lion (*Leo*) of the Tribe of Judah and defeats the serpent (*Serpens*)... exactly as foretold in the Heavenly Scroll! John the Revelator revealed this fulfillment in the Book of Revelation as he too was given a vision of The Heavenly Scroll and the fulfillment of it.

Revelation 5 - *The Opening of the Scroll of the Mazzaroth*
5 Then I saw in the right hand of the one who was seated on the throne a scroll written on the front and back (3D scroll of heavenly pictographs) and sealed with seven seals (the 7 visible planets were seen as seals over The Heavenly Scroll, also the 7 lampstand Heavenly Menorah). 2 And I saw a powerful angel proclaiming in a loud voice: "Who is worthy to open the (Heavenly) scroll and to break its seals?" 3 But no one in heaven or on earth or under the earth was able to open the scroll or look into it (because it speaks of only 1 man). 4 So I began weeping bitterly because no one was found who was worthy to open the scroll or to look into it. 5 Then one of the elders said to me, "Stop weeping! Look (at The Heavenly Scroll and understand the pictograph of Leo), the Lion of the tribe of

Judah, the root of David, has conquered (the serpent which is the meaning of Leo); thus (because he has fulfilled the scroll) he can open the scroll and (break) its seven seals (and read it, proving he alone is the one of whom it speaks. That testimony destroys all other demi-gods specifically the image of Jesus Christ)."

We see in this chapter of Isaiah a direct reference to the name of the coming Messiah who will return and deliver "Zion" at that time. The name of the Messiah is a compound sentence name. That sentence or expression that the name of the Messiah proclaims is "Yahuah is my salvation". Yahseph and Miriam were instructed to name their child Yahusha for "Yahuah will save His people from their sin".

Yahu'sha is a contraction of the two Hebrew words 'Yahuah Yasha' or Yahuah Salvation. It is contracted with the short poetic form of Yahuah or 'Yahu' combined with the word for salvation 'yasha'... YAHUah+yaSHA = Yahu'sha. Meaning "Yahuah is my salvation".

So anytime you see the phrase "Yahuah is my salvation" you can replace that phrase with its contracted form, Yahu'sha, without changing the meaning of the sentence.

> So in Isaiah Chapter 12 we read that "*in that day (at the end of the Age) you will say 'Behold! Yahusha*"... pointing directly to the name of the Messiah and King.

Yahusha was TRANSPOSED into *the Kingdom of Yahuah*

Now that we know Yahusha was created and his existence began like every other human being, in his mother's womb; we must understand what "resurrection" truly is. It is the transposition of our physical bodies into our spiritual bodies and our literal "birth" as sons of Yahuah into His Kingdom. Yahusha was literally the first son of Yahuah to be perfected in life through training and transposed into **the Kingdom of Yahuah**. The Apostle Sha'ul summed this up very well:

> **Romans 1**
> 1 Sha'ul, a servant of Yahusha the Messiah, called to be an apostle and set apart for the gospel of Yahuah (which is the Kingdom of Yahuah)— 2 the gospel He (Yahuah) promised beforehand through his prophets in the Holy Scriptures (the Torah and Prophets ARE the Holy Scriptures) 3 regarding his Son (who would by example set the Way into that kingdom), who as to his earthly life was a descendant of David (a human being or "son of man"), 4 and who, through the Spirit of holiness (the seed of Yahuah) was appointed the Son of Yahuah in power *by his resurrection from the dead*: Yahusha the Messiah our King (Yahusha was born human the son of Joseph and Mary. Yahusha was appointed the son of Yahuah by the resurrection).

Hebrews 1:1-4

1 In the past (6 covenants) Yahuah spoke to our ancestors through the prophets at many times and in various ways, 2 but in these last days (in **the Yahushaic Covenant**) Yahuah has spoken to us by his Son (Moses called Yahusha the greatest prophet of all who would properly teach the Law), whom Yahuah <u>appointed</u> (through resurrection) heir of all things, and for whom also Yahuah made the Universe (this is Yahuah's purpose). 3 The Son is the radiance (reflection) of Yahuah's glory and the exact representation of Yahuah's being (Yahusha was transposed into the full image of Yahuah as His literal son), upholding all things (as King) by Yahuah's powerful word (the Law). After he had provided purification for sins, he sat down at the right hand of the Majesty in **the Kingdom of Yahuah**. 4 So he became (after his transposition and birth as a elohim in the exact representation of Yahuah's being) as much superior to the angels as the name he has inherited is superior to theirs.

Chapter 5

The Plan of Salvation through a Mediating High Priest

The Mediator and the "New Bride"

There is a vital disconnect in the family of Yahuah in these last days. A misunderstanding of the Plan of Salvation. We are being taught that Yahuah had to come to Earth as a man and die! This is necessary (*so they say*), because of His own Law preventing a husband from remarrying the same bride. Only the death of the husband releases Yahuah from this "Law". The problem is, not only is it impossible for an Eternal being to die (that is what makes Him a God and eternal in the first place, but Yahuah made a vow never to come to Earth as a man. He swore He would never break that vow... and swore twice for emphasis! Yahuah does not break His vows so we have a problem!

> **Hosea 11**
> 9 I will not carry out my fierce anger, nor will I devastate Ephraim again. For I am Yahuah, and not a man

> **Numbers 23:19**
> 19 "Yahuah is not a man, that He should lie, Nor a son of man (*Yahusha is called the son of man 87 times*), that He should repent (*Yahusha went to Yahchanan to be Mikveh'd for remission of sin*); Has He said (*He would never come to Earth as a man*), and will He not do it (*keep this vow*)? Or has He spoken, and will He not make it good (*on His promises*)?

In Numbers 23:19, Yahuah made a vow saying He was not a man nor the son of man (*an idiom for human being*), then He proclaimed "will He not do it (*fulfill His vow not to come to Earth as a man*), and will He not make it good (*on this vow*). Yahusha's favorite title <u>for himself</u> was "son of man", saying he was a human being. 87 times Yahusha declared to us he was not a god, he was a human being. Yahusha, the son of man, went to Yahchanan to be Mikveh'd for "remission of sin" in other words <u>to fulfill all righteousness</u> in him, bringing him to perfection. Yahuah clearly denied incarnation as did Yahusha on many occasions. Yahuah is the Father and God of Yahusha, so says scripture on many occasions. So Yahuah <u>did not come to Earth as a man</u>, break His vows, and die (*impossible for a God*). We need only to listen to our elder brother speak these very simply truths:

> **John 20:17**
> Yahusha said, "Do not hold on to me, for <u>I have not yet ascended to the Father</u>. Go instead to <u>my brothers</u> and tell them, 'I am ascending <u>to my Father and your Father, to my God and your God</u>.'"

The Plan of Salvation that was first written in the stars, then prophesied to come was through a human being who would be perfected then risen Diving to MEDIATE between Yahuah and mankind.

> **John 17:3 3**
> Now this is eternal life: that they know you (*Yahuah*), <u>the only true God</u>, and (*come to You through*) Yahusha (*the Mediator*) who is the Messiah (*Anointed King of Israel*),

whom you have sent (*in fulfillment of Your promises as foretold through the prophets*).

1 Timothy 2:5
For there is one God (*Yahuah*) and <u>one mediator</u> between Yahuah and mankind, ***the man*** (*not the God*) Yahusha the Messiah!

The Plan of Salvation through a Mediator

I want to quickly summarize the meaning of The Plan of Salvation, and *how* Yahuah has provided for the salvation of His children. It was never prophesied or promised that Yahuah would come to Earth and die. That is "another Gospel message" than the one preached by the Prophets, Yahusha, and his disciples! Those who preach incarnation are to be cursed for blaspheming The Most High!

> **Galatians 1**
>
> 6 I am astonished that you are so quickly deserting the one (*Yahuah*) who called you to live in the grace of The Yahushaic Covenant, and are turning to a different gospel— 7 which is really no gospel at all. Evidently some people are throwing you into confusion (*with incarnation*) and are trying to pervert the gospel of Yahusha the Messiah (*that he was a human being 1 John 4*). 8 But even if we or an angel from heaven should preach a gospel other than the one we preached to you, let them be under Yahuah's curse! 9 As we have already said, so now I say again (*for emphasis*): If anybody is preaching to you a gospel other than what you accepted, let them be under Yahuah's curse!

Those who teach incarnation are cursed for calling Yahuah a liar, saying **He broke His vow** never to come to Earth as a man in Numbers 23:19.

> **John 5:1-20**

> This is the conquering Spirit (*of Yahuah*) that has overcome the world, even our faith (*in the promises of Yahuah*). 5 Who is it that overcomes the world? <u>Only the one who believes that Yahusha is the son of Yahuah</u> (*not Yahuah in the flesh*) ... Whoever believes in the Son of Yahuah (*and denies incarnation*) accepts this testimony (*that Yahusha was born (water) by the seed of David (bloodline) and begotten diving through resurrection by the Spirit of Holiness... water, blood, and Spirit* **Romans 1:2-3**). Whoever does not believe Yahuah (*that Yahuah is not a man nor the son of man*) **has made Yahuah out to be a liar** (*saying Yahuah came to Earth as a man*), because they have not believed the testimony Yahuah has given about his Son (*that he was born human, inherited the title Melchizedek, and begotten divine*).

More on the testimony of water, blood, and spirit later.   Yes, Yahuah married both The House of Israel and the House of Judah. We read how both houses were unfaithful to Yahuah, and by Law He issued them a certificate of divorce.   This was part of the Plan of Salvation to illustrate that we cannot be in a direct marriage covenant with Yahuah, and create a "need" for the Messiah to mediate a "New Covenant" where he is the Bridegroom and we are Yahusha's Bride.   Yahuah then had His prophets foretell of a Messiah, a Mediator, whom Yahuah would choose among men, perfect, and bring to perfect obedience.   Yahuah would enter into a "Father/Son" covenant with that Messiah.   That man would be risen Divine through resurrection (not human birth) <u>to Mediate a New Covenant</u> as Eternal High Priest, and atone for the unfaithfulness of the children of Yahuah.   That is the Plan revealed the Heavenly Scroll and in the Earthly scrolls.

Romans 1

2 which (*a Mediator*) Yahuah promised beforehand (*Yahusha did not pre-exist*) through His prophets in the holy Scriptures (*both Heavenly and Earthly Scrolls*), 3 concerning His (*first born*) Son (*from the dead **Revelation 1:5***), who was born (*human*) of a descendant of David (*by both parents*) according to the flesh (*it takes two human parents to pro-create "according to the flesh"*), 4 who was declared the (*Divine*) <u>Son of Yahuah with power by the resurrection from the dead</u>, according to the Spirit of holiness (*Yahuah's Spiritual Eternal Seed*), Yahusha the Messiah

Hebrews 5

8 though Yahusha was a (future) Son (*of Yahuah upon resurrection **Romans 1:3***), <u>yet he learned obedience</u> (*to Yahuah*) by the things which he suffered (*due to disobedience*). 9 <u>And having been perfected</u> (*he was not born perfect or a god*), Yahusha became the author of eternal salvation to all who obey him (*and follow his righteous example and abide in covenant with him as his bride*)

The doctrine of incarnation says that Yahuah came to Earth as a man, was imperfect, disobedient, and had to be perfected in obedience... Blasphemy!

Qualified to Mediate the Covenant and Atone for Our Sins as Eternal High Priest

Yahuah prepared a special bloodline for the coming Messiah to inherit, whereby, he would be qualified to be a "Mediator" between Yahuah and those He chooses as a New Bride (*not the old brides*).   That bloodline was the Zadok bloodline of High Priests.   Yahuah would then orchestrate a lineage to the throne of David through Solomon (through Yahusha's father Joseph), and this man would be born a unique genetic mixture of the Royal Bloodline of David and the House of Zadok.   This firstborn son of Yahuah would inherit the title Melchizedek the "Ruling Zadok", and be given the throne of David and serve in the Office of Zadok High Priest eternally.

Yahuah would then, as a sign of his place in the Plan of Salvation, have this son born a miraculous birth, by planting the seed of Joseph into Mariam's womb outside of physical sexual union (mankind can do this today through in vitro fertilization.   This Messiah would be born to a Davidian Prince (Joseph) and a Hasmonean Princess Miriam from the line of Zadok… and Melchizedek was born into this world John Chapter 1 as the prophetic word became a reality being fulfilled in the "flesh" and lived among us!

Concerning the righteous line of High Priest prepared for the Messiah; Zadok was a patrilineal descendant of Eleazar who was the son of Aaron the high priest. (*2 Samuel 8:17; 1 Chronicles 24:3*). The lineage of Zadok is presented in the genealogy of Ezra (*his descendant*) as being of ninth generation and direct patrilineal descent from Phineas the son of Eleazar (***Ezra 7:1, see 1 Chronicles 5:3***0) where he is placed ninth in descent from Phineas.

> **Ezra 7:1-4**
> ...Zadok, The son of Ahitub, son of Amaryah, son of Azaryah, son of Mirayoth, son of Zerachyah, son of Uzzi, son of Bukki, son of Avishua, son of Phineas

Similarly, the Hebrew Bible relates how, at the time, Phineas (son of Eleazar) appeased Yahuah's anger through his piety. He merited the divine blessing of Yahuah to be the prophesied lineage of the coming Melchizedek:

> **Book ot Numbers 25:13**
> Phineas the son of Eleazar the son of Aaron the priest. Behold I give to him my covenant of peace, and will be his, and his progeny after him, (a) covenant of everlasting priesthood in turn of his zealousness for his God, and he atoned for the sons of Israel

This is extremely important when tracing the right of Yahusha to be the Eternal High Priest. Yahusha must have come from the lineage of Zadok, which is the bloodline of High Priest prepared for him. This is "how" Yahusha was entrusted to mediate the Covenant of Peace, server as the Eternal High Priest, and exercise the right to atone for sin! It was not because Yahusha was a "god"! This is clearly laid out in Scripture and defined in Numbers 25:13 above. Those under the Spirit of the False Messiah (incarnation) have been given over to a depraved mine and cannot understand Scripture! They do not teach us the Truth, when the Truth is right in from of their eyes.

If Yahusha cannot be proven to be a Zadok High Priest, then he cannot mediate the "New Covenant of Peace", he cannot serve as Eternal High Priest, and atone for humanity. Nothing about Yahusha was "super spiritually appraised because he was some kind of demi-god", everything was laid out in detail by Yahuah through bloodlines.

Hebrews 4:15

14Therefore, since we have a great high priest who has passed through the heavens (*fulfilled The Heavenly Scroll*), Yahusha the (firstborn) son of Yahuah (*from the dead Revelation 1:5*), let us hold fast our confession (*that Yahusha came in the flesh 1 John 1:4*). 15 For we do not have a high priest who cannot sympathize with our weaknesses (*he was not a god*), but a high priest who has been tempted in all things as we are (*he was human, Yahuah cannot be tempted by Evil James 1:13*), yet without sin (*in the office of High Priest in context Zechariah 3*). 16 Therefore let us draw near (to Yahuah through the Mediator) with confidence (that we are accepted into His family as children, the Bride of His firstborn son)

Hebrews 1:4

So Yahusha became as much superior to the (other) messengers, as the name (*Melchizedek*) he has inherited (through blood lineage) is superior to theirs.

To learn more about the bloodlines of our King and High Priest, please read my book Melchizedek and The Passover Lamb.   Visit my website www.sabbathcovenant.com for more information.

The Witness of Yahuah that Yahusha is the Messiah

Yahuah would then bare witness of this Messiah, with 3 concurring witnesses, water, blood, and spirit:

- **Water**: he would be born human through his mother's womb **Psalms 22:9-10**

- **Blood**line: he, by the seed of David, would inherit and restore the Throne of David (through Joseph), and would inherit and restore the Priesthood of Zadok (through Miriam)

- **Spirit:** he would be begotten divine through resurrection by the seed of Yahuah, the Ruach.

John 5

4 This is the conquering Spirit that has overcome the world, even our faith (*in the promises of Yahuah*). 5 Who is it that overcomes the world? Only the one who believes that Yahusha is the son of Yahuah (*not Yahuah in the flesh?*) 6 This (*Yahusha*) is the one who came by **water** (*the womb of a woman*) and **blood** (*of the seed of David*)—Yahusha the Messiah. He did not come by **water** only, but by **water** and **blood**. And it is the **Spirit** who testifies (*that Yahusha is the son of Yahuah by the power of the resurrection*), because the **Spirit** is the truth.

7 For there are three (*witnesses*) that testify (*that Yahusha is The son of Yahuah*): 8 the Spirit of Holiness, the

water and the blood; and these three are in agreement (that Yahusha is The Son of Yahuah). 9 We accept (*the lying*) human testimony (*of incarnation, the Spirit of the False Messiah*), but Yahuah's testimony is greater because it is the testimony of Yahuah, which he has given about his Son Yahusha (*born human through* **water** *by the seed of the* **blood***line of David, begotten Divine by the* **Spirit** *of Holiness* ***Romans 1:2-4***).

10 Whoever believes in the Son of Yahuah accepts this testimony. Whoever does not believe Yahuah (that Yahuah is not a man nor the son of man) **has made Yahuah out to be a liar** (saying Yahuah came to Earth as a man), because they have not believed the testimony Yahuah has given about his Son (*that he was born human, Inherited Melchizedek, and begotten divine*).

11 And this is the testimony: Yahuah has given us eternal life, and this life is (found) in (*covenant with*) his Son (***John 17:3***). 12 Whoever has the (Spirit of the) Son (*that Yahusha was born human begotten divine through resurrection*) has (*eternal*) life; whoever does not have (the testimony about) the Son of Yahuah does not have (*eternal*) life.

Romans 1:3
2 which (*a Mediator*) Yahuah promised beforehand (*Yahusha did not pre-exist*) through His prophets in the holy Scriptures (*both Heavenly and Earthly Scrolls*), 3 concerning His (*first born*) Son (*from the dead* **Revelation**

1:5), who was born (*human*) of a descendant of David (*by both parents*) according to the flesh (*it takes two human parents to pro-create "according to the flesh"*), 4 who was declared the (*Divine*) Son of Yahuah with power <u>by the resurrection from the dead (**Revelation 1:5**)</u>, according to the Spirit of holiness (*Yahuah's Seed)*, Yahusha the Messiah

Yahuah and Yahusha Enter into an Adoption Covenant

In the Plan of Salvation, Yahuah would enter into covenant with His firstborn son (*to be his Father*) to forgive the sins of all His children... this adoption covenant is detailed in **Zachariah Chapter 3**.   You will tell me, Sha'ul, we never heard this prophecy before!   This is because those who teach under **The Spirit of the False Messiah** cannot teach this prophecy.   It contradicts their false doctrine, clearly showing Yahusha is NOT Yahuah; and in fact had his sin forgiven him through Mikveh!   They will tell us that this is referring to our Messiah's great grandfather Yahusha III.   This is not so, as this prophecy is clearly speaking of **The Branch**, and illustrating an event that never occurred in Yahusha III's life.   Yet it is illustrating a critical event that DID occur in our Messiah's life.

The prophecy, in Zachariah Chapter 3, gives us a front row seat to the conversation that happened between Yahuah and Yahusha <u>in the desert</u> after Yahusha was Mikveh'd by John (*and declared The Passover Lamb, then fled like the scapegoat into the desert to seek Yahuah's anointing as Messiah/Branch*).   Yahusha, then, fled into the desert with the sins of the world just placed on his shoulders by the High Priest John; for 40 days/nights looking for confirmation from his Father.   This event is detailed in Mark Chapter 1.

> ### Mark 1
> 1 This is the beginning of the Good News about Yahusha the Messiah, the Son of Yahuah (*not Yahuah*), 2 as the prophet Isaiah wrote: "I will send my messenger ahead of

you, who will prepare your way."   3 "This is a voice of one who calls out in the desert: 'Prepare the way for the Messiah. Make the road straight for him (*through Mikveh*).'"   4 John was Mikveh'ing people in the desert, and preaching a Mikveh of changed (*circumcised*) hearts and lives (*living sacrifices*) for the forgiveness of sins.   5 All the people from Judea and Jerusalem were going out to him (*they knew he was the true High Priest*). They confessed their sins and were baptized by him in the Jordan River.   6 John wore clothes made from camel's hair, had a leather belt around his waist, and ate locusts and wild honey.   7 This is what John preached to the people: "There is one coming after me who is greater than I; I am not good enough even to kneel down and untie his sandals.   8 I immerse you with water, but he will immerse you with the Set Apart Spirit of Yahuah."   9 At that time Yahusha came from the town of Nazareth in Galilee and was Mikveh'd by John in the Jordan River. 10 Immediately, as Yahusha was coming up out of the water, he saw heaven open. The Set Apart Spirit came down on him like a dove (as an earnest guarantee of his future resurrection),   11   and a voice came from heaven: "(*today*) You are my Son, whom I love, and I am very pleased with you." (*as Yahusha fulfilled all righteousness*)   12   Then the Spirit sent Yahusha into the desert (*in fulfillment of the scapegoat*).   13 He was in the desert forty days and was tempted by Satan. He was with the wild animals, <u>and the angels came and took care of him</u>.

Lying on the desert floor starving, dehydrated, and on the verge of death, we know Satan came to Yahusha and tempted him to take Jerusalem by force.   This is where the vision in Zachariah Chapter 3 picks up.   We have Yahusha lying on the desert floor suffering from dehydration and starvation looking like a "stick snatched from the fire of the hot sun", and Satan mad because Yahusha refused his offer.

Now let's listen in to the conversation where Yahuah confirms that Yahusha is the Messiah, and they agree on Yahushua's role in the Renewed Covenant.   We see the "covenant" between Yahuah and Yahusha laid out very clearly.   Yahuah promised Yahusha that if he is faithful to his end of the agreement, then Yahuah would forgive all His sons of their sin! This is the critical prophecy and overwhelming PROOF that Yahusha is the Messiah. It is also proof to Jews that Yahusha is named <u>by name as the Branch</u>.   But because we have been taught incarnation, we deny the ONE prophecy that could change the entire conversation...

> **Zechariah 3** – *Yahuah's consecration of Yahusha as High Priest, King of Kings, and Eternal Judge*
> 1 Then he showed me Yahusha, the high priest, standing before the angel of Yahuah, and Satan standing at his right side to accuse him (**Mark 1:13**). 2 Yahuah (*through His proxy messenger*) said to Satan, "Yahuah rebuke you, Satan! Yahuah, who has chosen Jerusalem, rebuke you (*because Satan offered Yahusha to take Jerusalem by force*)! Is not this man a burning stick snatched from the fire?" (*Yahusha was starving and dying in the hot sun of the desert* **Matthew 4:1-11**) 3 Now Yahusha was dressed in

filthy clothes (*metaphor of sin Isaiah 64:6*) as he stood before the messenger of Yahuah. 4 The messenger said to those who were standing before him, "Take off his filthy clothes." Then Yahuah said to Yahusha, "See (*after taking off his filthy rags i.e. sin Isaiah 64:6*), I have taken away your sin (*through Mikveh*), and I will put fine garments (*of the High Priest*) on you." 5 Then I (*Yahuah*) said (*through the messenger*), "Put a clean turban (*of the High Priest*) on his head." So they put a clean turban on his head and clothed him (*in the garments of the High Priest*), while the messenger of Yahuah stood by.

*** New Covenant made directly with Yahusha****

6 The messenger of Yahuah gave this charge to Yahusha: 7 "This is what Yahuah Almighty says: 'If (*Yahuah makes a conditional promise*) you will walk in obedience to me and keep my requirements (*as High Priest*) you will govern my house (*i.e. King over creation*) and have charge of my courts (*Eternal Judge*), and I will give you a place (*right hand of Yahuah*) among these standing here. 8 "'Listen, High Priest Yahusha, you and your associates seated (*who came*) before you (*probably Adam, Enoch, Moses, Elijah, etc.*), who (*those seated before him*) are men symbolic of things to come (*they were all shadows of The Messiah, but were not the Branch*): I am going to bring (*you*) my servant (*from this point forward*), **the Branch** (*he is The Messiah*). 9 See, the stone I have set in front of Yahusha! There are seven (*number of perfection*) eyes on that one stone (*to witness*), and I will engrave an inscription on it,' says

Yahuah Almighty, 'and I will remove the sin of this land in a single day' (*the day Yahusha, in obedience, dies as Passover Lamb*)

This is the most important passage of scripture in the entire Bible. Yet, no one teaches it because our teachers are filled with The Spirit of the False Messiah... incarnation.   This one prophecy proves Yahusha is the Messiah, and literally spells out his role and how we are saved by Yahuah through Yahusha's obedience to our Father.   This is the reason Yahusha went to Yahchanan to be Mikveh'd, to "fulfill all the righteous requirements of the Law" in him, and bring him to perfection, just like Yahusha proclaimed:

> **Matthew 3:15**
> Yahusha replied, "Let me be Mikveh'd now; it is properly required in The Law, for us to do this to fulfill all righteousness (have his sin washed away with living water)."

That is what Mikveh is for, and why John (Yahchanan) was in the desert, he was commission to "set the path straight for the Branch" and immersing him for the remission of sin.   No other reason!   Yahusha was setting the proper example we all must follow to have our sin washed clean by Yahuah with living water. We just witnessed in **Zachariah Chapter 3** exactly what Yahusha's role was in the Renewed Covenant.   He was the Messiah (*the Branch*) and had to from that point forward (*after Mikveh as High Priest*) walk in complete obedience to the Law and set the righteous example that we are to follow.   And if he would do that, Yahuah promised to cover the death decrees in the Law, that is called Grace.

Yahuah Chooses a New Bride for His son

Scripture reveals how Yahuah would hand pick a "New Bride" for His firstborn son.   Not the old ones, but this one would be "chosen" not based on bloodline alone and be a small remnant from both the old brides.   It would be taken from among the House of Israel and the House of Judah... this **New Bride** would be called **Remnant Israel**.   It would be wed to Yahuah's son, not to Yahuah.

> **Romans 9:24**
>
> 24 even us (*Remnant Israel in context*), whom he also called, not only from among the Jews (*The House of Judah*) but also from among the Gentiles (*where The House of Israel is scattered*)?

Sha'ul goes into great detail about this New Bride and how there is a new criterion that makes this Bride "New".   It is a totally new group who are chosen not based on bloodline alone. For more information on this New Bride, please see the link on my website: Yahuah's gifts to Remnant Israel

Yahuah would literally chose a bride for His firstborn son, and marry His son to this New Bride.   His chosen children would then be given the opportunity to "abide in" covenant with His firstborn son.

> **John 15:7**
>
> 6 "If anyone does not abide in Me, he is thrown away as a branch and dries up; and they gather them, and cast them into the fire and they are burned.

It is through <u>a Mediator</u>, now, that we become "one" with Yahuah in family as ADOPTED sons/daughters, not through a direct marriage to Yahuah (He is our Father not our Husband)! We are one with Yahuah by being married to His son!

John 17:3 3

Now this is eternal life: that they know you (*Yahuah*), the only true God, and (*come to You through*) Yahusha who is the Messiah, whom you have sent (*in fulfillment of Your promises as foretold through the prophets to be the Mediator*).

1 Timothy 2:5

For there is one God (*Yahuah*) and one mediator between Yahuah and mankind, the man Yahusha the Messiah

John 17:19-21

"And for their sakes I sanctify myself (*through the Truth of Scripture*), that they also might be sanctified through the truth. Neither pray I for these alone, but for them also which shall believe on me through their word (enter into covenant); That they all may be one; as thou, Father, art in (*covenant with*) me, and I in (*covenant with*) thee, that they also may be one in (covenant with) us (*through me*): that the world may believe that thou hast sent me (*to mediate*)."

John 1:12

Yet to all who did receive Yahusha as the Messiah, to those who believed in (*the covenant that bears*) his name, he gave the right to become children of Yahuah.

Hebrews 2

...11 For both He who sanctifies (*Yahuah*) and those who are sanctified (*Yahusha and the rest of the sons*) are all from one Father; for which reason <u>Yahusha is not ashamed to call them brothers</u>, 12saying, "I WILL PROCLAIM YOUR NAME TO MY BRETHREN, IN THE MIDST OF THE CONGREGATION I WILL SING YOUR PRAISE." 13 And again, "I, Yahusha, WILL PUT MY TRUST IN YAHUAH." And again, "BEHOLD, I AND THE (*REST OF THE*) CHILDREN WHOM YAHUAH HAS GIVEN ME (*as a Bride*)."...

His firstborn son would become the Bridegroom and the rest of His children would become the Bride of the Messiah. This is the meaning behind the Annual Wedding Celebration we call The Appointed Times or Holy Days.

> The Spring Feasts are the engagement between the Messiah and His Bride. The Fall Feasts are "The Wedding Supper of the Lamb", where the Bridegroom Yahusha marries this New Bride called Remnant Israel.

This was foretold in The Heavenly Scroll from the foundation of the world, as this Messiah would be portrayed as crucified, a lamb seen slaughtered at the foundation of the world as witnessed in The Heavenly Scroll.

Revelation 13:8
All inhabitants of the earth will worship the beast--all whose names have not been written in the Lamb's book of life, the Lamb who was slain from the creation of the world.

His firstborn son would have to shed his own blood, as bloodshed is required to consummate a marriage covenant.   In Psalms below we see that as the sun and moon rises and sets daily and night after night... knowledge concerning The Plan of Yahuah is proclaimed without voice or speech from one end of the Earth to the other to all mankind from The Heavenly Scroll.

Psalm 19
19 The heavens (*H8064: shamayim - the stars and constellations of the Zodiac*) are telling of the glory of Yahuah; And their expanse is declaring the work of His hands. 2 Day to day (*the Zodiac*) pours forth speech, And night to night (*the Zodiac*) reveals knowledge. 3 There is no speech, nor are there words; Their (*stars and constellations of the Zodiac*) voice is not heard. 4 Their line (*ecliptic plane through which the sun appears to travel when viewed from Earth*) has gone out through all the earth, And their utterances to the end of the world. In them (*the constellations*) He has placed a tent for the sun, 5 Which (*the Sun*) is as (*a shadow or metaphor*) a bridegroom (the Messiah) coming out of his chamber (to run the course of a wedding and marry the Bride); It rejoices as a strong man (Messiah) to run his course (Plan of Salvation).   6 The Sun's rising is from one end of the

heavens, And its circuit (*Zodiac or Path*) to the other end of them; And there is nothing hidden from its heat.

David is clearly describing the Zodiac, the chart of the sun moving across our skies, and the "line of the sun" (called the ecliptic) that goes throughout all the earth; as it runs its course each year through the Signs of the Zodiac (*called constellations or starry hosts*). David properly understood the message contained in the Zodiac. The sun rises from one end of heaven, and then its "circuit or Zodiac" is like a "bridegroom coming out of his chamber" as The Heavenly Wedding is foretold. The Feast Cycle is a celebration in detail of this wedding. This is fulfilled in Yahusha the Messiah. Yahusha proclaims himself the "bridegroom", and says those who "hear His voice" (*speaking of the Zodiac* **Psalms 19:2**) rejoice; and it is Yahusha's joy to be the fulfillment of that message. Yes, the Zodiac is the original Gospel message proclaiming the Messiah.

John 3:29
[29] He who has the bride is the bridegroom; but the friend of the bridegroom, who stands and hears Him, rejoices greatly because of the bridegroom's voice (*proclaimed in The Heavenly Scroll* **Psalms 19**). Therefore, this joy of mine is fulfilled (*Yahusha fulfilled the message contained in The Heavenly Scroll*).

Matthew 25
[4] The wise ones, however, took oil in jars along with their lamps. [5] The bridegroom was a long time in coming (*2,000 years at the end of the Age of Pisces*), and they all became

drowsy and fell asleep. ⁶At midnight the cry rang out: "Here's the bridegroom! Come out to meet him!"

Revelation 19
⁹ And the angel said to me, "Write this: Blessed are those who are invited to the marriage supper of the Lamb." And he said to me, "These (*words written in The Heavenly Scroll*) are the true words of Yahuah."

In other words, David sees the Sun as a prototype for The Messiah.   This physical metaphor of the sun as the bridegroom pointing to The Messiah is repeated throughout scripture.   This is, in fact, true as the Sun was created as a witness of the coming of the Messiah, and what the Messiah would do.   This striking declaration In **Psalms 19** clearly tells us that Yahuah built into the Zodiac the story of redemption, and through the stars He has been witnessing His Plan to all humanity in a unique view only from Earth.

This firstborn son is Yahusha. Yahusha entered into a covenant personally with Yahuah, and fulfilled his obligations to Yahuah. Yahuah promised to make him His Eternal High Priest, Judge, and King over creation which Yahuah would give to him as an inheritance.   The rest of the children of Yahuah then enter into covenant with the Mediator as his Bride becoming children of Yahuah.   Yahuah then becomes our Father not our Husband through marriage between the Messiah and his Bride.

How did Yahusha Defeat Death?

This is the real question we are seeking to answer. Did Yahusha raise himself from the grave? Was he literally a God, Yahuah in the flesh? The answer to this question should be quite obvious. Death is the penalty of sin. All humans must die (for all have sinned) and pay that penalty, even Yahusha. "God" cannot die, that is what makes Him "eternal". It is a contradiction and blasphemy. Even true, fully begotten "sons of Yahuah" which are born of the dead (Rev 1:5) cannot die! Only fully humans... with no 'god' in them are capable of dying.

> **Luke 20:36**
> and they can no longer die; for they are like the angels. They are God's children, since they are children of the resurrection.

We see below that Yahusha cried out to the ONE GOD (who did not die) to save him from death. We also see, the Yahuah saved Yahusha from death NOT because he was a "god", but because of his piety (reverent submission to the Will of Yahuah to honor their agreement in Zachariah Chapter 3).

> **Hebrews 5**
> 6just as He says also in another passage, "YOU ARE A PRIEST FOREVER ACCORDING TO THE ORDER OF MELCHIZEDEK." 7In the days of His flesh, He offered up both prayers and supplications with loud crying and tears to the One able to save Him from death, and He was heard

because of His piety. 8Although He was a Son, He learned obedience from the things which He suffered....

So not only was Yahusha not a "god" or "God in the Flesh" which is blasphemy, but he was not yet a fully begotten son of Yahuah! He, like all mankind, had been Mikveh'd and given an earnest guarantee of his future resurrection.   Yahusha had to pay the price of sin... which is death of the physical flesh.   We have been so conditioned by the Spirit of the False Messiah that blasphemy is commonplace in our mouths, and the Truth sounds like blasphemy!   While the truth is boldly proclaimed in the pages of scripture that Yahusha was born human to two parents by the seed of David, then fully begotten Divine by the power of the resurrection... we have been given over to a spirit of stupor... and simply cannot "see" with our own eyes.

1 John 4 – *The Spirit of the False Messiah is "incarnation"*
1 Beloved, do not believe every spirit, but test the spirits to see whether they are from Yahuah, because many false prophets have gone out into the world (*claiming to be the incarnation of God*).

Birthday's of the Savior God's worshiped on December 25th

Hermes	Buddha	Krishna	Horus	Hercules	Adonis
Greece	Nepal	India	Egypt	Greece	Phoenician
December 25th	December 25th	December 25th	December 25th	December 25th	December 25th
200 BC	563 BC	900 BC	3000 BC	800 BC	200 BC

Dionysus	Zarathustra	Jesus	Mithras	Tammuz
Greece	Greece	Rome	Persia	Babylon
December 25th	December 25th	December 25th	December 25th	December 25th
500 BC	1000 BC	3 BC	600 BC	400 BC

According to Scripture our Messiah Yahusha was born Feast of Trumpets (September) 3 BC

2 By this you know the Spirit of Yahuah: every spirit that confesses that **Messiah Yahusha has come in the flesh** (*a man*) is from Yahuah; 3 and every spirit that **does not confess Yahusha has come in the flesh** (*but says Yahuah came in the flesh*) is not from Yahuah; this is the spirit of the antichrist (*or False Messiah*) ... 12 No one has seen Yahuah at any time! (*Because Yahusha is not Yahuah in the flesh or a demi-god*).

2 John 7 - *Beware of Antichrist Deceiver*
7 For many deceivers have gone out into the world (*teaching incarnation the Spirit of the False Messiah*) who **do not confess Yahusha the Messiah as coming in the flesh** (*but teach that Yahuah came in the flesh*). This (*spirit*) is a deceiver and an antichrist. 8 Look to yourselves, that we do not lose those things we worked for, but that we may receive a full reward. 9 Whoever transgresses (*blasphemes the Spirit of Yahuah*) and **does not abide in the doctrine** of the Messiah (*that he came in the flesh, not a god*) does not have (*the Spirit of*) Yahuah. He who abides in the doctrine of the Messiah (*that he came to Earth as a human being*) has both the Father and the Son. 10 If anyone comes to you and does not bring this doctrine (but rather teaches incarnation), do not receive him into your house nor greet him; 11 for he who greets him shares in his evil deeds (*of committing blasphemy*)

We are taught in Christianity that "Jesus paid the price for us, he bore our sin, he kept the Law so we don't have to keep it, he died so we can live, he was God the Father become the Son in the Flesh".   Just like that, just utter the name "Jesus" ... and you are in the clear, no need to do anything else, you can be lawless and sin all you like; Grace will cover you because God died for you. That is another Gospel message!

What Yahusha did do, was he was obedient to his role as messiah (*defined by Yahuah in Zachariah Chapter 3*) and show us the way by example that we must follow ourselves.   Yahusha "bore our sin" in fulfillment of the scapegoat and as a sin offering in that Yahuah accepted his offering and through that sacrifice we now can approach Yahuah's throne personally.   He didn't "die for our sin" (*we still have to die physically for the sin in our own bodies*) and he didn't do it all for us.   We have to follow in his example if we too are to defeat death like he did.   We must follow his example of **Mikveh** (*ritual cleansing of sin*), **circumcision** (*of heart our commitment to keep his law*), and bringing an **offering** of our lives to the altar on Passover (*we are living sacrificial lambs*).

> **John 14:6**
> Yahusha answered, "I am (*his example is*) the way and (*his example is*) the truth and (*his example is*) the life. No one comes to the Father except through me (*in covenant with him by following his example*).
>
> **John 10:3-4**
> For I have given you an example (*a true way that leads to eternal life*), that you should do as I have done.

1 Peter 2:2121
But if you suffer for doing good (*obey the Law*) and you endure it (*you will be conformed to the image of Yahusha, Romans 8:29 and 2 Corinthians 3:18, who was perfected through suffering*), this is commendable before Yahuah. 21 To this (*to be conformed to the image of His son*) you were called, because the Messiah suffered (*on Passover*) for you (*and tore the veil giving you access to the Altar of Yahuah*), leaving you an example (*of what to do as he fulfilled the spiritual meaning of Passover*), that you should follow in his steps (*being Mikveh'd, demonstrating a circumcised heart, and bring your own offering on Passover to the Altar of Yahuah*).

Yahusha did not do it all for us, he obeyed Yahuah, and set the righteous example for us to follow.   In doing so, Yahuah promised to forgive our sin and cover the death decree against us as Sha'ul said... IF we follow his example!

The death decree that Yahuah covers is called 'The Second Death' (*or rather the final spiritual death decree*).   He does not cover the first physical death decree, you still must die!   The spiritual death decree (*or second death*) is 'passed over' for all who follow Yahusha's example and put their faith in (*and properly celebrate*) **Passover**.   Very few people know what I'm talking about and keep Passover properly.   We follow the example of Rabbinical Judaism... not Yahusha.   Yahuah does not issue the final death decree, and we defeat death and live again **if** we "do this in remembrance of his example".   So we all, like Yahusha, must physically die and pay the price of sin as we inherited death in our bodies (not physical die on Passover, we give our lives on the altar as living sacrifices).   It is Spiritual Death that we do not suffer because after we die, like Yahusha, we defeat death and are raised to eternal life by Yahuah.   Let me explain.

Every one dies for their own sin!

I said that Yahusha did not pay our penalty of sin in our body, and he did not cover the first death decree... you still are going to die. Every physical body must die a natural death (*or be translated through transposition, <u>which is just another form of physical death</u>*).   We know that Yahuah's own laws prevent anyone (*including Yahusha*) from being judged for another man's sin. Each man is judged for his sin alone:

> **<u>Deuteronomy 24:16</u>**
> "The fathers shall not be put to death for the children, neither shall the children be put to death for the fathers: <u>every man shall be put to death for his own sin</u>."

We all are going to pay for our sin through physical death just like Yahusha did.   Yahuah would never violate His own law, and put Yahusha to death for our sin!   Yahusha was a "sin offering" only in the respect that he obeyed Yahuah and Yahuah promised to forgive our sin AFTER we die and pay the price for it.   Yahusha died as all men do, he was not born into sin, our physical bodies die for our <u>own sin</u>.   For all have sinned Romans 3:23. There was no exception in that statement.   Original Sin is a false doctrine. Death, not sin, is passed on from Adam into our genetic code. Then we all fall for "sin" and that death sentence we inherited is justified.

In fact, per **Zachariah Chapter 3,** Yahusha had his sin forgiven through Mikveh just like we do.   The entire doctrine of "Original Sin" is a false doctrine.   What the Bible teaches is that through one MAN'S act of disobedience to the Law of Yahuah (Adam), "sin" was brought into the world (*not our body*), and as a result of Adam's sin his body began to die.   From that point forward, DEATH was passed to all men genetically and sin was in the world.

> **Romans 5:12**
> "Wherefore, as by one man... sin entered into the world, and death by sin (*so death comes by your own sin not genetically*); and so death passed upon all men, for that all have sinned *(Yahusha died)*"

The Bible says that death (*not sin*) is passed on in the body, we are not born into "original sin". We are born into a body that is predisposed to sin.   Sin was brought into the world (*not our body*) through one act of disobedience.   Death however is passed to all men genetically as we are all born to die.   In this way the "law" of sin and you die by decree, called the **Law of Sin and Death** reigned over humanity, and we lived in bondage to the fear of death.   It is this threat of death that held us captive not the Law of Yahuah:

> **Hebrews 2:14-15**
> 14 so that by his death he, Yahusha, might break the power of him who holds the power of death—that is, the devil — 15 and free those who all their lives were held in slavery by their fear of death (*not in slavery to the Law as Christianity teaches*)

2 Kings 14:6
"But the children of the murderers he slew not: according unto that which Yahuah commanded, saying, the fathers shall not be put to death for the children, nor the children be put to death for the fathers; but every man shall be put to death for his own sin."

Ezekiel 18:20
"The soul that sinneth, it shall die. The son shall not bear the iniquity of the father, neither shall the father bear the iniquity of the son: the righteousness of the righteous shall be upon him, and the wickedness of the wicked shall be upon him."

Ezekiel.33:20
"Yet ye say, the way of Yahuah is not equal. O ye house of Israel, I will judge you every one after his ways."

Jeremiah 31:29-30
"In those days they shall say no more, the fathers have eaten a sour grape, and the children's teeth are set on edge. But every one shall die for his own iniquity: every man that eateth the sour grape, his teeth shall be set on edge."

As we read before the Law was weakened by our flesh, it is we who are not perfect!   We were the weak link in the Law, and our weaknesses made the Law incomplete and prevented the Law from delivering eternal life as promised.   The Law had to be made complete through grace (*by covering the death decrees*), in order for the Law to achieve its righteous outcome which is eternal life.

Proverbs 3
1My son, do not forget my Torah, but let your heart keep my commandments; 2 For length of days and years of life and peace they will add to you.

Deuteronomy 11
20"You shall write them (*the Torah*) on the doorposts of your house and on your gates, 21 so that your days and the days of your sons may be multiplied on the land which Yahuah swore to your fathers to give them, as long as the heavens remain above the earth.

It is in this way Yahusha "fulfilled" the Law; he bridged the gap of our own weaknesses by covering the death decrees. Now, in covenant with Yahusha, the Law is complete and delivers eternal life for obedience as promised. This is called **The Law of the Spirit that Leads to Life**. However, this fleshly body predisposed to sin and designed genetically to die... must pay the price for our sin.

> The penalty of sin is death which is in our genetic structure because of Adam. So the sentence of "physical death" is justified because we all individually fall for the temptation of sin in this world.

The Law of Sin and Death vs. The Law of the Spirit of Life

This is extremely important to understand, because Yahusha showed us The Way a human being can live a life pleasing to Yahuah, that results in the resurrection from the dead. If we follow that path, we too as humans can defeat death in the exact same way!

The main theme of The Yahushaic Covenant is that Yahusha defeated the 'Law of Sin and Death' by fulfilling the requirements of the Passover Lamb. Now those in covenant with him live in freedom (*from the threat of death*) in what is called the 'Law of the Spirit of Life'. Before we go any further, first let me define terms:

- **The Law of Yahuah** – An all-encompassing term for the commands/law, ordinances, and decrees of Yahuah. So when we say "the Law" we are referring to all 3 aspects combined:

    Deuteronomy 5
    30 "Go, tell them to return to their tents. 31 But you stay here with me so that I may give you all the commands, decrees and ordinances you are to teach them to follow in the land I am giving them to possess."

As we read above, the Law contains **commands**, **decrees**, and **ordinances**, so let me quickly define each one:

- **Commands also called Laws** - Simply speaking these are the 10 commandments, the dietary Laws, the judicial laws, the Laws of ritual purity, the sacrificial laws, and so forth.

- **Ordinances** – these are the ordained times such as The Sabbath, and the ordained festivals (spring and fall feasts).

- **Decrees** – these are the divine judgments or judicial decrees within the Law that levy judgment against us for violating the commands and ordinances within the Law. Only the decrees were "nailed to the stake" as our transgressions were forgiven by Yahuah and covered by the blood of the lamb Yahusha as agreed upon in Zachariah Chapter 3.

- **The Law** - So together, the commands, decrees, and ordinances make up what we call 'the Law'. The Law first existed in what Sha'ul the Apostle refers to as 'the Law of Sin and Death'. The Law, was then transposed by Yahusha into 'the Law of the Spirit of Life'. Let me explain and clearly define these terms used by Sha'ul the Apostle...

The Law of Sin and Death

is the Law of Yahuah with active death decrees for disobedience as it existed in written form passed down from Adam through Moses. The first (*and every subsequent "law"*) came with a corresponding judicial decree for breaking that law. The first Law was given in Eden with "you shall not eat of the apple" (*law*) and then the decree "or you shall surely die". That is where the

Law of sin and you die was first introduced. Over time as new laws were added, so were new judicial decrees for each new law Yahuah revealed as he progressively disclosed the 'constitution' of his Kingdom. Since we all have sinned, we were being held captive by the death decrees and in bondage to the fear of death.

The Law of the Spirit of Life

is the Law of Yahuah with the death decrees covered by the blood of the Lamb (*this is called Grace*). The covering of the death decree which Sha'ul called a 'certificate of debt' (*we owed with our lives*) was a free give that we did not deserve. This is the definition of 'Grace'. By covering the death decrees and forgiving the 'certificate of debt' we owed Yahuah, we are restored to a state of perfect obedience and freeing us from slavery to the fear of the death decrees. Our sin is forgiven through Mikveh and the decrees covered by our faith in Yahusha as the Passover Lamb.

> In effect the Law has not changed, it was just made whole or 'complete' through grace (the covering of the death decrees in the Law).

With the understanding of terms, it becomes clear what Sha'ul the Apostle is saying in Romans 1.

Romans 8

1 Now there is no condemnation (*referring to the Death Decrees/Certificate of Debt*) for those in The Yahushaic Covenant. 2 For the Law of the Spirit of life in (*covenant with*) Yahusha the Messiah, has made me free from the

Law of Sin and Death (*the death decrees in the Law are covered and paid in full*).   3 For what the Law could not do (*bring eternal life as promised*) because the Law was made weak by our flesh (*because we broke the Law and the decrees in the Law condemned us to death for disobedience*), Yahuah did (*provided Eternal Life as a free gift to those who try to keep the Law and fail i.e. Grace*) by sending His own (*firstborn*) Son in the likeness of sinful flesh (*as a man fully human*), on account of sin (*to defeat it by living obedient to the Law and dying innocent*): Yahusha condemned   sin in the flesh (*our genetic death sentence*),   4 that the righteous requirement of the Law might be fulfilled in us (who are Mikveh'd into the Yahushaic Covenant and brought into total obedience to the Law) who do not walk according to the flesh (disobedient to the Law) but according to the Spirit

This is the reason Yahusha went to John to be Mikveh'd, to "fulfill all the righteous requirements of the Law" in him, and bring him to perfection.

Matthew 3:15

Yahusha replied, "Let me be Mikveh'd now; it is properly required in The Law, for us to do this to fulfill all righteousness (have his sin washed away with living water)."

Then Yahusha fled into the desert where Yahuah consecrated him High Priest personally and said:

Zechariah 3

3Now Yahusha was dressed in filthy clothes as he stood before the angel. 4 The angel said to those who were standing before him, "Take off his filthy clothes." Then he said to Yahusha, "See, I have taken away your sin (*earlier through Mikveh*), and I will put fine garments on you."

Yahusha was setting the proper example that we all must follow to have our sin washed clean by Yahuah with living water. Most people think walking according to the Spirit is somehow walking in some super spiritual state, letting the Spirit guide us while we completely ignore the Law. The Spirit Sha'ul is referring to is the Spirit of loving obedience to the Law prophesied in Ezekiel 36: 26, 27).

> **Ezekiel 36: 26, 27**
> Walking according to the new Spirit I will give you a new heart (*for my Law and write my Law on it*) and put a new spirit (*of loving obedience*) in you; I will remove from you your heart of stone (*legalistic observance of the Law out of fear of death*) and give you a heart of flesh. And I will put my (*loving*) Spirit in you and move you to follow (*the Spiritual Intent*) my commands and be careful to keep (*the Intent of*) my laws.

Now, continuing with Romans 8...
> 5 For those who live according to the flesh set their minds on the things of the flesh (*and abolish the Law of Yahuah*), but those who live according to the Spirit (*of loving obedience to the Law*), the things of the Spirit (*the Law is Spiritual* **Romans 7:14**). 6 For to be carnally minded is death (*you'll be judged by the decrees in the Law*), but to

be spiritually minded is life and peace (*because in loving obedience to the Law the decrees against you are covered by the blood of the lamb resulting in peace and a spirit of comfort*). 7 Because the carnal mind is hatred against Yahuah; for it is not subject to the Law of Yahuah, nor indeed can be. 8 So then, those who are in the flesh cannot please Yahuah (*because they hate the Law of Yahuah and abolished it in their hearts*).

Romans 7:14

13Therefore did that which is good (the Law) become a cause of death for me? May it never be! Rather it was sin, in order that it might be shown to be sin by effecting my death (*through the death decrees*) through that which is good, so that through the commandment sin would become utterly sinful. 14For we know that the Law is spiritual, but I am of flesh, sold into bondage to sin.

Romans 2:13

For it is not those who hear the Law who are righteous in Yahuah's sight, but it is those who obey the Law who will be declared righteous.

Yahusha Sends "*the Comforter*"

As we just read in Romans 8:6, to be spiritually minded is life and peace!   This Spirit Sha'ul is referring to, is the **comforter** that Yahusha and Ezekiel prophesied would come upon us.   We have a spirit of comfort, now that the death decrees are covered, and we no longer live in bondage to the fear of sin and death.   Sha'ul is saying that Yahusha "nailed the death decrees that demand our death" in the Law, to the stake (*covering them with the blood of the Lamb*).   Now that Yahusha was obedient unto death, the Law of Yahuah has become the **Law of the Spirit of Life** as Yahusha has removed our enmity (*fear of death*) toward the Law.

Through Yahusha the Messiah, those in covenant with him are found in perfect obedience to the Law (*the righteous requirements are fulfilled in us, just like they were in Yahusha when he was Mikveh'd to "fulfill all righteousness in him"!*).   This is because Yahuah forgives our transgression, and covers the 'certificate of debt' against us that justified our physical death.   The promise for obedience to the Law is eternal life, so once that certificate of debt is forgiven... we defeat death through resurrection exactly like Yahusha did!   Now, in the Yahushaic Covenant, the Law has been transposed to the Law of the spirit of loving obedience that leads to eternal life.   Sha'ul discusses this in detail in Colossians.

> **Colossians 2**
> 13 When you were dead in your transgressions (*held captive to the death decrees*) and the uncircumcision of

your flesh (*lost among the Gentile nations*), Yahuah made you alive together (*in covenant*) with Yahusha, having forgiven us all our transgressions (*covered the death decrees*), 14 having canceled out <u>the certificate of debt consisting of decrees against us</u>, which was hostile to us; and Yahuah has taken <u>the certificate of debt</u> (*death decrees in the Law, NOT THE LAW*) out of the way, having nailed the certificate of debt (*that justifies our physical death*) to the stake with Yahusha.

If Yahusha was "God"... We are Dead in Our Sins!

This cycle of "being born to die, and dying guilty of sin to justify that death" had to be broken by a man, just as it began with a man. If Yahusha was a demi-god or God in the flesh, the entire concept of overturning Adam's act would have no value. In order to defeat death, a man whose body was genetically engineered to "die" (*which was justified because "all have sinned"*) had to die innocent in the eyes of Yahuah by walking obedient to His instructions and being perfected. That is the glorious message behind the Gospel; that it is possible for a human being (who sinned) to be perfected and die innocent in the eyes of Yahuah through faith and Mikveh!

Death, then, cannot hold an innocent man, because death is the penalty of sin. Yahuah has to issue the final death decree for them to stay dead (*the Second Death*). Yahuah predestined a human Messiah (*foretold in both The Heavenly and Earthly Scrolls*), to come and live and serve as High Priest. This man would be perfected through discipline by follow the instruction of Yahuah to become righteous, then Mikveh'd clear of sin, and would live from that point forward in complete obedience to His Law as High Priest. That is how Yahusha defeated death... Yahusha accomplished his role defined in ***Zachariah Chapter 3*** (being the heir to the promise to the House of Zadok to mediate a covenant of peace, reign eternally as High Priest, and make atonement)... then Yahuah honored His promise, and death was defeated in ONE DAY when Yahuah forgave the sins of the land as Yahuah fulfilled his end and proclaimed "*it is finished*!".

==Yahusha was literally saved by his faith in himself as the Passover Lamb having been perfected through obedience and Mikveh==. That is The Way to Yahuah that we all can follow that will result in our resurrection as well.   As we follow Yahusha in the resurrection "path".

> **Matthew 19:28**
> 28 And Jesus said to them, "Truly I say to you, that <u>you who have followed Me, in the regeneration</u> when the Son of Man will sit on His glorious throne, you also shall sit upon twelve thrones, judging the twelve tribes of Israel. 29 "And everyone who has left houses or brothers or sisters or father or mother or children or farms for My name's sake, will receive many times as much, and <u>will inherit eternal life</u>....

What is "that path we follow"?

> **Hebrews 5:8-9**
> 8 though Yahusha was a Son, yet he learned obedience (*to Yahuah*) by the things which he suffered. 9 And having been perfected (*by Yahuah through obedience and suffering throughout his life and ultimately on Passover*), Yahusha (*his example*) became the author of eternal salvation (*forefather of everlasting life* **Isaiah 9:6-7**) to all who obey Yahuah (*and follow Yahusha's example* **John 1:12**).

In other words, Yahusha's life, of being perfected by the Law of Yahuah, became the true way to eternal life <u>by example</u>.

> His way is the **true way** that leads to eternal **life**. **The Truth, the way, and the life**.

The messiah Yahusha was <u>that man</u> to break the 'Law of Sin and Death' and then die innocent and defeat death in the process. Through the Messiah, one act of the obedience of <u>one man</u> (*not God*) resulted in salvation from death. We see that DEATH (not "sin") came through Adam genetically... and by "man" (not "God") came the resurrection of the dead!

> **1 Corinthians 15**
> 20 But now the Messiah is risen from the dead (*by Yahuah*), and has become the first fruits of those who have fallen asleep (*first born son of the resurrection **Romans 1:3-4***). 21 For since by man (*Adam*) came death, by Man (*not God*) also came the resurrection of the dead. 22 For as in (one human) Adam all die, even so in (*one human*), the Messiah, all (*the sons of Yahuah*) shall be made alive (*begotten by Yahuah as sons through resurrection*).

The Law of the Spirit of Life i.e. a man living in complete obedience to the Law, having his sin forgiven through **Mikveh**, demonstrating a contrite spirit and **circumcised** heart, and giving his life as a living sacrificial **offering** to serve Yahuah has received the promise of eternal life. Yahusha, the man, became the example for all the sons of Yahuah and he is called the "forefather of everlasting life" and made righteous in the eyes of Yahuah. Later in this book, I am going to show that ==The Way through The Narrow Gate of Passover is Mikveh, circumcision, and offering.==

Now, to all of us who follow in his footsteps in obedience to Yahuah, we too are declared righteous.   Not by faith alone, but by a process of obedience to the Law, suffering through faith, and expressing our faith by keeping Passover in light of Yahusha's sacrifice.

In doing so, Yahusha's "blood" or sin offering is accepted by Yahuah to cover <u>the second death decrees</u> on our behalf and we too are found innocent after we die… and we too will defeat death through resurrection:

> **James 2:16-26**
> 16 Faith and Deeds (*works of the Law*).   Faith alone does not save, nor does deeds alone.   You must have both.   …17 In the same way, faith by itself, if it is not accompanied by action, is dead. 18 But someone will say, "You have faith; I have deeds."   Show me your faith without deeds, and I will show you my faith by my deeds. 19 You believe that there is one God (*The Shema*). Good! Even the demons believe that—and shudder.   … 24 You see that a person is considered righteous by what they do and not by faith alone…26 As the body without the spirit is dead, so faith without works of the Law is dead.

Yahusha, being fully human, denied the fleshly desire to "sin" after his Mikveh in the office of High Priest, and obeyed Yahuah even to the point of willingly going to his own death (*which was not Yahusha's own will*).   It is the ultimate demonstration that Yahusha set aside his selfish will to live, and obeyed Yahuah's will that he die, IF he loved his brothers enough to pay that price.

> This was Yahuah's plan from the beginning! Written in the stars before the foundation of the world... To literally perfect a human being (Yahusha) through suffering, making Yahusha our "pioneer of our salvation" our "forefather of everlasting life" our ultimate example... all meaning the same thing.

Yahuah orchestrated our salvation through his human messiah NOT by coming to Earth and dying! This was His plan from the beginning written in the stars. It was prophesied in Genesis where the seed of a woman would crush the head of the serpent. It was foretold through all his prophets, His Ordained Times, and countless shadow pictures such as Joseph, David, Joshua, Sampson, and so forth. That plan of Yahuah's was fulfilled in Yahusha:

Hebrews 2

14 Since the children have flesh and blood (*and are held captive to the Law of Sin and Death*), he too shared in their humanity (*he was human too and captive to genetic death*) *so that by his death (the death of a human not God)* he, Yahusha, might break the power of him who holds the power of death—that is, the devil— 15 and free those who all their lives were held in slavery by their fear of death. 16 For surely it is not angels he helps, but Abraham's descendants. 17 For this reason (*to break the Law of Sin and Death*) he (*Yahusha*) had to be made like them fully human in every way, in order that he might become a merciful and faithful high priest (*who are chosen from among men*) in service to Yahuah.

The Messiah had to be 100% Human!

Sha'ul is teaching above in Hebrews 2, the exact same message I am trying to convey.   Since the children of Yahuah are first born flesh and blood, the Messiah <u>had to be born flesh and blood to atone</u> for them and break the power of death.   Nowhere in Scripture does it say it takes 'God' to die to save us.   Nowhere in Scripture did Yahuah promise to come to Earth and die; that is impossible.   For this reason, the messiah HAD TO BE HUMAN, not God or a demigod.

As I defined earlier, Yahusha came "in the flesh".   The word ***<u>flesh</u>*** means... natural/physical origin (not Spiritual), born of natural origin ONLY, mere human/natural birth only... APART FROM DIVINE INFLUENCE...

> g4561 '***sarki***'   - Thayer:
> 2a) the body of a man
> 2b) used of natural or physical origin, generation or relationship
> 2b1) born of natural generation
> 4) the flesh, denotes mere human nature**, the earthly nature of man apart from divine influence**, **and therefore prone to sin and opposed to God**

He could not have been Yahuah *"in the flesh"* because the very definition of that word is a contradiction.   He had to be and was human.... fully human in every way so says **Hebrews 2:17**.   Because if he wasn't fully human in every way... he could not undue what was done by Adam who was human.   Yahusha is the "second chance Adam". A man brought sin and death into the world... it would take a man to take them out of the world.

Now, having proven himself as a human that could obey and withstand the temptation of his flesh... Yahusha was chosen by Yahuah from among all mankind as High Priest to serve Him for eternity (fulfilling the promise to the House of Zadok... see my book **Melchizedek and the Passover Lamb**). <u>Yahusha HAD to die, not only for us but for himself (to pay the price of the genetic structure he inherited from Adam, he was 100% human and his death proved it</u>).

He too was in a human body predisposed to death genetically and that body had to be put to death for Yahusha to enter The Kingdom of Yahuah. He had to make that sacrifice as the human High Priest. Let's look at Hebrews 5 in more detail to show that Yahusha had to make the Passover Sacrifice for himself as well. We see that Yahusha as High Priest is chosen from among men in vs. 3 "he is obligated to offer sacrifices for sins, as for the people, so also for himself".

How Could a Man Do All the Work of Salvation?

... "IT HAD TO BE GOD"... actually, it is the exact opposite!

I get asked all the time "*how could a man do all the work of salvation? It HAD TO BE GOD*" I am told.   Not only is that untrue, because it is impossible for Yahuah to die, be tempted by evil in the process, or "come in the flesh".   It is also clearly stated that the Messiah had to be a human, and the sacrifice of death for humanity had to come at the hands of a human high priest for the people and for himself.   He (a human being) had to overturn what Adam (a human being) brought into this world.   A man brought sin into this world, and a man had to take it out.

> **Hebrews 5**
> 1 For every high priest (*Yahusha was the High Priest of Israel by bloodline of Zadok, consecrated High Priest by Yahuah Zachariah Chapter 3*) taken <u>from among men</u> is appointed (*by Yahuah **Zachariah Chapter 3***) on behalf of men in things pertaining to Yahuah, in order to offer both gifts and sacrifices for sins; 2 he can deal gently with the ignorant and misguided, since he himself also is beset with weakness; 3 and because of it he is obligated to offer sacrifices for sins, as for the people, <u>so also for himself</u>. 4 And no one takes the honor to himself, but receives it when he is called by Yahuah, even as Aaron was. 5 So also Yahusha did not glorify himself so as to become a high priest, but Yahuah who said to Yahusha "YOU ARE MY SON, TODAY I HAVE BEGOTTEN YOU"; 6 just as Yahuah says also in another passage, "YOU ARE A PRIEST FOREVER

ACCORDING TO THE ORDER OF MELCHIZEDEK." 7 In the days of Yahusha's flesh (*when he was fully human in every way* **Heb. 2:17**), Yahusha offered up both prayers and supplications with loud crying and tears to the One (*God, Yahuah, The Shema*) able to save Yahusha from death (*Yahusha did not rise from the dead, he was risen by Yahuah*), and Yahusha was heard because of Yahusha's piety (*NOT because he was a demi-god! But because of his reverent obedience to the Law see Zachariah Chapter 3*). 8 Although Yahusha was a Son (*not Yahuah*), Yahusha learned obedience (*to the ONE GOD*) from the things which he suffered. 9 And having been made perfect (*Yahusha was not born perfect being simply a man*), Yahusha became (*he was not always, he BECAME after his submission and death on Passover*) to all those who obey Yahuah and follow Yahusha's example, the source of eternal salvation (*his example is our source*), 10 being designated by Yahuah as a high priest (*from among men verse 1*) according to the order of Melchizedek (*see my book **Melchizedek and The Passover Lamb***). 11 Concerning Yahusha we have much to say, and it is hard to explain, since you have become dull of hearing. (*that is a true statement especially today*).

So what Sha'ul is saying above, is that it took a human high priest to offer the final sacrifice for himself and for all those in covenant with him. As we read in Zachariah Chapter 3, Yahusha fulfilled his responsibility, to show the way by example and be obedient to his role as the Branch. As a result, Yahuah too fulfilled His promise (*in Zachariah Chapter 3*) and "forgave the sin of the land in one day" including Yahusha's. When Yahusha said "it is finished" Yahuah covered the second death decree and released all those being held in bondage to death. We see in the Gospel account that the graves gave up their dead at that moment. What we don't realize is that we all followed Yahusha that day in the resurrection just like he told the thief on the stake next to him.

You see, the resurrection is an event that occurs outside of the boundaries of time (*in the realm of the Spirit*) and we witnessed the first resurrection of the dead on that day. When Yahusha said it is finished and Yahuah covered the second death decree (*which was holding us in bondage to death*) and death was defeated. More info on the resurrection in my book **The Yahushaic Covenant Volume 1 – *The Mediator*...**

Human Sacrifice or Love Offering?

We never quite get the real story from our modern day teachers filled with the Spirit of the False Messiah teaching "incarnation", and anti-messianic "Jews" who deny the messiah leaving us all "questioning the sacrifice of Yahusha". We have erred in our understanding of the Plan of Salvation, and run the very real risk of falling out of covenant with Yahuah in our ignorance (*lack of knowledge*). Worse yet, we are being led to commit blasphemy against the Spirit of Yahuah by modern translations to declare Yahuah is Yahusha and that Yahuah had to come to Earth and die.

The problem is that we have not found an anointed teacher and are listening to "self-appointed" ones with no understanding. Leading us astray. It is of the utmost importance that we understand the sacrifice of Yahusha, his humanity at the time, and "why" he was qualified to make atonement! He was not Yahuah in the flesh, Yahuah did not come and die, and a God cannot atone for humanity!

Human sacrifice forbidden

Does Yahuah forbid one human from sacrificing another human... yes. But as with everything in scripture, we cannot sound-bite that restriction! We must use wisdom and seek out the "intent" of that restriction, given that it appears the entire Plan of Salvation depends on what "appears to be" a human sacrifice! Making Yahuah out to be a hypocrite; or Yahusha's sacrifice ineffective and an abomination.

There are several flaws that must be addressed:

1. **Blood does not cleanse of "sin"**... WATER does through Mikveh.
2. **Blood consummates marriage covenants** (*even human marriage with breaking the hymen*), and that is why Yahusha shed his blood.   His blood was shed to consume a marriage covenant, whereby we THROUGH Mikveh we are forgiven our sins in covenant.
3. **Yahusha's sacrifice was not a "human sacrifice"** (*where one man sacrifices another*), nor was it even a human sacrifice where Yahuah sacrifices a man at all!
4. **Yahusha "willingly went to his death"** to save the lives of his brothers!   There is no greater love.   It was one man willingly ready to die, and a choice by that man to do so for the right reasons.   He was not "sacrificed unwillingly" by another.   He literally orchestrated the events on that Passover.
5. **Yahusha's real sacrifice was his entire life**, not his death. His death was meaningless outside of his life, living the Torah by example, and giving his life as a *living sacrifice* to his Father; to consummate the marriage covenant by giving his life for his brothers.

There is a reason why one man cannot sacrifice another man. Man cannot give "life", and is forbidden therefore from taking a life... Man cannot promise to raise another man from the grave (nor grant eternal life).   This is why "human sacrifice" is forbidden.

Shedding blood to consummate covenants is required...

The "shedding of blood" is required to consummate any covenant, including human marriage (*which is a shadow of the covenant we enter into with Yahuah*).   Yahusha's "blood" does not cleanse from sin, it consummates the relationship with Yahuah (*required to have our sin forgiven through Mikveh*) by following Yahusha's righteous example!   Yahuah reserves the right to give life, take life, and grant eternal life. The restriction on human sacrifice does not apply to Yahuah (who has the power to both raise from the dead and grant eternal life, not to mention the life we have is his gift to us in the first place).   Yahuah is not "taking" anything that does not already belong to Him.   And he did not even "take" that from Yahusha, it was willingly offered in love.

Yahusha's life pleased Yahuah

Yahusha's sacrifice was efficient because it was not his death, it was his obedient life that overturned the power of sin/death brought into this world by Adam.   As it took one man "Adam" to introduce sin into this world, it took one man "Yahusha the second Adam" to take it out.   Yahusha, by willingly giving his entire life to Yahuah, living in obedience to the Law, then willingly giving that sacrificial life back to Yahuah (by dying to save his brothers), died innocent in the eyes of the Law.   Death's power is held in sin, so if a man every died innocent, then Death would be defeated.   A God cannot accomplish that requirement.   It had to be a man.

Chapter 6

Yahuah Shammah

The Capital City of the Kingdom of Yahuah

Jerusalem, the capital city of Israel, is a ***physical to spiritual parallel*** of the Capital City of **the Kingdom of Yahuah** which is called **Yahuah Shammah**.   Yahuah Shammah means Yahuah is there.   It is also known as the New Jerusalem and it is documented prophetically by Ezekiel Chapter 48 and described again in Revelation.

Biblical Description of Yahuah Shammah

According to John in the book of Revelation, the New Jerusalem is "pure gold, like clear glass" and its "brilliance [is] like a very costly stone, as a stone of crystal-clear jasper." The street of the city is also made of "pure gold, like transparent glass". The base of the city is laid out in a square and surrounded by a wall made of jasper.

It says in Revelation 21:16 that the height, length, and width are of equal dimensions - as were the Holy of Holies in the Tabernacle and First Temple - and they measure 12,000 furlongs (which is approximately 1500.3 miles). John writes that the wall is 144 cubits, which is assumed to be the width since the length is mentioned previously. 144 cubits are about equal to 65 meters, or 72 yards. It is important to note that 12 is the square root of 144. The number 12 was very important to early Israelites, representing the 12 tribes of Israel and 12 Apostles of Yahusha the Messiah. The four sides of the city represented the four cardinal directions (North, South, East, and West.) In this way, New Jerusalem was thought of as an inclusive place, with gates accepting all of the remnant 12 tribes of Israel from all corners of the earth.

There is no temple building in the New Jerusalem. Yahuah and the Lamb are the city's temple as the Temple has been transposed, and Yahuah is worshiped everywhere. Revelation 22 goes on to describe a river of the water of life that flows down the middle of the great street of the city from the Throne of Yahuah that

Yahusha sits on as proxy King. The tree of life grows in the middle of this street and on either side, or in the middle of the street and on either side of the river. The tree bears twelve fruits, or kinds of fruits, and yields its fruit every month. According to John, "the leaves of the tree were for the healing of the nations." This inclusion of the tree of life in the New Jerusalem harkens back to the Garden of Eden. The fruit the tree bears may be the fruit of life.

John states that the New Jerusalem will be free of sin. The servants of Yahuah will have Theosis (will be elohims), and they will bear the Mark or Seal of Yahuah which is "His name will be on their foreheads." Night will no longer fall, and the inhabitants of the city will "have no need for lamp nor light of the sun, for Yahuah gives them light." John ends his account of the New Jerusalem by stressing its eternal nature: "And they shall reign forever and ever."

Gates

There are twelve gates in the wall oriented to the compass with three each on the east, north, south, and west sides. There is an angel at each gate, or gatehouse. These gates are each made of a single pearl, giving them the name of the "pearly gates". The names of the twelve tribes of Israel are written on these gates. The new Jerusalem gates may bear some relation to the gates mentioned in Enoch, Chapters 33 - 35, where the prophet reports (at the extremities of the whole earth) "heavenly gates opening into heaven; three of them distinctly separated." [33, 3.] And so on for each of the four major compass directions.

The wall has twelve foundation stones, and on these are written the names of the Twelve Apostles. Revelation lacks a list of the names of the Twelve Apostles, and does not describe which name is inscribed on which foundation stone, or if all of the names are inscribed on all of the foundation stones, so that aspect of the arrangement is open to speculation. The layout of the precious stones is contested. All of the precious stones could adorn each foundation stone, either in layers or mixed together some other way, or just one unique type of stone could adorn each separate foundation stone.   This latter possibility is favored by tradition, as each gate presumably stands on one foundation stone, and each of the twelve tribes has long been associated with a certain type of precious stone. These historical connections go back to the time of Temple worship, when the same kinds of stones were set in the golden Breastplate of the Ephod worn by the Kohen Gadol, and on the Ephod the names of each of the twelve tribes of Israel were inscribed on a particular type of stone.

Geometry of Yahuah Shammah

In Revelation 21:16, the angel measures the city with a golden rod or reed, and records it as 12,000 stadia by 12,000 stadia at the base, and 12,000 stadia high. A stadion is usually stated as 185 meters, or 607 feet, so the base has dimensions of about 2220 km by 2220 km, or **1380 miles by 1380 miles**. In the ancient Greek system of measurement, the base of the New Jerusalem would have been equal to 144 million square stadia, 4.9 million square kilometers or *1.9 million square miles*.

If rested on the Earth, its ceiling would be inside the exosphere (the exosphere is the uppermost layer, where the atmosphere thins out and merges with interplanetary/outer space).

Chapter 7

The Temple or "Castle" of the Kingdom of Yahuah

Introduction

In keeping with Scripture and progressive revelation, this chapter will illustrate that Yahuah designed the physical Temple of Solomon in the previous covenants as a shadow picture or physical representation of the temple in **the Kingdom of Yahuah**. That spiritual Truth, alluded to by the design of the physical Temple of Yahuah, was that Yahuah's Temple was always the bodies of the sons of Yahuah.

This fact was the meaning behind Yahusha's declaration that he would tear down the Temple and raise it again in 3 days. This "Temple" the Messiah was referring to was his body. The Bible confirms that the resurrection of the Messiah was, in fact, the beginning of the construction of the true Temple of Yahuah as the Messiah is the Chief Cornerstone.

In this chapter we will examine the physical design of the Temple of Solomon demonstrating the design was a divine physical portrait of the human body. Then we will apply our understanding of "transposition" as it relates to **the Temple of Yahuah** from physical to spiritual Truth. Once we have fully established that the Temple of Solomon was a temporary physical structure illustrating a greater spiritual Truth, we can fully understand the physical and spiritual state in which Yahuah's Temple now exists in **the Kingdom of Yahuah**.

The Physical Design of the Temple of Solomon

The physical design of the Temple of Solomon was literally a human portrait. In keeping with progressive revelation, this physical world is literally a training ground and a teaching tool for the sons of Yahuah. We are being trained and taught spiritual Truths concerning **the Kingdom of Yahuah** by what we see and experience in the physical world. Every detail of the previous 6 covenants including the physical priesthood of Levi, the High Priesthood of Aaron, the sacrifice of the Passover Lamb, the scapegoat, **the Temple of Yahuah**, **the Altar of Yahuah**, were all given to us physically **as training aids**. The Spring and Fall Festivals were given as physical "rehearsals" to teach us about the spiritual plan of salvation.

Everything in the first 6 covenants was designed to point us to the Messiah and teach us about Yahuah's Spiritual Kingdom. It is only within the scope of this chapter to discuss the *physical to spiritual parallels* of the Temple of Solomon as it relates to **the Temple of Yahuah** in **the Kingdom of Yahuah**.

The 3 chambers of the Temple of Solomon

One evident *physical to spiritual parallel* is that both the Tabernacle of Moses and the Temple of Solomon contained three distinct and clearly defined sections. There was the Outer Court (Ulam), the Inner Court or Holy Place (Hekal), and the Holy of Holies or Most Holy Place (Beit HaMikdash).

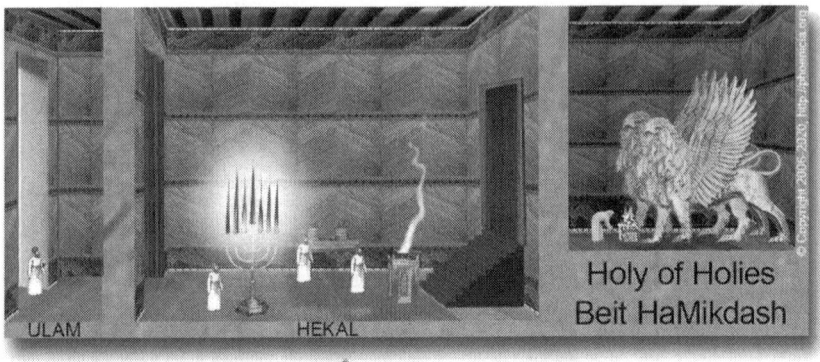

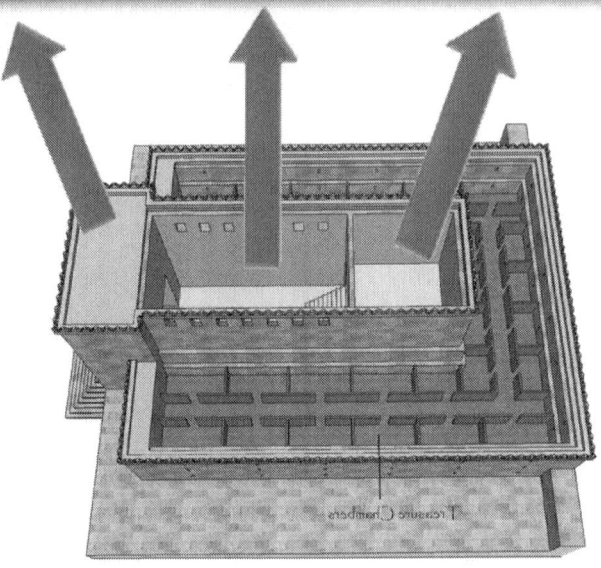

These three sections find perfect correspondence to man as he is also a tri-part being consisting of body, soul and spirit. The Apostle Sha'ul was speaking of our body temples below and the physical to spiritual parallel of the Temple:

> **I Thessalonians 5:23**
> Now may the Elohim (Sha'ul declares the Shema) of peace Himself (Yahuah) sanctify you (His Temple) entirely; and may your spirit (Holy of Holies) and soul (Inner Court) and body (Outer Court) be preserved complete, without blame at the coming of our King Yahusha the Messiah.

The Human Portrait in the Temple of Solomon

It is only my intention to communicate what Tony Badillo and others have illustrated.

> The Temple of Solomon was a physical portrait of a human body (***physical to spiritual parallel***).

Very specifically crafted as a 3 layered "Temple Man" carefully constructed to illustrate, physically, the ultimate spiritual Truth that **the Temple of Yahuah** is the human body.

The High Priest as Temple Man

The section below is taken from Tony Badillo's website http://www.templesecrets.info/. The picture below is the temple floor plan as seen from looking at the Temple from above. It is transformed into a figure of the Zadok High Priest; and within the figure are 13 red numbers

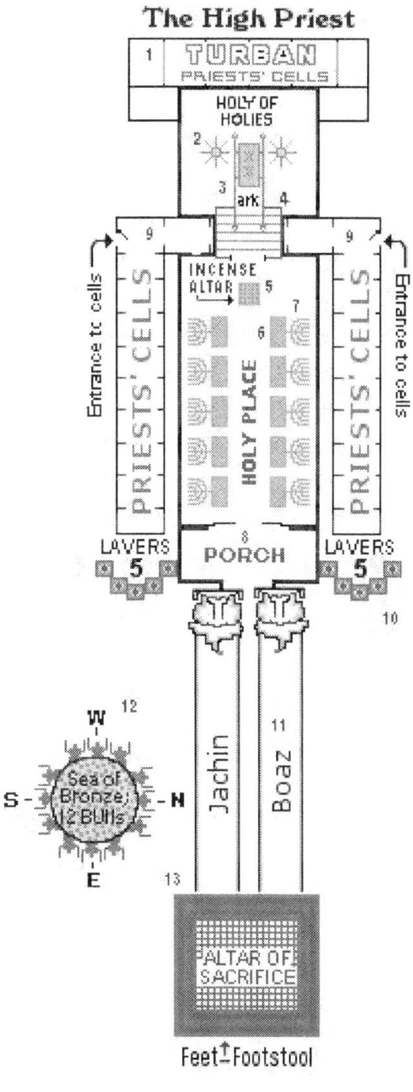
The High Priest
1
TURBAN
PRIESTS' CELLS
HOLY OF HOLIES
2
3
ark
4
9
9
Entrance to cells
Entrance to cells
INCENSE ALTAR
5
7
6
PRIESTS' CELLS
HOLY PLACE
PRIESTS' CELLS
LAVERS
5
8
PORCH
LAVERS
5
10
W
12
11
Sea of Bronze; 12 Bulls
S
N
Jachin
Boaz
E
13
ALTAR OF SACRIFICE
Feet-Footstool

briefly explained below. All are in sequence except nine (9).

1. ***PRIESTS' CELLS*** as a TURBAN[1] *west side* – Gold and silver bullion, I Kings 7:51, was likely stored here. These cells form the High Priest's head cover or turban mentioned in Exodus 28:4, 37. The common priest's cap or bonnet, Exodus 28:40, was more globular, resembling an inverted bowl.

2. ***PRIESTS' CELLS***, *south and north sides* – These are the arms. Only one ingress is given, I Kings. 6:8, but Ezekiel 41:11 includes a second. The entrances correspond to the onyx stones the High Priest wore on his left and right shoulders. Each was engraved with the names of six Israelite tribes, twelve names total, Exodus. 28:9 -12.

3. **TWO LARGE STARS** – These are two 10-cubit tall cherubs of gold plated olive wood, I Kings. 6:23, 28; they are the eyes within Temple Man's head, while the head is the Holy of Holies[2] .

4. **THE ARK of the COVENANT** – This is a gold plated chest with a solid gold cover and two small cherubs (small stars).The Ark is his nose; and its *poles* –when attached to its long sides and drawn

forward (I Kings. 8:8) – depict extended nostrils smelling the sweet smoke from the Incense Altar in the Holy Place.

5. **STAIRWAY** – A short staircase or ramp led from the Holy Place to a slightly elevated (six cubits) Holy of Holies. The stairway is his neck/throat and its top is his mouth.

6. **INCENSE ALTAR** – This small gold plated altar (I Kings 6:22) is national Israel's *heart*, and its sweet-smelling smoke is the prayers and spiritual life of national *ideal* Israel,

7. **TABLES OF THE SHOWBREAD** – On these gold plated tables (I Kings 7:48) were bread and wine, symbolizing flesh and blood, i.e., the humanity of national Israel.

8. **THE LAMP STANDS** (I Kings 7:48, 49) – Their total number was 10 stands/menorahs x 7 stems each = 70 lights, relating to the 70 Israelites of Exodus 1:5 (Jacob's offspring). This is national Israel as the *light to the world,* and the world is the 70 nations of Genesis 10. They may also symbolize the Sabbath multiplied 10 times, implying a messianic age of worldwide rest (meaning *peace).*

9. **THE PORCH**, Portico or vestibule – This antechamber, the *ulam,* (I Kings 6:3, II Chronicles 3:4) corresponds to the human pelvis (hips) and, therefore, *procreation* through the male and female genitalia.

10. **TEN LAVERS** – Five bronze water lavers were on the north and five on the south side. These signify the ten fingers of the hands. The lavers were for washing the blood off the sacrificial offerings, I Kings 7:38

11. **JACHIN, BOAZ** – The large bronze pillars were named *Jachin* and *Boaz* (II Chronicles.3:17) and form Temple Man's legs. These are two hybrid plants symbolizing Kings David and Solomon, war and peace.

12. **SEA OF BRONZE, TWELVE BULLS** – This was a huge basin full of water for the priests to wash their hands and feet (II Chronicles 4:2). It depicts the twelve tribes of Israel crossing the Red Sea. Its water symbolizes the Yahuah's spirit and also his seed.

13. **THE SACRIFICIAL ALTAR** – This (II Chronicles. 4:1) forms Temple Man's feet, while also symbolizing the metallic King Messiah's feet and *footstool,* as was the custom of that time, II Chronicles 9:18, Psalms 110:1.

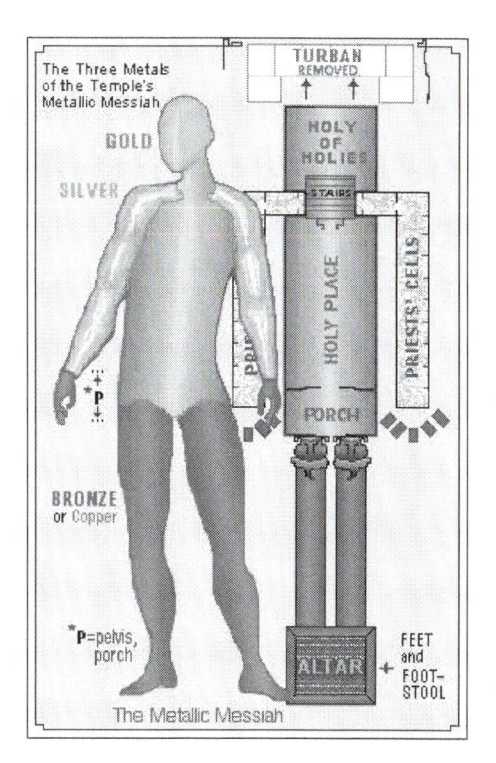

The point here is that the physical Temple that existed in the previous covenants prior to the 7th Yahushaic Covenant was designed as a physical metaphor or "shadow-picture" or portrait. The Temple of Solomon was a physical shadow designed to teach us the greater Spiritual Truth found in the Messiah that **the Temple of Yahuah is our body.**

Many men throughout history have studied the Temple of Solomon. It is considered one of the 7 Wonders of the World and Sir Isaac Newton (1642–1727), the noted English scientist, mathematician and theologian, studied and wrote extensively upon the Temple of Solomon. He dedicated an entire chapter of the Chronology of

Ancient Kingdoms to his observations regarding the temple. Newton was intrigued by the temple's sacred geometry and believed that it was designed by King Solomon with privileged eyes and divine guidance.

Transposition of the Temple of Yahuah

Now that we have looked into the physical design of the Temple of Solomon, and see a portrait of the human body, is there evidence in Scripture to support this **physical to spiritual parallel**. Is it true now, in the 7th and final Yahushaic Covenant, that the Temple was transposed from a physical place to its final Spiritual state never to be rebuilt physically again?

> Could it be that there will never be another physical temple built by the hands of man in Jerusalem? There hasn't been in 2,000 years!

This spiritual Truth concerning the state of **the Temple of Yahuah** is a consistent theme in Scripture which clearly defines **the Temple of Yahuah** as the human body in **the Yahushaic Covenant**:

John 2
19 Yahusha answered and said unto them, destroy this temple, and in three days I will raise it up. 20 Then said the Jews, Forty and six years was this temple in building, and wilt thou rear it up in three days? 21 But he spake of the temple of his body.

I Corinthians 6:19
Do you not know that your body is a temple of the Spirit of Yahuah who is in you, whom you have from Yahuah?

II Corinthians 6:16
What agreement has *the Temple of Yahuah* with idols? For we are the temple of the living Elohim; just as Yahuah said, "*I will dwell in them* and walk among them; and I will be their Elohim, and they shall be My people."

Ephesians 2:19-22
So then you are no longer strangers and aliens, but you are fellow citizens with the saints, and are of Yahuah's household, having been built upon the foundation of the apostles and prophets, the Messiah Yahusha Himself being the corner stone (of *the Temple of Yahuah*), in whom the whole building, being fitted together is growing into a Holy Temple of Yahuah; in whom you also are being built together into a dwelling of Yahuah in the Spirit (*the Kingdom of Yahuah*).

I Peter 2:5
You also, as living stones, are being built up as a spiritual house (Temple)…

We see this Spiritual Truth clearly in Revelation as the "physical Temple" was not seen in the City of Jerusalem, but rather that Temple is now spiritual:

Revelation 21
22 I did not see a temple in the city, because the Yahuah Almighty and the Lamb are its temple.

The Temple of Yahuah has been transposed from its physical shadow to its Spiritual Reality and is the human body, *the sum total of the sons of Yahuah*.

The Sons of Yahuah are Living Arks of the Covenant

In **the Kingdom of Yahuah**, the Ark of the Covenant has been transposed from physical to spiritual. The hearts/minds of the sons of Yahuah are now the Ark of the Covenant.

As we see, in **the Yahushaic Covenant**, the Torah or "Law" or "Commandments/Instructions" are now written within our "heart" which is now the spiritual Ark of the Covenant:

> **Romans 2:14-15**
> 14 (Indeed, when Gentiles, who do not have the law, do by nature things required by the law, they are a law for themselves, even though they do not have the law. 15 They show that the requirements of the law are written on their hearts, their consciences also bearing witness, and their thoughts sometimes accusing them and at other times even defending them.)

Inside each of us, is the spiritual equivalent of the physical portrait of the Ark of the Covenant! The tablets of **the Law of Yahuah** as given to Moses... Aaron's staff, and a portion of Manna (bread from Heaven). Sha'ul lists the physical items found within the physical Ark of the Covenant:

> **Hebrews 9:4**
> ⁴ which had the golden altar of incense and the gold-covered ark of the covenant. This ark contained the gold jar of **manna**, **Aaron's staff** that had budded, and the **stone tablets** of the covenant.

The Ark of the Covenant is within each of us in **the Kingdom of Yahuah**. The blood of Yahusha, the Passover Lamb, is poured on top of the Ark spiritually inside us to cover our sins as we keep Passover in light of Yahusha's sacrifice.

Inside the Ark (in our heart) is:

- **The Commands of Yahuah**. They are "written on our hearts" or placed inside the Ark of the Covenant. We keep them out of love.

- **The staff of Aaron**. Yahuah is our shepherd (Yahusha by proxy), Yahuah "Rohi".

- **The Manna**. We are fed spiritually "manna from heaven" as we are filled with the Spirit of Yahuah

Chapter 8

The Altar of the Kingdom of Yahuah

Introduction

Now that the spiritual Kingdom of Yahuah has been announced by Yahusha and the 7th Covenant has been consummated by the blood of the true Passover Lamb, let us examine **the Altar of Yahuah** in **the Kingdom of Yahuah**.

In the last chapter we clearly demonstrated that **the Temple of Yahuah** is the human body, the sum total of the sons of Yahuah; Yahusha being the Chief Cornerstone of that Temple. The physical temple in Jerusalem was but a prototype or shadow of this greater Truth revealed by the Messiah. We discovered that each of the sons of Yahuah are living **Arks of the Covenant**. Just as with all things previous in 6 physical covenants:

- The Passover Lamb
- The Levitical Priesthood
- The Aaronic High Priesthood
- The Temple
- The Altar
- The Law
- The Ark of the Covenant
- The Sacrifices

The Altar was transposed to **the Kingdom of Yahuah** in **the Yahushaic Covenant**. Therefore, in what way was **the Altar of Yahuah** transposed from physical shadow to spiritual reality?

Transposition of the Altar of Yahuah

***What is the Altar of Yahuah in the body temple?* The "heart and mind" is the Altar in the body temple.**

The Altar of Yahuah now resides in the body temple as the "hearts and minds" of those so chosen by Yahuah as sons! It is still very much a "working altar" with the proper daily oblation (daily sacrifices) being offered up to Yahuah in those Chosen Few by Melchizedek our Eternal High Priest.

In fact, it is still in keeping and putting our faith in Passover that Yahusha (as High Priest) faithfully makes the proper sacrifices before the throne of Yahuah. Expressing our faith in Passover by keeping it is the spiritual equivalent of "sacrificing a lamb". As we keep Passover in faith, Yahusha's "blood" is poured out on the altar of our hearts and minds covering the death decrees in the Law that held us captive to the fear of death. We see below, Yahusha set the righteous example of keeping Passover and the significance of keeping Passover going forward in "remembrance" or "faith" in him.

We see Yahusha clearly say the Passover will find its fulfillment spiritually in *the Kingdom of Yahuah* and only then will Yahusha eat Passover again with us.

> **Luke 22**
> [7] Then came the day of Unleavened Bread on which the Passover lamb had to be sacrificed. [8] Yahusha sent Peter and John, saying, "Go and make preparations for us to eat the Passover."... [14] When the hour came, Yahusha and his

apostles reclined at the table. ¹⁵ And he said to them, "I have eagerly desired to eat this Passover with you before I suffer. ¹⁶ For I tell you, I will not eat it again until it (Passover) **finds fulfillment in *the Kingdom of Yahuah*.**" ¹⁷ After taking the cup, he gave thanks and said, "Take this and divide it among you. ¹⁸ **For I tell you I will not drink again from the fruit of the vine until *the Kingdom of Yahuah comes*.**"   ¹⁹ And he took bread, gave thanks and broke it, and gave it to them, saying, "This (Passover meal) is my body given for you; do this (keep Passover) in remembrance of me (Yahusha commands us to keep Passover in *the Yahushaic Covenant* and that is how we express our faith in him)."   ²⁰ In the same way, after supper he took the cup, saying, "This (Passover) cup is the new covenant in my blood (*the Yahushaic Covenant* was consummated by blood on the Passover), which is poured out for you. ²¹ ...   And I confer on you a kingdom (we are co-heirs), just as my Father conferred one on me (His Kingdom), ³⁰ so that you may eat and drink (Passover) at my table **in my kingdom** (Passover is kept in *the Kingdom of Yahuah*) and sit on thrones, judging the twelve tribes of Israel.

The Apostle Sha'ul confirms that Passover is kept as we put our faith in the sacrifice of Yahusha thereby his blood is spread over *the Altar of Yahuah* (in our hearts and minds) covering our sin:

1 Corinthians 11
²³ For I received from the King what I also passed on to you: Yahusha the Messiah, on the night he was betrayed, took bread, ²⁴ and when he had given thanks, he broke it

and said, "This (Passover meal) is my body, which is for you; do this (keep Passover) in remembrance (faith) of me." ²⁵ In the same way, after supper he took the cup, saying, "This (Passover) cup is the new covenant (the transposition of Passover literally inaugurated **the Yahushaic Covenant**) in my blood; do this (keep Passover), whenever you drink it, in remembrance of me." ²⁶ For whenever (once a year as commanded by Yahuah) you eat this bread and drink this cup, you proclaim (your <u>faith,</u> which is the spiritual sacrifice, in) the King's death until he comes (and his blood is poured out over the Altar of your heart).

²⁷ So then, whoever eats the bread or drinks the cup of the King's in an unworthy manner (eating ham on Easter for example, violating Yahuah's command and Yahusha's instruction to keep Passover) will be guilty of sinning (you will not have the proper sacrifice for sin offered by the eternal High Priest on Yahuah's altar which is your heart and mind) against the body and blood of the King. ²⁸ Everyone ought to examine themselves (purify **the Altar of Yahuah**) before they eat of the bread and drink from the cup. ²⁹ For those who eat and drink without discerning (that) the body of the Messiah (is the Passover Lamb not the Easter pig) eat and drink <u>judgment on themselves</u> (because the blood is only poured out to cover sin on the Altars of those who keep Passover)

Above, Sha'ul is talking about examining ourselves before we keep Passover. He is speaking of the ***physical to spiritual parallel*** of ritually cleansing the Altar in the Torah:

Holman Bible Dictionary
http://www.studylight.org/dic/hbd/view.cgi?number=T51 57

> The altar for sacrifice was purified so that it would be prepared for worship (Leviticus 8:15; Ezekiel 43:26). The objects of gold used in the tabernacle and Temple were also pure in this sense; this would be true of the incense in Exodus 37:29. The Levites were to purify themselves for service in the tabernacle (Numbers 8:21). When that which was unclean or impure came into contact with that which was holy, danger resulted and could even lead to death. This is probably the background for the preparation made for the ==theophany==, a manifestation of Yahuah's presence, in Exodus 19:1 and for the death of Uzzah when he was unprepared (not purified) to touch the ark of the covenant, a most holy object (2 Samuel 6:1-11). Malachi 1:11-12 contrasts the pure offerings of Gentiles with blemished offerings given by Yahuah's people; such a state necessitated purification (Malachi 3:3-4). Purity qualified one to participate in worship, an activity central to the life of ancient Israel. Breaking that purity was a serious matter.

In the book of Hebrews, we see the Apostle Sha'ul address the reality that, instead of the Law being abolished, the Law has literally been transferred to **the Kingdom of Yahuah** to define the role of Melchizedek the Eternal High Priest.

The main point I want to establish here is that the Law pertaining to the High Priesthood that <u>gives authority to offer sacrifices on the Altar</u> (the hearts/minds) on behalf of the sons of Yahuah has been *transposed* to define the role and to give authority to Yahusha as High Priest:

> **Hebrews 7:12**
> "for when there is a transfer (of position from Earth to Heaven or transposition) of the priestly office (of Levi to Melchizedek), out of necessity there is ALSO A TRANSFER of the LAW of the priesthood (by which the Priesthood has authority)"

And now, Yahusha as High Priest makes those sacrifices on behalf of **only those whose faith is put in Passover** in light of his sacrifice. That was the entire "point" of the physical portrait of Passover. It was a rehearsal designed to teach us the greater spiritual Truth found in Yahusha's sacrifice. We are instructed not only by Yahuah in His Law to keep Passover but also by Yahusha and the Apostle Sha'ul. ==Passover was the beginning of **the Yahushaic Covenant** and was transposed to **the Kingdom of Yahuah** spiritually==.

> In keeping with transposition, the Passover shadow was pointing to Yahusha and *faith in Passover* is as essential today as it ever was or even more so.

We see below the description of Yahusha, the High Priest in the Order of Zadok, being called by Yahuah to assume the role of making sacrifices on behalf of men before Yahuah.

As we showed earlier, those sacrifices are made on behalf of those who **do this** or keep Passover in remembrance of his sacrifice:

> **Hebrews 5** - *The Perfect High Priest*
> 1 For **every** high priest taken from among men (Yahusha was a man when chosen by Yahuah as heir to High Priest Yahusha III) is appointed on behalf of men in things pertaining to Yahuah (the High Priest, including Yahusha, is not Yahuah but is a mediator), in order to offer both gifts and sacrifices for sins (this is Yahusha's eternal role, these offerings/sacrifices are defined in the Law which has been transposed to serve him in **the Kingdom of Yahuah**); 2 he can deal gently with the ignorant and misguided, since he himself also is beset with weakness; 3 and because of it he is obligated to offer sacrifices for sins, as for the people, so also for himself. 4 And no one takes the honor to himself, but receives it when he is called by Yahuah, even as Aaron was. 5 So also (like every human High Priest) Yahusha did not glorify himself so as to become a high priest (he was chosen by blood in the Order of Zadok being the heir to Yahusha III, he is the High Zadok or Melchizedek), but He who said to Him
>
> "YOU ARE MY SON, TODAY I HAVE BEGOTTEN YOU"; 6 just as He says also in another passage, "YOU ARE A PRIEST FOREVER ACCORDING TO THE ORDER OF MELCHIZEDEK."

So now Yahusha is offering the daily oblation (sacrifice) for sin on **the Altar of Yahuah** and offers his slain body as the final Passover

Sacrifice.   This is performed for those <u>who put their faith in and keep Passover</u> as he commanded.

The "Altar" has not disappeared as many assume, and in error claim there are currently no daily sacrifices being made. **The Altar and the sacrifices being made on it, are still alive and very active**.   It has simply been transposed to its final spiritual state in *the Kingdom of Yahuah* along with Passover.

We see a "picture" of this spiritual reality in Revelation as Yahusha is seen as *the Passover Lamb* that had been slain in on *the Altar of Yahuah* in Revelation 5.

> **Revelation 5**
> ⁶ Then I saw a Lamb, looking as if it had been slain, standing at the center of the throne... 11 "Worthy is the (spotless) Lamb, who was slain (on Passover), to receive power and wealth and wisdom and strength and honor and glory and praise!"

So Yahusha, the final Passover Lamb, is offering his spiritual body as THE sacrifice for sin before the throne of Yahuah **continually** (daily oblation) now in *the Kingdom of Yahuah*.   This sin offering is made effectual only for those who obey Yahuah and Yahusha's command to <u>keep Passover</u> in light of and expressing faith in his sacrifice.   This Altar is not the physical altar used by the physical priesthood of Aaron and Levi.   The Altar in *the Kingdom of Yahuah* is intimately connected spiritually throughout *the Temple of Yahuah,* which has been transposed, and now is the sum total of the sons of Yahuah!

Isaiah gives us a glimpse of this very truth.   We learn that in the Spiritual Kingdom of Yahuah, we will turn our eyes directly to the

Holy One of Israel not "physical altars made with our hands and fingers":

> ### Isaiah 17
> In that day (in the future Kingdom of Yahuah) people will look to their Maker and turn their eyes to Yahuah, the Holy One of Israel. [8] They will not look to the (physical) altars, the (altars made with the) work of their hands...

The Physical Altar Metaphor

This spiritual Truth concerning the True **Altar of Yahuah** was the reason why Yahuah commanded *the physical altar was not to be made of "stone" cut by human hands* but only by <u>stones cut by Yahuah</u>:

> ### Exodus 20:25
> 'If you make an altar of stones for me, do not build it with cut stones, for you will defile it if you use a tool on it.'

Why such restrictions on the construction of the physical altar? Because the physical altar was pointing to the reality that the physical altar was a shadow picture of the human heart and mind which was not made by man but by Yahuah Himself. Our hearts and minds are spiritual parallels of those stones uncut by human hands... the physical stones in the physical altar were a ***physical to spiritual parallel*** designed to teach us this fact:

> ### I Peter 2:5
> You also, as living stones, are being built up as a spiritual house...

We have established the reality of the Temple and Altar in the true Spiritual realm where **the Kingdom of Yahuah** exists and how this physical world around us was designed as a teaching tool. Let us examine now the sacrifices defined by the Law. Have they been "abolished" or are they being made "daily" by the Eternal High Priest Melchizedek exactly as defined in the Law?

The Transposition of Sacrifices on the Altar

The sacrifices and burnt-offerings were appointed to represent (***physical to spiritual parallel****s*) the offering-up of <u>our affections</u> to Yahuah. The animals offered by the physical shadow, whether lamb, or ram, or goat, or bullock, were the **types of principles in the mind of the worshipper.** We offer these in loving devotion to Yahuah; they are spiritually represented by the physical fire of the offering. Yahuah's acceptance of those offerings was declared by the words so often used respecting the different sacrifices. "It is an offering made by fire, of a sweet aroma unto Yahuah."--Leviticus 3:5.

Animal sacrifices were always intended (as all things physical) as a teaching tool whereby we can come to an understanding of spiritual things i.e. physical to spiritual parallels. What Yahuah was teaching us in these physical examples is what He truly desires spiritually:

> **Psalm 40:6-8**
> [6] (Physical) Sacrifice and meal offering You have not desired; My ears You have opened; (Physical) Burnt offering and (Physical) sin offering You have not required. [7] Then I said, "Behold, I come; In the scroll of the book it is written of me. [8] I delight to do Your will, O my Elohim; <u>Your Law is within my heart</u>."

Transposition of all things is the "key" to understanding this physical world in which we live.

The Apostle Sha'ul taught the transposition of the Law as it related to physical sacrifices in **the Yahushaic Covenant**:

Hebrews 10

1 For the Law, since it has *only* a shadow of the good things to come *and* <u>not the very form of things</u> (the very form of things is in the spirit not physical), can never, by the same (physical) sacrifices which they offer continually year by year, make perfect those who draw near. ² Otherwise, would they not have ceased to be offered, because the worshipers, having once been cleansed, would no longer have had consciousness of sins? ³ But in those (physical) *sacrifices* there is a reminder of sins year by year. ⁴ For it is impossible for the blood of bulls and goats to take away sins. ⁵ Therefore, when He comes into the world, He says,

> ### Psalm 40:6-8
> "SACRIFICE AND OFFERING YOU HAVE NOT DESIRED, BUT A BODY YOU HAVE PREPARED FOR ME; ⁶ IN WHOLE BURNT OFFERINGS AND *sacrifices* FOR SIN YOU HAVE TAKEN NO PLEASURE. ⁷ "THEN I SAID, 'BEHOLD, I HAVE COME (IN THE SCROLL OF THE BOOK IT IS WRITTEN OF ME) TO DO YOUR WILL, O ELOHIM.'"

⁸ After saying above, "SACRIFICES AND OFFERINGS AND WHOLE BURNT OFFERINGS AND *sacrifices* FOR SIN YOU HAVE NOT DESIRED, NOR HAVE YOU TAKEN PLEASURE *in them*" (which are offered physically according to the Law until Yahusha came), ⁹ then He said, "BEHOLD, I HAVE COME TO DO YOUR WILL." He (Yahusha) takes away (the responsibility to offer physical sacrifices from) the first in order (of the Levitical Priests) to establish (the spiritual sacrifices in) the second (order of the

Priesthood of Melchizedek). ¹⁰ By this will we have been sanctified through the (daily) offering of the body of the Messiah Yahusha (who was sacrificed) once for all (as The Passover Lamb). ¹¹ Every priest (of Levi) stands daily ministering and offering time after time the same (physical) sacrifices, which can never take away sins; ¹² but He (Yahusha as Melchizedek the Spiritual High Priest), having offered one (spiritual) sacrifice for sins for all time (as he stands before the spiritual Altar of Yahuah daily or continually as a Lamb that has been slaughtered), SAT DOWN AT THE RIGHT HAND OF YAHUAH, ¹³ waiting from that time onward UNTIL HIS ENEMIES BE MADE A FOOTSTOOL FOR HIS FEET. ¹⁴ For by one offering He has perfected for all time those who are sanctified (because he lives eternally offering his body as the daily sacrifice before Yahuah). ¹⁵ And the Holy Spirit also testifies to us; for after saying,

> ¹⁶ "THIS IS THE COVENANT THAT I WILL MAKE WITH THEM AFTER THOSE DAYS, SAYS YAHUAH:
> I WILL PUT MY LAWS UPON THEIR HEART,
> AND ON THEIR MIND I WILL WRITE THEM,"
>
> *He then says*,
>
> ¹⁷ "AND THEIR SINS AND THEIR LAWLESS DEEDS
> I WILL REMEMBER NO MORE."

¹⁸ Now where there is forgiveness of these things, there is no longer *any* (physical) offering for sin (because the sacrificed body of Yahusha is ever before the Throne of Yahuah).

Revelation 5:6
Then I saw a Lamb, looking as if it had been slain, standing at the center of the throne

A New and Living Way

[19] Therefore, brethren, since we have confidence to enter the holy place by the blood of Yahusha, [20] by a new and living way which He inaugurated for us through the veil, that is, His flesh, [21] and since *we have* a great priest over the house of Yahuah (offering the spiritual sacrifices prescribed by the Law on our behalf), [22] let us draw near with a sincere heart in full assurance of faith (in the Passover), having our hearts (*the Altar of Yahuah*) sprinkled *clean* (by the blood of the Passover Lamb when we express our faith by keeping Passover in remembrance of him until he comes again) from an evil conscience and our bodies washed with pure (living) water (Mikveh). [23] Let us hold fast the confession of our hope (as we keep Passover in remembrance of Yahusha) without wavering, for He who promised (that the Passover Lamb covers the death decrees in the Law) is faithful (to set us free from bondage to the threat of death); [24] and let us consider how to stimulate one another to love and (to do) good deeds (of the Law, because now we have been set free from the Law of Sin and Death and live by the Law of the Spirit of Life)

Transposition of the Law that Governs the Sacrifices

The Apostle Sha'ul describes the "change" that occurred in both the physical law and physical priesthoods. Sha'ul used the Greek word "***metathesis***" in Hebrews 7:12 when explaining how the Law and the Priesthood of Levi defined by **the Mosaic Covenant** "*changed*" in **the Yahushaic Covenant**. Metathesis is Strong's 3331 and means "*transferred to Heaven*"... ***transposition***.

3331	metathesis met-ath'-es-is	from metatithemi 3346; transposition, i.e. transferal (to heaven), disestablishment (of a law from physical to spiritual):--change to, removing, translation.

Hebrews 7:12
For when the priesthood is *changed*, of necessity there takes place a *change* of law also.

The word "change" above means "transferred to heaven" so the proper translation is:

Hebrews 7:12
For when the (physical) priesthood (of Aaron/Levi) is *transferred to heaven* (to Melchizedek), of necessity (because the Law is what gives the authority to make

sacrifices) there takes place a *transposition* of the Law (to heaven to serve Yahusha now as High Priest) also.

It is not my intention in this chapter to teach on all the various sacrifices and what they represent. Every section in this book should really be developed fully into a book of its own. Again, this book is meant more as *Cliff Notes*. In this book series, we will eventually look at the most "abominable" sacrifice that could be made. Before we can identify that "abominable" sacrifice we must first establish the "true" sacrifice that this "abominable" sacrifice replaces on the altar of our hearts and minds in the Body Temple. **That true sacrifice is Passover.**

Passover the true sacrifice for sin

As we see below, the sacrifice of Passover as well as the keeping of Passover wasn't "abolished" by the Messiah; it too was transposed over to Yahusha as "the Passover Lamb of Yahuah". The sacrifice of **the Passover Lamb** is only effective now for those who have the blood of THAT sacrifice on their hearts (Altars).

We renew that "sacrifice" annually in loving obedience in keeping Passover in light of Yahusha's sacrifice. "Easter" is not "Passover" as we will soon realize clearly later in this book series. Easter is not an **Appointed Time of Yahuah**, it is not a sacred assembly of Yahuah's, it is not the day on which the Messiah's sacrifice was made nor was it his resurrection day.

There is no commandment for Easter. It is a pagan sacrifice of a pig and a pagan holy day originating not in the Bible but in Babylon.

ONLY, and I cannot stress this enough, **ONLY** those who have properly put their faith in Passover and express that faith in their actions by keeping Passover (*believe Yahusha was that Lamb*) as commanded by Yahuah and instructed by Yahusha and taught by his disciples <u>are covered by the Blood of the Lamb</u>.

The keeping of Passover to be saved from death was established clearly by the original Passover when Isaac was spared by a substitutionary ram (a male lamb). Then again in Egypt when the Angel of Death "passed over" those who had the blood of the lamb on their doorposts.

Yahusha made this clear as he kept Passover the day he died. John the Baptist made this point crystal clear when he saw Yahusha at his Mikveh and declared "Behold! The Passover Lamb of Yahuah". The Apostle Sha'ul makes this point clear instructing us in "how" to keep Passover, Peter stressed it, John the Revelator showed us this in the Spirit;

> Passover is truly the scarlet thread (blood) of redemption running from cover to cover in the Word of Yahuah beginning with 'the lamb being slaughtered before the foundation of the world... in the Heavenly Scroll

Luke 22:19

19 And when He had taken some bread and given thanks (at Passover), He broke it and gave it to them, saying, "This (Passover Dinner) is My body (Passover Lamb) which is given (sacrificed) for you; do this (keep Passover) in remembrance of Me."

John 1:29
"Behold the (Passover) Lamb of Yahuah, which taketh away the sin of the world."

John 1:36
"and he looked at Yahusha as He walked, and said, "Behold, the (Passover) Lamb of Yahuah!"

1 Corinthians 5: 7-8
"Get rid of the old yeast that you may be a new batch without yeast--as you really are. For the Messiah, our Passover Lamb has been sacrificed. Therefore let us keep the Festival (of Passover/Unleavened Bread), not with the old yeast, the yeast of malice and wickedness, but with bread without yeast, the bread of sincerity and truth."

1 Peter 1: 18-25
"For you know that it was not with perishable things such as silver or gold that you were redeemed from the empty way of life handed down to you from your forefathers, but with the precious blood of the Messiah, a (Passover) lamb without blemish or defect"

Revelation 5:6
"Then I saw a (Passover) Lamb, looking as if it had been slain.

Revelation 5:12

"In a loud voice they sang: "Worthy is the (Passover) Lamb, who was slain, to receive power and wealth and wisdom and strength and honor and glory and praise!"".

Revelation 5:13

"Then I heard every creature in heaven and on earth and under the earth and on the sea, and all that is in them, singing: "To him who sits on the throne and to the (Passover) Lamb be praise and honor and glory and power, for ever and ever!"

So we see the "proper" sacrifice for sin on **the Altar of Yahuah** is **the Passover Lamb of Yahuah**, the Messiah Yahusha. We are to keep **and** put our faith in Passover each year as we "do this" in remembrance of the Messiah's sacrifice. Keeping Passover is our spiritual sacrifice to Yahuah and in doing so, we are "covered by the Blood of the Lamb" and will be Passed Over the Second Death. This is the story of salvation told in the Bible.

Today, however, Christianity no longer puts their faith in Passover but rather "Easter". We will cover this **abomination** in detail later in Chapter 14 as we define **the Abomination of Desolation**. In this chapter I am simply demonstrating the transposition of physical sacrifices defined in the Law (now "written on our hearts") and the transposition of His Altar. In doing so I demonstrate that the TRUE sacrifice for sin ***is keeping Passover***. Not "Easter".

True sacrifices in the Spiritual Kingdom of Yahuah

The physical sacrifices defined in the Law are physical to spiritual parallels of true Spiritual sacrifices to Yahuah. These true sacrifices in the spiritual realm are our affections toward Yahuah expressed through our actions (faith without works is dead faith). This is not a new concept limited to the New Testament. King David proclaimed this reality in Psalms; clearly illustrating the spiritual Truth later to be revealed in **the Yahushaic Covenant**. The true Altar of Yahuah is in the heart and mind of the Body Temple and TRUE sacrifices are made on that altar not a physical one:

> **Psalms 51:17**
> "The (true) sacrifices of Yahuah are a broken spirit (Spiritual); (offered on) a broken and a contrite heart (the true Altar), O Yahuah, thou wilt not despise.

The Apostle Sha'ul in his letter to the Roman Church, again, illustrates this spiritual truth concerning true sacrifices in the Spiritual Kingdom of Yahuah:

> **Romans 12:1**
> "I beseech you therefore brethren, by the mercies of Yahuah, that you present your bodies a living sacrifice, holy and acceptable to Yahuah, which is your spiritual worship."

It is in the keeping of Passover that we express our faith in the Passover Lamb and keep the memory of Yahusha's sacrifice alive. That is the spiritual equivalent of "sacrificing the Passover Lamb and pouring the blood of the Lamb over **the Altar of Yahuah**" which is our hearts/minds. Many say they have "faith in the blood of the Lamb" and then keep Easter. True faith in the blood of the Lamb is expressed by "works" of the Law and Yahuah and Yahusha and Sha'ul all commanded we keep Passover!

> **James 2:18**
> But someone may well say, "You have faith (alone) and (condemn me because) I have works (trying to work my way to heaven legalistically); show me your faith without the works, and I will show you my faith by my works."

We cannot "say" we have faith in Yahusha and then not keep Passover as Yahusha commanded. That is dead faith and if we don't keep Passover then our faith in **the Passover Lamb** is DEAD and your sin is not covered as we did not offer the spiritual sacrifice required. If we don't express our faith by our works of keeping the Passover, the blood of the Passover Lamb is not poured out over **the Altar of Yahuah** on our behalf. Everyone (even demons) know Yahusha is the Passover Lamb, but how many express that faith in Yahusha by being obedient to his command to keep Passover? Faith expressed through actions of obedience makes us perfect.

We see that we are justified not by faith alone, but by faith combined with works:

> **James 2:14-26**
> ¹⁴ What *does it* profit, my brethren, if someone says he has faith but does not have works? Can faith save him? ¹⁵ If a brother or sister is naked and destitute of daily food, ¹⁶ and one of you says to them, "Depart in peace, be warmed and

filled," but you do not give them the things which are needed for the body, what *does it* profit? ¹⁷ **Thus also faith by itself, if it does not have works, is dead.** ¹⁸ But someone will say, **"You have faith, and I have works." Show me your faith without your works, and I will show you my faith by my works.** ¹⁹ You believe that there is one Elohim. You do well. Even the demons believe—and tremble! ²⁰ **But do you want to know, O foolish man, that faith without works is dead?** ²¹ Was not Abraham our father justified by works when he offered Isaac his son on the altar? ²² Do you see that faith was working together with his works, and **by works faith was made perfect**? ²³ And the Scripture was fulfilled which says, "Abraham believed Yahuah, and it was accounted to him for righteousness." And he was called the friend of Yahuah. ²⁴ **You see then that a man is justified by works, and not by faith only.** ²⁵ Likewise, was not Rahab the harlot also justified by works when she received the messengers and sent *them* out another way? ²⁶ **For as the body without the spirit is dead, so faith without works is dead also.**

In Chapter 12 I will fully establish the reality of the Law in **the Kingdom of Yahuah**.

Chapter 9

The Seal of the Kingdom of Yahuah

Introduction

The Seal of Yahuah or the protective shield over the minds of His servants is known as **the Shema**. Shema is the Hebrew word for "hear" and comes from the definition of **the Seal of Yahuah** in the Torah "Hear O Israel". That seal is the knowledge of Yahuah, the declaration that He alone is Elohim and there is no other. A claim Yahuah is very clear about making... *He alone is Elohim and there is no other. He alone is Creator and He did it alone all by Himself. He alone is our savior, our redeemer*:

Isaiah 44

24 "This is what Yahuah says— your Redeemer, who formed you in the womb: I am Yahuah, who has made all things, who alone stretched out the heavens, who spread out the earth by myself.

Isaiah 24

15 Therefore in the east give glory to Yahuah; exalt the name of Yahuah, the Elohim of Israel! 8 "I am Yahuah; that is my name (not Yahusha, not LORD, and certainly not Jesus)! I will not give my glory to another or my praise to idols (no other, not even to His first born son! The name Yahusha even cries out *"Yahuah is our savoir"*).

Jude 1:25

25 to Yahuah Our Savior, who alone is wise, be glory and majesty, dominion and power, both now and forever.

Isaiah 42

5 This is what Yahuah says— he who created the heavens and stretched them out, who spread out the earth and all that comes out of it, who gives breath to its people, and life to those who walk on it:

Isaiah 45

5 I am Yahuah, and there is no other; apart from me there is no Elohim. ...
18 For this is what Yahuah says— he who created the heavens, he is Elohim; he who fashioned and made the earth, he founded it; he did not create it to be empty, but formed it to be inhabited— he says: "I am Yahuah, and there is no other."

Isaiah 46

5 "To whom will you compare me or count me equal? To whom will you liken me that we may be compared (not even His messiah)? 8 "Remember this, fix it in mind (seal your mind with it), take it to heart (write it on your heart), you rebels. 9 Remember the former things, those of long ago; I am Elohim, and there is no other; I am Elohim, and there is none like me. 10 I make known the end from the beginning, from ancient times, what is still to come. I say: My purpose will stand, and I will do all that I please.

The Seal of Yahuah is very well defined as **His Name** written on our foreheads. That is a metaphor for those who know His Name and **understand** that He alone is Elohim and there is no other. He is not a trinity nor is He a bi-entity. To fully understand *the Seal of Yahuah* we must understand and employ the intended *physical to spiritual parallel*s given to us and how they were explained over time through progressive revelation and then transposed into His Kingdom. I will explain these in detail.

The Seal of *the Kingdom of Yahuah* is clearly defined both in the Torah and *the Yahushaic Covenant*. Let us first define exactly what that seal is. **The Seal of Yahuah** *is quite literally* **His Name** *and* **the knowledge that He alone is Elohim** *and it is "written" on the foreheads as a SEAL over the minds of those who will inhabit His Kingdom*:

Revelation 3

12 *Him who overcomes I will make a pillar in the temple of my Elohim* (those sealed will become *the Temple of Yahuah*). *Never again will he* (Yahuah) *leave it* (that Spiritual Temple). *I will write on him* (who overcomes) *the name of my Elohim* (Yahuah)

Revelation 7:3

3 "*Do not harm the land or the sea or the trees until we put a seal on the foreheads of the servants of our Elohim* (Yahuah)."

Revelation 9

4 *They were told not to harm the grass of the earth or any plant or tree, but only those people who did not have the seal of Elohim* (Yahuah) *on their foreheads.*

Revelation 22

4 They will see his face, and his name (Yahuah) will be (written/sealed) on their foreheads.

This seal is defined in detail in the Torah in Deuteronomy Chapter 6 below, in keeping with progressive revelation, **physical to spiritual parallel**s, and transposition I will explain the meaning of these physical metaphors in (parenthesis):

Deuteronomy 6

6 "Now this is the commandment, the statutes and the judgments which Yahuah your Elohim has commanded *me* to teach you, that you might do *them* in the land where you are going over to possess it (the future Kingdom of Yahuah), ² so that you and your son and your grandson might fear Yahuah your Elohim, to keep all His statutes and His commandments (the governing constitution in the Kingdom of Yahuah) which I command you, all the days of your life, and that your days may be prolonged ==(the promise for obedience found in the Law is Eternal Life)==. ³ O Israel, you should listen and be careful to do *it*, that it may be well with you and that you may multiply greatly, just as Yahuah, the Elohim of your fathers, has promised you, *in* a land flowing with milk and honey (the future Kingdom of Yahuah). ⁴ "==**Hear (Shema), O Israel! Yahuah is our Elohim, Yahuah is one (Elohim)! ⁵ You shall love Yahuah your Elohim with all your heart and with all your soul and with all your might.**== ⁶ These words, which I am commanding you today, shall be (written) on your heart (in *the Yahushaic Covenant* see Jeremiah 31:33). ⁷ You shall teach them diligently to your sons and shall talk of them when you sit in your house and when you walk by

the way and when you lie down and when you rise up. 8 You shall bind them as a sign on your hand (the works of your hand) and they (His Law) shall be as frontals (or spiritual seal) on your forehead.

When questioned by the Pharisees (teachers of the Law) about what is the single greatest commandment, Yahusha declared the Shema, **the Seal of Yahuah** by literally quoting Deuteronomy Chapter 6:

> **Mark 12:28-34**
> 28 One of the teachers of the law (Torah) came and heard them debating. Noticing that Yahusha had given them a good answer, he asked him, "Of all the commandments, which is the most important?"   29 "The most important one," answered Yahusha (then he quoted Deuteronomy 6), "is this: *'Hear, O Israel, Yahuah our Elohim, Yahuah is one. 30 Love Yahuah your Elohim with all your heart and with all your soul and with all your mind and with all your strength*.' 31 The second is this: 'Love your neighbor as yourself.' There is no commandment greater than these." 32"Well said, teacher," the man replied. "You are right in saying that Yahuah is one and there is no other but Him. 33 To love him with all your heart, with all your understanding and with all your strength, and to love your neighbor as yourself is more important than all burnt offerings and sacrifices."

Yahusha also proclaimed *the Seal of Yahuah* to be essential to eternal life, just as it was defined in Deuteronomy 6 and confirmed in Revelation:

John 17:3

³ And this is eternal life, that they may know You (Yahuah), **the only true Elohim (the Shema), AND** (be in covenant with) Yahusha (the) Messiah whom You (Yahuah) have sent (as the Passover Lamb to purchase that eternal life by covering the decrees in the Law that demand our death for transgressing His commandments and ordinances).

The Meaning of Frontals

We see that Yahuah's Law and specifically the declaration and knowledge *that Yahuah is ONE Elohim* (not a trinity or bi-entity) *and there is no other Elohim* is said to be as **frontals or a protective shield on our foreheads**:

> **Deuteronomy 6:8**
> "they (His Law) **shall be as frontals** (or spiritual seal) **on your forehead**(Spiritual Mind).

The Frontal Bone is literally the protective shield in the cranium (physical metaphor) that protects the Frontal Lobe of the brain:

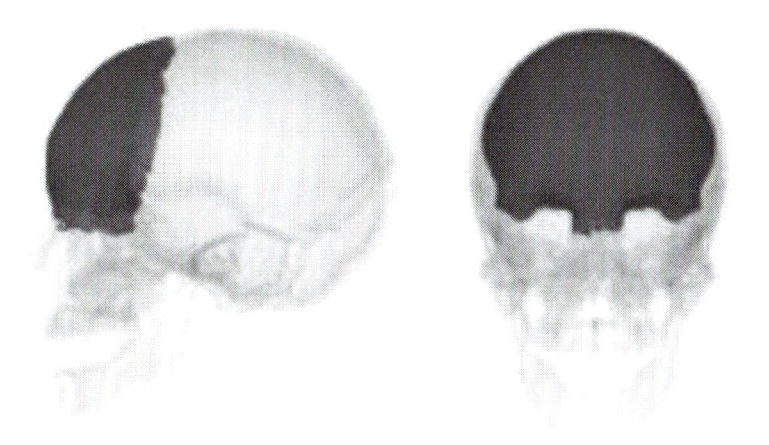

This ***physical to spiritual parallel*** employed by Yahuah in Deuteronomy can only now be understood in the context it was meant. Science has defined the purpose of the Frontal Lobe of the human brain and we can see why that lobe MUST be sealed by Yahuah.

The Frontal Lobe has been identified and described as follows, according to Dr. Donald Stuss of the Rotman Research Institute:

> *The frontal lobe is a critical center and it controls the "essence" of our humanity. The frontal lobes, which are also called the cerebral cortex, are the seat of emotions and judgments related to sympathy, which is the ability to feel sorrow for someone else's suffering, and empathy, which is the ability to understand another's feelings and problems. They are also the seat of understanding humor, including subtle witticisms and word plays. The frontal lobe also recognizes sarcasm and irony. And they are where recognition of deception occurs guiding our judgment between right and wrong. The cerebral cortex, or frontal lobes, is indeed the seat of our essence and nature.*

We need to always keep in the foremost of our mind that Yahuah's purpose is to govern the Universe with His sons. The Frontal Lobe is critical in all aspects of judgment, empathy, knowing right from wrong. Yahuah literally provides a "protective shield" called **the Seal of Yahuah** which protects that very part of our mind that enables us to have empathy toward others, recognize deceptive philosophies, and determines our essence and nature.

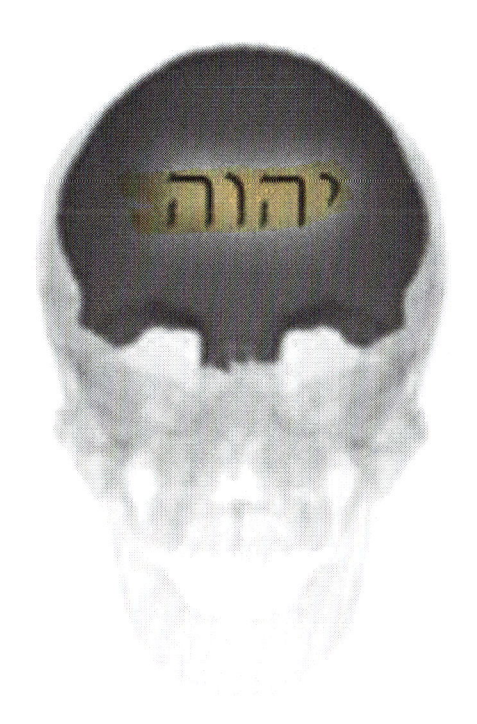

In effect those who have this seal have in the foremost of their mind the truth that Yahuah is ONE Elohim and that His Law defines what is right and wrong and that it is love (empathy) for others that are the foundation of that Law. This is exactly what was declared by Yahusha when asked.

Yahusha demonstrated this SEAL and declared it THE GREATEST COMMANDMENT of all as he quoted Deut 6:

> **Mark 28-34**
>
> 28 One of the teachers of the law (Torah) came and heard them debating. Noticing that Yahusha had given them a good answer, he asked him, "Of all the commandments, which is the most important?" 29 "The most important one," answered Yahusha (then he quoted the Shema in

Deut. 6), "is this: 'Hear, O Israel, Yahuah our Elohim, Yahuah is one. 30 Love Yahuah your Elohim with all your heart and with all your soul and with all your mind and with all your strength.' 31 The second is this: 'Love your neighbor as yourself.' There is no commandment greater than these."

We see Yahusha confirm that **the Seal of Yahuah** is the Greatest Commandment of all. He went on to explain that in that understanding that *Yahuah is the ONE and ONLY Elohim,* our minds are sealed with the Love required to enter His Kingdom: Love Yahuah and your neighbor.

Yahusha was not giving us two new commandments here that the "Church would be built upon" as the "Old Laws" were abolished. Not at all, Yahusha was simply summarizing the 10 Commandments which were themselves a summary of the full set of 613 Laws. The Pharisees understood that and declared Yahusha a "true teacher of the Law".

The first 5 Commandments instruct us, in detail, how to express our love toward Yahuah. The last 5 Commandments instruct us (in detail) how to express our love toward our neighbor.

We see below that both the Seal and Sign of **the Kingdom of Yahuah** are expressed in the 10 Commandments:

How to love Yahuah	How to love your neighbor
1. You shall have no other Elohims before me (the Seal of *the Kingdom of Yahuah*)	6. You shall not murder (your neighbor).
2. You shall not make for yourself an image in the form of anything in heaven above or on the earth beneath or in the waters below.. (the Seal of *the Kingdom of Yahuah*)	7. You shall not commit adultery (with your neighbor's wife).
3. You shall not misuse the name of Yahuah your Elohim. (the Seal of *the Kingdom of Yahuah*)	8. You shall not steal (from your neighbor).
	9. You shall not give false testimony against your neighbor.
4. Remember the Sabbath day by keeping it holy. (the Sign of *the Kingdom of Yahuah*)	10. You shall not covet your neighbor's house. You shall not covet your neighbor's wife, or his male or female servant, his ox or donkey, or anything that belongs to your neighbor.
5. Honor your father and your mother, so that you may live long in the land Yahuah your Elohim is giving you (because your parents are given as proxies in Yahuah's stead so loving them is loving Him.)	

The Pharisee understood that Yahusha was summing up the Law which was summed up into the 10 Commandments.

The False Seal or Mark of the Beast

NOTE: Please see my book **The Antichrist Revealed!** where I explain in great detail what The Mark, the monogram, the pictogram, and the name of the Beast are. In that book I prove ==the Mark of the Beast is the sign of the cross.==

It is very difficult (if not impossible) to reach someone who has elevated the image of a man in their hearts above Yahuah, and marked themselves with the one mark on the forehead that is contrary to **the Mark of Yahuah**. The Apostle Sha'ul and the Prophet Daniel (both) warned us of this very thing in a letter to the assembly of believers in Rome; where this deception was later to be formalized at the Council of Nicaea,

> **Romans 1**
> 21 Because that, when they knew Yahuah, they glorified Yahuah not as Elohim, neither were thankful; but became vain in their imaginations, and their foolish heart was darkened (to believe a lie, the Spirit of Error). 22 Professing themselves to be wise, they became fools, 23

And changed the glory of the incorruptible Yahuah into *an image* made like to corruptible man (Jesus Christ).

Instead of sealing their minds with the knowledge that Yahuah alone is Elohim and there is no other, they elevated an "image of the Babylonian Tammuz/Apollo" called this image "Jesus Christ" and worshipped this image as God. Without the protective seal over their frontal lobe they cannot recognize the Great Deception and are given over to it.

The Prophet Daniel prophesied this would happen:

Daniel 8

11 Yes, it (image of the Beast) even considered itself as great as the prince of the army (the Messiah, the Prince of the Army of Yahuah); the regular burnt offering (daily sacrifice) was taken away from him (Easter replaced Passover in this image of Jesus), and the place of his sanctuary (the human body) was thrown down. *12* Through sin (transgression of the Law), the army (of the false messiah) was put in its power, along with the regular burnt offering (a sacrificial pig of Ishtar replaced Yahusha the Passover Lamb). It flung truth on the ground (sold a lie instead, it is based on the Spirit of Error) as it acted and prospered.

I explain this in detail in my book ***the Antichrist Revealed!*** What false spirit (called the Spirit of Error and the Spirit of the False Messiah) prevails in the Beast (Christian Church) that led to the Messiah being worshipped above Yahuah as God?

The Spirit of the Anti-Christ is CLEARLY defined below:

1 John 4
1 Beloved, do not believe every spirit, but test the spirits to see whether they are from Yahuah, because many false prophets have gone out into the world (claiming to be the incarnation of God). 2 By this you know the Spirit of Yahuah: every spirit that confesses that Messiah Yahusha has come in the flesh (a man) is from Yahuah; 3 and every spirit that does not confess Yahusha has come in the flesh (but says Yahusha is Yahuah or the Trinity) is not from Yahuah; **this is the *spirit* of the antichrist** (or False Messiah. The False Messiah is an image of a man worshipped above Yahuah as God) ... 12 No one has seen Yahuah at any time! (Because Yahusha is not Yahuah in the flesh or a demi-god).

We see that the Spirit of the False Messiah is anyone who does not admit that Yahusha was simply a human and not a God. The **Spirit of the Antichrist** is the denial that Yahusha was 100% (a fleshly man) and not *"God incarnate"*. It is the doctrine that Yahuah came to earth as Jesus Christ, and that Jesus Christ is God incarnate.

We see in Revelation again a stern warning against what is the largest religion on Earth. Note, I cover this in detail in my book **The Antichrist Revealed!** to prove my comments in parenthesis below are valid:

> **Revelation 13** - *The Beast out of the Earth*
> 11 Then I saw another beast (Christianity), coming out of the earth. He (leader of the second beast) had two horns like a lamb (the Pope's Mitre hat), but he spoke like a dragon (Satan is the Spirit behind Christianity). 12 He (the

Pope) exercised all the authority of the first beast (Jesus Christ) on his behalf (<u>Authority of the Church</u>), and (Christianity) made the earth and its inhabitants worship (in their hearts) the first beast (Jesus Christ), whose fatal wound had been healed (giving us a clue that this false messiah would be a false image of the true one). 13 And he (second Beast/Christianity) performed great and miraculous signs, even causing fire to come down from heaven to earth in full view of men. 14 Because of the signs he (Christianity) was given power to do on behalf of the first beast (Jesus Christ), he (Christianity) deceived the inhabitants of the earth (the largest religion on Earth is Christianity). He (Christianity) ordered them (humanity) to <u>set up an image</u> (in their hearts above Yahuah) in honor of the beast (Jesus Christ) who was wounded by the sword and yet lived (another reference that he is a FALSE image of the true Messiah). 15 He (second Beast/Christianity) was given power to give breath (Spirit of the False Messiah) **to the image of the first beast**, so that it could speak (to the hearts of man declaring Jesus is God incarnate) and cause all who refused to worship the image to be killed (Christianity has been waging a war on the True Sabbath Keeping Saints for 2000 years).

I will cover all of this in my book ***The Antichrist Revealed!***.

The "seal" of the Christian Church is the Trinity which is represented by "the cross".   This "cross", however, was the very "seal" over the foreheads of the Priests of Tammuz (the second member of the Pagan Trinity in whose image Jesus Christ was created).

We see the "cross" adorn the dress of ancient Babylonian priests of Tammuz:

Statues of the Babylonian Queen who created the Babylonian religion that Christianity is founded upon has the cross or Mark of the Beast emblazoned on her forehead:

The cross and the Trinity is the universal sign of all pagan sun worshipping religions on Earth.   It is the symbol or "seal" of the sun worshipping religion of Rome

SUN GODS: Isis, Horus, & Seb

It is a "seal" written on the foreheads of those initiates into the false religion:

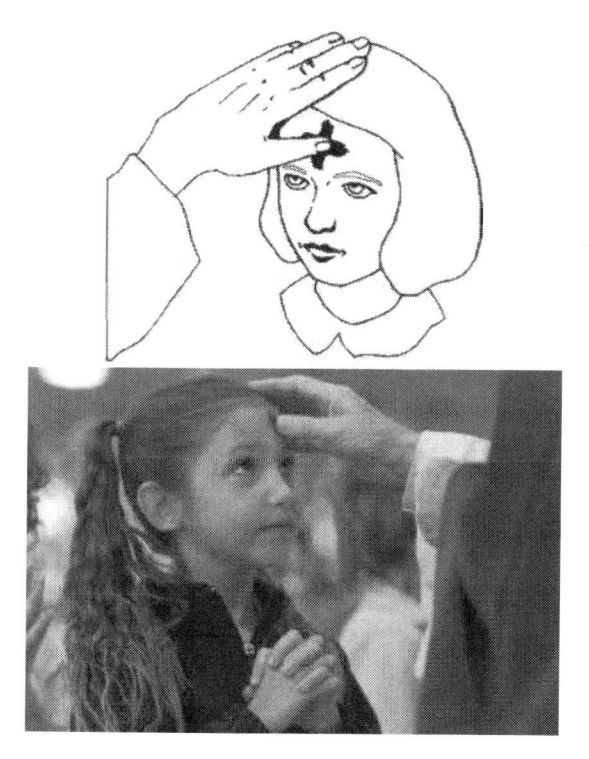

269

I explain all of this in great detail in my second and third books in this series; ***The Mystery Religion of Babylon*** and ***Christianity the Great Deception***. If you are reading this book and have not yet read the previous 4 books, there is much you probably do not understand. Please go back and read these first 4 books and everything I am saying now will make much more sense to you.

They who don't have the mark Ҳ could not buy or sell

In Revelation 13:17 we see that those who do not take the mark of Jesus Christ (Ҳ) are prohibited from commerce within his realm. Is this referring to some futuristic physical "mark" or biochip in our forehead and hand as is being taught today? Or have we simply overlooked the obvious because we are unwilling to acknowledge that Jesus Christ is the beast and Christianity is the second beast? If we simply take an honest look throughout history, we see that Christianity has outlawed "buying and selling" specifically for all those who do not bow down to the authority of the Pope and accept the specific mark on their forehead Ҳ.

The Book of Revelation is misunderstood by many as applying only to the last 7 years of *"tribulation"*, when in fact it was given 2000 years ago and covers a 2000-year span of Christian dominance. We see below, the *Mark of the Beast* is the sign of the cross Ҳ, and those who do not have that mark were forbidden to "buy or sell" throughout history. It is admitted below that the mark of the X is the "**seal on the forehead**" which is in opposition to the **Seal of Yahuah**:

> Jamieson-Fausset-Brown Bible Commentary
>
> > The *mark, or the name*—Greek, "the mark (namely), the name of the beast." The mark may be, as in the case of <u>the sealing of the saints in the forehead</u>, <u>not a visible mark</u>, <u>but symbolical of allegiance. So the sign of the cross in Popery.</u> The Pope's interdict has often shut out the

excommunicate from social and commercial intercourse.

Clarke's Commentary on the Bible

And that no man might buy or sell, save he that had the mark – "If any," <u>observes Bishop Newton,</u>

"*dissent from the stated and authorized forms (of Christianity); they are condemned and excommunicated as heretics; and in consequence of that they are no longer suffered* **to buy or sell**; *they are interdicted from traffic and commerce, and all the benefits of civil society.*

<u>Roger Hoveden relates of William the Conqueror,</u>

that he was so dutiful to the pope that he would not permit any one in his power **to buy or sell** *any thing whom he found disobedient to the apostolic see (the Pope).*

<u>The canon of the Council of Lateran, under Pope Alexander III.,</u>

made against the Waldenses and Albigenses, enjoins, upon pain of ==anathema==*, that no man presume to entertain or cherish them in his house or land,* **or exercise traffic with them** *(that do not follow Papal authority).*

The Synod of Tours, in France, under the same pope, orders,

*"under the like intimidation, that no man should presume to receive or assist them, no, not so much as hold any communion with them, **in selling or buying**; that, being deprived of the comfort of humanity they may be compelled to repent of the error of their way."*

It was ordered by a bull of Pope Martin the Fifth,

*"that no contract should be made with such, and **that they should not follow any business and merchandise**: save he that had the mark; took the oath to be true to the pope, or made a public profession of the Popish religion: or the name of the beast; Papists, so called from the pope"*

"In the tenth and eleventh centuries the severity against the excommunicated was carried to so high a pitch, that nobody might come near them, not even their own wives, children, or servants; they forfeited all their natural legal rights and privileges, and were excluded from all kinds of offices."

Now that we know the identity of the first beast, that it is the "image of a man" we have elevated in our hearts as God above Yahuah … and John identified that man by his mark, his monogram, and by a pictogram and it is Jesus Christ the serpent. The second beast is easily identified… it is Christianity. It is the religion that evolved around the first beast that causes the Earth to worship the first beast. Remember that Christianity is the largest religion on Earth. It is the very one that sits on 7 hills etc.

and by definition is the "widest gate" on earth! It is not the "narrow gate" that leads to salvation.

When you insert their true identities into passages in the Book of Revelation those passages come alive! For more information on the identity of the False Messiah, please read my book ***The Antichrist Revealed!*** available on www.sabbathcovenant.com.

Chapter 10

The Standard or "Sign" of the Kingdom of Yahuah

Introduction

Every kingdom or government has a standard or sign that is raised high above for all to see. In Earthly kingdoms and governments that standard is a physical flag. A flag is the physical shadow of the Sabbath. Those that carry this flag or sign of that kingdom/government are called Standard Bearers or Ensigns:

A **standard-bearer** is a person (soldier or civilian) who bears an emblem called an ensign or standard, i.e. either a type of flag or an inflexible but mobile image, which is used (and often honored) as a formal, visual symbol of a state, prince, military unit, etc. This can either be an occasional duty, often seen as an honor (especially on parade), or a permanent charge (also on the battlefield); the second type has even led (in certain cases) to this task being reflected in official rank titles such as Ensign.

The weekly Sabbath is a 'moedim' or rehearsal. A physical shadow of a greater spiritual truth. The Sabbath is Yahuah's stamp over his creation and illustrates the duration of His Plan for mankind. That plan is a 7000-year plan over which time Yahuah is training His sons to rule His creation. The first 6000 years, we labor under the curse of Adam. Then that curse is lifted in the last "day" or thousand years. So every 7 days, all of humanity rehearses the Plan of Yahuah. Those who know Yahuah, then celebrate the coming Kingdom on Earth every 7th day. Fire is a physical shadow of Yahuah's wrath which is kindled during the first 6 days (thousand years) then it is not during the last day. That is why we do not "kindle a fire" and we rest on the 7th Day.

The Scriptural Truth concerning the Sabbath

Yahuah kept **the Sabbath**, the ONLY Holy Day or ritual kept by the Living Creator. It is Yahuah's Covenant with creation and his stamp over His creation. He then sanctified the 7th day (set it apart from all other days as His Day of Rest) and then commanded all mankind for eternity to keep **the Sabbath** to demonstrate they too are "set apart" from His Creation! Yahuah then declared **the Sabbath** to be an everlasting "sign" between Himself and His sons on earth. If you consider yourself a "son" you better keep **the Sabbath** or you are fooling yourself!

> ### In Exodus 31:16
> 16 The people of Isra'el (all sons of Yahuah) are to keep the *Sabbath*, to observe *the Sabbath* through all their generations as a perpetual (everlasting) covenant.

The Sabbath is the Everlasting Covenant. Yahuah then went so far as to establish **the Sabbath** as **the Sign of the Kingdom of Yahuah**. It is this sign that signifies you actually know your Creator and are set apart from Creation with Him.

> ### Exodus 31
> 12 *Yahuah* said to Moshe, 13 Tell the people of Isra'el, 'You are to observe my Sabbaths; for this is a sign between me and you through all your generations; so that you will know that I am *Yahuah*, who sets you apart for me. 17 It is a sign between me and the people of Isra'el forever; for in six days *Yahuah* made heaven and earth, but on the seventh day he stopped working and rested.'

Breaking the Everlasting Covenant of the Sabbath

The Sabbath is so important to Yahuah that humanity breaking it is the cause of **the Great Tribulation,** where Yahuah destroys the face of the Earth and those who break His Sabbath and do not keep His Laws:

> **Isaiah 24**
> See, Yahuah is going to lay waste the earth and devastate it; he will ruin its face and scatter its inhabitants… ³ The earth will be completely laid waste and totally plundered. Yahuah has spoken this word. ⁴ The earth dries up and withers, the world languishes and withers, the heavens languish with the earth. (because) ⁵ The earth is defiled by its people; they have disobeyed the laws of Yahuah, violated the Feasts of Yahuah and <u>broken the everlasting covenant of the Sabbath</u>. ⁶ **Therefore** a curse consumes the earth; its people must bear their guilt. Therefore earth's inhabitants are burned up, and very few are left.

Only Sabbath Keepers inherit Yahuah's Creation

Yahuah then prophesied through Isaiah that he would set this same Sabbath "sign" among the gentiles and call out His Chosen from among them and they would keep His Sabbath among the gentile nations.   As I stated, that "sign" is defined as the Sabbath…   He will send His Sabbath Keeping sons to "raise the standard" and display the Sign to the nations.   Yahuah will gather His elect among all nations and bring them back to Himself where they will keep the Sabbath for all eternity

> **Isaiah 66**
> 19 "I will set *a sign* (the Sabbath) among them, and I will send some of those who survive to the nations—to Tarshish, to the Libyans and Lydians, to Tubal and Greece, and to the distant islands that have not heard of my fame or seen my glory. They will proclaim my glory (as Creator) among the nations (By displaying THE SIGN of the Sabbath to them). 20 And they will bring all your people, from all the nations, to my holy mountain in Jerusalem as an offering to Yahuah.

In the next verse, Yahuah then declared that after he re-creates Heaven and Earth after the Millennial Kingdom on the Last Great Day/Day of Yahuah (8th prophetic day after the Sabbath Millennium) that all living in **the Kingdom of Yahuah** will keep **the Sabbath** forevermore. We know from Revelation that this current Heaven and Earth will be destroyed by fire and Yahuah will create a "new Heaven and Earth" after the prophetic 7th Day or Sabbath Millennium. This is the time frame Isaiah is speaking of and he makes it crystal clear that throughout eternity... all mankind will be keeping **the Sabbath**.

> Those who disobeyed Yahuah (violated His Sabbaths in context) are found DEAD as those Sabbath Keepers literally step over their abominable disobedient bodies to enter *the Kingdom of Yahuah*.

Isaiah 66:22-24

(previous verses talked about a sign, the Sabbath, being set among the gentiles and those who keep the sign are brought out of the nations) 22   "For just as the new heavens and the new earth that I am making will continue in my presence," says Yahuah, "so will your descendants and your name continue. 23   "Every month on Rosh-Hodesh and every week on Shabbat, *everyone living* will come to worship in my presence (they won't be worshipping on Sunday)," says Yahuah. 24 "As they (who bear His Sabbath Sign) leave (from worshipping Yahuah on the Sabbath), they will look on the corpses of the people who rebelled against me (in context rebelled against His Sabbath) for their worm will never die, and their fire will never be quenched; but they will be abhorrent to all humanity."

We are to Obey Yahusha's Sabbath Keeping Example

Now, we are "told" *that a new day of rest* came with the New Covenant. There is zero proof of that in scripture, and for 500 years the early church kept **the Sabbath** until the Sun god worshipping Emperor Constantine change **the Sabbath** to his god's day... Sunday. Then he imposed Sunday worship by the threat of death in the inquisition! 2000 years later, Sunday is set as a "tradition", so much so, that it is no longer even challenged. It is however, an abomination to Yahuah and a violation of His Commands.

We see in 1 John that we are to "walk as Yahusha walked" and live by the example the Messiah set on Earth...

> **1 John 2**
> 3 We know that we have come to know Yahuah if we keep his commands. 4 Whoever says, "I know him," but does not do what he commands is a liar, and the truth is not in that person. 5 But if anyone obeys his commandments, love for Yahuah is truly made complete in them. This is how we know we are in (covenant with) Yahuah (through Yahusha): 6 Whoever claims to live in (covenant with) Yahusha *must live as Yahusha did*.

The example Yahusha set, that we are to follow, is an obedient son of Yahuah to His Commandments. Yahusha kept the Sabbath; he kept Passover and every other commandment and festival of Yahuah. **This is our example**. Constantine is not our example. The Pope, the pastor of your Christian Church, no one else is your example.   For all the double talk Christians do in claiming to walk in the footsteps of "Jesus" they don't even come close to walking as Yahusha so set the example!   In fact, they don't even try!   They abolished everything Yahusha stood for, and everything he did on Earth.

It is well documented that Yahusha kept the Sabbath:

Mark 6:2
And when the Sabbath had come, He began to teach in the synagogue.

Luke 4:16
So he came to Nazareth, where he had been brought up. And as his custom was, he went into the synagogue on the Sabbath day, and stood up to read.

Luke 6:6
Now it happened on another Sabbath, also, that he entered the synagogue and taught.

Luke 13:10
Now he was teaching in one of the synagogues on the Sabbath.

Luke 4:31
Then he went down to Capernaum, a city of Galilee, and was teaching them on the Sabbaths.

In fact, Yahusha understood **the Sabbath Covenant** and that he would return to rule as King to fulfill the Sabbath Covenant in the 7th prophetic day or 7th Millennium known as the Millennial Reign:

Mark 2:27-28

And he said to them, "the Sabbath was made for man (it is the coming of Yahuah's rest from the curse of Adam), and not man for the Sabbath. Therefore the Son of Man is also King of the (coming) Sabbath.

Only Sabbath Keepers Enter Yahuah's Kingdom of Rest

The Apostle Sha'ul cleared it up word for word: "If you don't keep the 7th Day Sabbath EXACTLTY like Yahuah did, you will not enter His Rest/Eternal life".

Below, Sha'ul clearly says you cannot be saved if you violate **the Sabbath**. Remember, all the men of Yahuah in the Bible and the true assembly of believers kept **the Sabbath** for 500 years after the Messiah's death until Constantine changed it by threat of death in the inquisition and eventually had most of them killed for not keeping Dias Solis the Vulnerable day of the Sun god.

We see in Hebrews 4 even in the NT or New Covenant **the Sabbath** is key to salvation.

> Hebrews 4 - *A Sabbath-Rest for the People of Yahuah*
> 1 Therefore, since the promise of entering his (the Sabbath) rest still stands, let us be careful that none of you be found to have fallen short of it (by failing to Keep the Sabbath). 2 For we also have had the gospel preached to us, just as they did; but the message they heard was of no value to them, because those who heard did not combine it with faith (Keep the Sabbath in light of the Messiah). 3 Now we who have believed (and are in covenant with Yahusha) enter that rest (Keep the Sabbath in light of faith in the Passover Lamb of Yahuah, whose name is Yahusha), just as Yahuah has said, "So I declared on oath in my anger, 'They shall never enter my rest.' "And yet his work has been finished since the creation of the world (Yahuah

Himself kept the Sabbath in Genesis 1 and commanded we do to, the 4th Commandment). 4 For somewhere he has spoken about <u>the seventh day</u> (Saturday, not Sunday) in these words: "And on <u>the seventh day</u> Yahuah rested from all his work." 5 And again in the passage above he says, "They shall never enter my rest." (Referring to those disobedient to His Sabbath command)   6 It <u>still remains that some </u>(the remnant sons of Yahuah) <u>will enter that </u>(Sabbath) <u>rest</u>, and those who formerly had the gospel preached to them did not go in, because of their disobedience (to the Sabbath). 7 Therefore Yahuah, again (Sha'ul repeats for emphasis), set a certain day, calling it Today (start keeping the Sabbath today!), when a long time later he spoke through David, <u>as was said before</u>: "Today, if you hear his voice, do not harden your hearts. (against His Sabbath)" 8 For if Joshua (son of Nun) had given them (the Israelites) rest (from the curse of Adam when they entered the Promised Land of Canaan), Yahuah would not have spoken later about another day (the true Sabbath Rest is yet to come in the 7th Millennium).   9 **There remains, then, a Sabbath-rest for the people of Yahuah**; 10 **for anyone who enters Yahuah's rest also rests from his own work, <u>just as Yahuah did from His</u>** (You must keep the Sabbath just as Yahuah did on the 7th Day). 11 Let us, therefore, make every effort to enter that rest (<u>by being obedient to the Sabbath</u>), so that no one will fall (short of salvation and not enter Yahuah's Rest) by following their example of disobedience (to the Sabbath).

The Christian Church tries to twist the scripture above into saying something else in actual support of Sunday worship. the Sabbath is defined as the 7th Day; the Sign between Yahuah and His sons. The "sign" of the Christian Church between Satan and his chosen is, and has always been, <u>Sunday dating back to Babylon</u>.

So the reality is, from cover to cover, **the Sabbath** is the only Holy Day kept by Yahuah, it was set apart from every other day and made Holy along with anyone who keeps it.   All who keep the Sabbath are "set apart" as Yahuah stated... it is one of the 10 Commandments, Yahusha kept it, all the disciples kept it, the church for 500 years after the death of Yahusha kept it, and it is written in both Testaments **that it is critical to Salvation.**

Don't Keep the Sabbath? You do not Know Yahuah!

So if you keep Sunday you are simply a liar if you say you know Yahuah. 1 John says if you say you know Yahuah and do not keep His Commandments (Sabbath is the 4th Commandment) then <u>*you are a LIAR.*</u> It is through obedience to His Commandments you are made complete. If you have any doubts about what that means, then the example you are given is Yahusha who was a Sabbath keeping, Torah observant, Jewish High Priest. Yahusha is our example, not the Pope's feeble decrees.

> **<u>1 John 2</u>**
> 3 We know that we have come to know Yahuah if we keep his commands. 4 Whoever says, "I know him," but does not do what he commands is a liar, and the truth is not in that person. 5 But if anyone obeys his word, love for Yahuah is truly made complete in them. This is how we know we are in (covenant with) him (through Yahusha): 6 whoever claims to live in (covenant with) Yahusha must live as Yahusha did.

If you really knew the Living Creator, you would be obedient to His Commandments, and His Messiah's example. If you TRULY know Yahuah and demonstrate it by the "sign", you will be gathered from among the nations to worship Him on **the Sabbath** forevermore. If you do not keep **the Sabbath** you will die and not enter **the Kingdom of Yahuah**.

There is no salvation for those who do not keep Yahuah's commandments. "Grace" is the blood of THE PASSOVER (not Easter) Lamb covering the <u>DECREES</u> in the Law that demand our death for disobedience to the Commandments and Ordinances. Everything I just wrote about above... the exact same case I can make for the Passover. It, too, is a commandment; Yahusha kept it, commanded we keep it, and died on it as the Passover Lamb of Yahuah. So all those who claim "Grace" and do not keep Passover, there is no "Passover" for you... Yahusha is **the Passover Lamb of Yahuah** and commanded you to keep Passover in light of his sacrifice... "do this (keep Passover) in remembrance of me" was the ONLY commandment Yahusha gave. It was his "last words to us" on the eve of Passover as he kept Passover with his disciples the night before he died....

So, if you keep Sunday and Easter... you do not know Yahuah. You have fallen for another gospel because your frontal lobe has not been Sealed with the Shema and you do not have the ability to recognize deception. That is what the Bible teaches and explicitly says. There is no justifying it or getting around it. No human tradition is a valid replacement, those who say *"you are being legalistic"* I say this... you don't know Yahuah or you would have NEVER said that of His Commandments! People who blaspheme Yahuah with such statements are themselves just as legalistic only they are legalistic for the sun worshipping rituals of Babylon... Christmas, Easter, Sunday, etc. They are pagan hypocrites.

They simply replaced the Sabbath and are just as legalistic toward SUNDAY. They just replace Passover and are just as legalistic toward EASTER. They just simply replaced the Festivals of

Yahuah for their pagan days of worship and holidays and are legalistic toward them just the same. They have the Spirit of the False Messiah who is Jesus.

Those who have been deceived by Christianity call a true son of Yahuah "legalistic" for keeping His Commandments when they are JUST AS LEGALISTIC in their adherence to the Babylonian sun god's rituals (Sunday/Easter/Christmas/Good Friday/Valentine's Day, All Saint's Day/Halloween, etc. etc.). Christians just simply replace the truth with a lie and worship an image of a man (keeping his day) above the Creator. There is no difference in "legalism". Christians are just upset that there is another set of laws found in the Bible and they are in open rebellion against the Truth.

> The difference is, if you keep Passover as commanded by Yahuah and Yahusha... *Grace applies to your inability to keep His Law totally.* If you keep Easter, that is not a valid sacrifice for your sin; and YOU remain guilty of violating the entire Law. You are "lawless" with no Grace to cover you at all. Christians follow *the lawless one* (the one in whose name the Law was abolished) Jesus Christ.

Choose this day whom you will serve. If your desire is to enter **the Kingdom of Yahuah**, then you must raise the standard of that Kingdom and display His Sign to the world around you... keep His Sabbaths Holy. In **the Kingdom of Yahuah**, every son of Yahuah is and "Ensign" or bearer of the standard of His Kingdom which is the Sabbath.

Those who break the commandments of Yahuah are denied entry into His Kingdom, rounded up by the angels of Yahuah and destroyed:

> **Matthew 7:21-23**
> "Not everyone who says to Me, King, King, shall enter the kingdom of heaven, but he who does the will of my Father (keeps His Commandments) in heaven. Many will say to Me in that day, Lord, Lord (calling Yahusha by the title for Ba'al), have we not prophesied in Your name (Jesus not Yahusha), and cast out demons in Your name, and done many wonders in Your name? And then will I (Yahusha) declare to them (who call him by the title Lord and by the false name Jesus), I never knew you, depart from Me, you who practice lawlessness" (you who are without *the Law of Yahuah*).
>
>> **Matthew 13:41**- *English Standard Version*
>> *The Son of Man will send his angels, and* **they will gather out of his kingdom** *all causes of sin and* **all law-breakers**,

Sunday is the Standard or Ensign of the 'Beast'

Sunday is a human tradition dating back to Babylon that has no scriptural support in the OT or NT. The church admits this fact:

> "You may read the Bible from Genesis to Revelation, and you will not find a single line authorizing the sanctification of Sunday. <u>The Scriptures enforce the religious observance of Saturday</u>, a day which we never sanctify." **James Cardinal Gibbons, The Faith of Our Fathers (1917 ed.), pp. 72,73.**

In fact, Sunday "rest/worship day" violates explicit Biblical commands and the example set by the Messiah and Yahuah Himself. Every man in the Bible (even Yahuah) kept **the Sabbath**. From Yahuah to Adam to Noah to Abraham to Isaac to Jacob to David to all the Prophets to Yahusha to all the disciples and every member of the early church for 500 years after the death of the Messiah as late as the 5th Century AD. **They all kept** <u>**The 7th Day Sabbath**</u>. Not one of the true sons of Yahuah ever kept Sunday.

We see this admitted in church and historical records, below is from the 5th Century AD (500 years after Yahusha came), Socrates admitted the obvious truth; Sunday is based on an "ancient Babylonian tradition" revived in Rome while <u>all churches around the world kept the Sabbath day</u> not Sunday, only in ROME (birthplace of Christianity) was Sunday kept in honor of Ba'al a.k.a. Mithra a.k.a Zeus.. the Sungod in context of The Cult of Sol Invictus (Cult of the Invincible Sun)

> *"Nor is there less variation in regard to religious assemblies. For although almost all churches <u>throughout the world</u> celebrate the sacred mysteries on the Sabbath of every week, yet the Christians of Alexandria and at Rome, <u>on account of some ancient tradition</u>, have ceased to do this."* ... **Socrates Scholasticus Church History book 5**

That "ancient tradition" was Babylonian Sun worship. If you keep Sunday you cannot call yourself a "son of Yahuah" as **not one of the men in the Bible kept Sunday.** There is no example for you to follow for Sunday worship in the Bible! That is the Babylonian day of worshipping the Sungod Ba'al. To put it plainly, Sunday worship/rest is idolatry in the eyes of Yahuah and a blatant act of disobedience to His Commands (the 4th to be exact).

First let's admit the obvious historical fact. Man (Roman Emperor Constantine) changed the "day of rest" from the 7th Day Sabbath to the 1st day of the week Sunday.

The power or authority to rewrite the commandments of Yahuah was never given to any man, <u>not even the Messiah</u>. Constantine decreed (March 7, 321) dies Solis—day of the sun, "Sunday"—as the Roman day of rest just prior to the Council of Nicaea to ensure his religion's holy day, The Cult of Sol Invictus, was enforced:

> *"On the venerable day of the Sun let the magistrates and people residing in cities rest, and let all workshops be closed. In the country however persons engaged in agriculture may freely and lawfully continue their pursuits because it often happens that another day is not suitable*

for grain-sowing or vine planting; lest by neglecting the proper moment for such operations the bounty of heaven should be lost." ... **decree by Roman Emperor Constantine**

Then Constantine went so far as to curse Yahuah, Yahusha, and all the men in the Bible as an "abomination" or *anathema* to his new god Hesus Horus Krishna (a.k.a Jesus H. Christ) for keeping Yahuah's Commandments and resting on the Sabbath:

Christians must not judaize (Yahusha was a Jew, the Sabbath is not a "Jewish" day of worship it is Yahuah's Holy Day) by resting on the Sabbath, but must work on that day, rather honoring the Lord's (Lord is Ba'al in English) Day; and, if they can, resting then as Christians. But if any shall be found to be judaizers (by Keeping the Sabbath), **let them be <u>anathema</u> from Christ.** *(**Canon 29 [A.D. 360]**). (**The Church Council of Laodicea circa 364 CE**)*

Wow, and people today still believe Constantine followed the Jewish Messiah?

> The Christian Church even admits that there was no commandment to change ***the Sabbath*** to Sunday anywhere in scripture. The Church goes further to admit that if you believe in the Bible you would be keeping ***the Sabbath***.

By being obedient to Sunday worship you are following the example set by the Pope of Rome not the Messiah of Israel.

> *"If Protestants would follow the Bible, <u>they should worship God on the Sabbath Day, that is Saturday</u>. In keeping Sunday they are following a law of the Catholic Church."*
>
> **Albert Smith, chancellor of the Archdiocese of Baltimore, replying for the cardinal in a letter of Feb. 10, 1920.**

What the Chancellor of the Archdiocese of Baltimore is saying to his "Cardinal" is simple... Sunday is not in the Bible and contradicts the commanded Sabbath of Yahuah. Albert Smith is admitting is that *"Protest*ants" are simply *protest*ing Catholics but still <u>Catholic non-the-less in fundamental doctrine</u>. They display the "sign" of the religion of Rome not the sign of the sons of Yahuah.

When addressing the issue of the Sabbath vs. Sunday, we must always keep in the forefront of our minds that the Roman Empire's religion before, during, and even after the Roman Emperor Constantine was <u>The Cult of Sol Invictus</u> (the worship of the invincible sun which began in Babylon). In fact, the Catholic Church even admits that Constantine never accepted the Jewish Messiah!

> *From Constantine's point of view, there were several factions that needed satisfying, and he set out to develop an all-embracing religion during a period of irreverent confusion. In an age of crass ignorance, with nine-tenths of the peoples of Europe illiterate, stabilizing religious splinter groups was only one of Constantine's problems. The smooth generalization, which so many historians are content to repeat, that Constantine "embraced the Christian religion" and subsequently granted "official toleration", is <u>**contrary to historical fact**</u>" and should be*

> *erased from our literature forever...* (***Catholic Encyclopedia, Pecci ed., vol. iii, p. 299, passim***).

You see, it was never given to Constantine the authority by Yahuah to grant "official tolerance" to pagan religions and incorporate them into a religion and then, through syncretism, blended it with the Holy Scriptures! The result of syncretism is the false religion of Christianity. We even read that in historical documents of that time that, keeping "Sunday" was a compromise made by Christianity to accommodate **pagan** religions:

> *At this time in early church history it was necessary for the church to either adopt the Gentiles' day or else have the Gentiles change their day (to Yahuah's Day). To change the Gentiles' day would have been an offense and a stumbling block to them. The church could naturally reach them better by keeping their (pagan) day (Sunday)."--**William Frederick, Three Prophetic Days, pp. 169-170.***

Constantine founded Christianity on purely political bases to stabilize his empire and unite pagan religions not because he became a follower of Yahusha and child of Yahuah. Constantine never changed his religion; he just forced his sun worship upon the entire world. In truth, history has proven that four years prior to the Council of Nicaea, Constantine was ***initiated into the Cult of Sol Invictus***; the sun worshipping religion that evolved out of Babylon. The pagan day of worship was called Dies Solis or Day of the Sun because they worshipped the planets (creation over the Creator).

Christianity is notorious for "wordsmithing" and twisting scripture:

> **Westminster Confession of Faith, Chapter 21, "Of Religious Worship, and the Sabbath Day". Section 7-8 reads:** *As it is the law of nature, that, in general, a due proportion of time be set apart for the worship of God; so, in his Word, by a positive, moral, and perpetual commandment binding all men in all ages,* **he hath particularly appointed one day in seven** *(this is a lie), for a Sabbath, to be kept holy unto him: which, from the beginning of the world to the resurrection of Christ, was the last day of the week; and, from the resurrection of Christ, was changed into the first day of the week, which, in Scripture, is called the Lord's day, and is to be continued to the end of the world, as the Christian Sabbath.*

No. Yahuah did not set aside "one day in Seven" that is a lie! He set aside **THE 7th Day**! The first "lie" is that Yahusha rose on Sunday when in fact he was raised on **the Sabbath**! Yahusha rose on the 7th Day. The "Lord's Day" or more accurately "Day of the Lord" in scripture actually says "Day of Yahuah" and refers to the END OF DAYS when Yahuah destroys the Earth – NOT SUNDAY - See Amos 5:18, Joel 2:31, 1Thes. 5:2. The Apostle John in Revelation uses this term. His entire letter is describing the end of days, end time events. He wasn't saying, "let's see, I think it **was on Sunday that I had this vision**". No, he was saying, "I have been a witness of future events on the Day of Yahuah" – referring to judgment. Change the name Yahuah to "the LORD", give that same title to the Messiah, call him "Jesus" then twist the reckoning of time and scriptures, and **only then** can you arrive at Sunday being "the Lord's Day' or the resurrection day. All these lies regarding Sunday are clever manipulation of humanity by a religion that has no foundation in scripture. Oh how easily we are misled and how very easily we put up with it! This trickery, sleight of hand, and wordsmithing is notorious in the Christian Church.

> "Christian Sabbath" is a man-made term <u>not found in Scripture</u> or taught by anyone until 5th century.

Only by circular reasoning can this statement be made – (i.e. the Lord's Day must mean Sunday since that is the day Jesus rose from the grave.) – in fact Yahusha **was not** raised on Sunday at all! He was raised 3 days and 3 nights after the Passover when he was killed. That resurrection day was the weekly *Sabbath*!

We have literally been given another Gospel (Trinity/Sunday/Easter/Jesus) not in scripture (which is Yahuah/Yahusha/Sabbath/Passover):

> **2 Corinthians 11:4**
> ⁴ For if someone comes to you and preaches a Messiah other than the Messiah we preached, or if you receive a different spirit from the Spirit you received, or a different gospel from the one you accepted, **you put up with it easily enough**.

Yahuah Raised Yahusha on the Sabbath Day!

The Messiah was impaled on a tree on the Passover on the 15th of Abib, a Wednesday, and rose from the grave on **the Sabbath** exactly 3 full days/nights later. This is both a Biblical fact and historical fact. Sunday worship is "justified" by a lie of Easter/Sunday originating in Babylon. The fact is that Friday night (supposed time of Jesus crucifixion) to Sunday morning (supposed time of his resurrection) is only a day and a half! Yahusha is therefore made a FALSE PROPHET by this lie because he specifically prophesied that he would be in the grave 3 days **AND** 3 nights. So either Yahusha is a false prophet and no messiah, or we have been taught a pagan lie of Easter/Sunday instead of the truth of Passover/Sabbath. Three days and three nights is "the sign he is the Messiah" that he gave. There is no logic known to man, not even Einstein, could get 3 days and 3 nights from Friday evening to Sunday morning. **Are we so ignorant and uneducated that we cannot even count to 3?** Or do we just simply not care?

Basically *"we keep Sunday because we keep Sunday"*! We don't care what the Bible says, or what Yahuah Commanded, or what day Yahusha taught in the temple, or what day he was resurrected, or what day Yahuah rested and sanctified. As long as "we are right in our own eyes". This is our only defense and reason for keeping Sunday because there is no justification for Sunday worship at all! History clearly shows **the Sabbath** was changed by a sun worshiping pagan emperor then forced on an uneducated realm by law then by death:

> *"The Church, on the other hand, after changing the day of rest from the Jewish Sabbath, or seventh day of the week, to the first, made the Third (fourth) Commandment refer to Sunday as the day to be kept holy as the Lord's Day."* **The Catholic Encyclopedia Topic: Ten Commandments, 2nd paragraph**

> *"We have made the change from the seventh day to the first day, from Saturday to Sunday, on the authority of the one holy, <u>catholic</u>, apostolic church of Christ."--* **Episcopalian Bishop Seymour said in "Why We Keep Sunday."**

The pagan Popes of Rome even go so far as to claim Yahuah's most Holy Sabbath as an "execration" or "curse" claiming it was the day he was buried when in fact it was the day of his resurrection!

> *Sylvester I (314-337 A.D.) was the pope during the reign of Constantine. Here is what he thought of the Bible Sabbath: "If every Sunday is to be observed joyfully by the Christians on account of the resurrection, then every Sabbath on account of the burial is to be execration [loathing or cursing] of the Jews."--***quoted by S. R. E. Humbert, Adversus Graecorum calumnias 6, in Patrologie Cursus Completus, Series Latina, ed. J.P. Migne, 1844, p. 143.**

Yahusha was neither buried on Friday nor was he resurrected on Sunday. He was buried on Passover (a Wednesday) and raised on the Sabbath according to the Biblical witness and <u>historical records</u>.

Again, it is openly admitted that the 7th Day Sabbath is the ONLY Holy Day in scripture and was changed to accommodate <u>the pagan sun worshippers of their day</u>:

> *At this time in early church history it was necessary for the church to either adopt the Gentiles' day or else have the Gentiles change their day. To change the Gentiles' day would have been an offense and a stumbling block to them. The church could naturally reach them better by keeping their day."--***William Frederick, Three Prophetic Days, pp. 169-170.**

That's right; to assimilate pagans into this new false religion, the decision was made to "keep THEIR pagan day".   Even the Pope admits as much, if you follow Yahuah you will keep **the Sabbath**, if you follow the Pope you will keep Dies Solis (the day of the Sun god) as it is his "divine right" given him by the Sun deity to <u>change the ordinances of Yahuah</u>:

> *"The Pope has the power to change times, to abrogate (abolish) laws, and to dispense with all things, even the precepts of Christ." "The Pope has the authority and often exercised it, to dispense with the command of Christ."* - **Decretal, de Tranlatic Episcop. Cap. (The Pope can modify divine law.) Ferraris' Ecclesiastical Dictionary.**

Make no mistake if you are Christian and do not keep **the Sabbath** IT IS BY PAPAL DECREE!

> *"Had she (Christianity, the Great Whore of Revelation) not such power, she could not have done that in which all modern religionists agree with her, **she could not have substituted the observance of Sunday**, the first day of the*

*week, **for the observance of Saturday**, the Seventh day, a change for which there is no Scriptural authority"*
Stephen Keenan, A Doctrinal Catechism 3rd ed. p. 174

The Christian Church... "by virtue of her (Christianity's) divine mission", changed the day from Saturday to Sunday.
The Catholic Mirror, official organ of Cardinal Gibbons, Sept. 23, 1893.

I could go on and on and on with this, it should be obvious by now what day is THE Holy Day of Yahuah and which simply isn't. Will you be an ensign for Yahuah's Kingdom? You will if you want to partake in it.

Chapter 11

The Citizens of the Kingdom of Yahuah

Introduction

In this chapter we are going to take a very clear look at exactly "who" inhabits **the Kingdom of Yahuah**. Is it anyone who simply utters the name "Jesus Christ"? That is what we are taught! All that is required to go to "heaven" by the false religion of Christianity; just accept "Jesus" into your heart and you are saved; so they say. The reality is that "accepting Jesus into your heart" means seating the image of the false messiah on the throne as Yahuah. By keeping Easter over Passover you are slaughtering the abominable pig on **the Altar of Yahuah**. Doing such a thing **is a death sentence**. That is committing **the Abomination of Desolation** as I demonstrate in my book *The Antichrist Revealed!*.

So then, who are the "citizens of **the Kingdom of Yahuah**"? Well, they are the chosen sons of Yahuah taken from among **the House of Israel** and from among **the House of Judah**. They are those who:

- Have been chosen from the bloodline of Israel called **Remnant Israel**

- Raise the standard of His Kingdom, **the Sign of the Sabbath**

- Have the protective **Seal of Yahuah** between their eyes

- Have been delivered from **the Law of Sin and Death** in covenant with Yahusha and now live according to **the Law of the Spirit of Life**

- Have had their bodies transposed from physical to spiritual and have been given eternal life and a place within **the Kingdom of Yahuah** to govern the Universe

In short, they are those who have followed THE WAY or example set by Yahusha their King and elder brother and they have been **Signed/Sealed/Delivered** into His Kingdom.

In the previous chapters of this book we have demonstrated that only those who keep **the Sabbath** enter His Kingdom. We have demonstrated that only those who have the mark i.e. **The Seal of Yahuah** enter His Kingdom. In this chapter I want to clearly define **Remnant Israel** and demonstrate that remnant is chosen from within the bloodline of Abraham that runs through Isaac and then Jacob <u>exclusively</u>.

When speaking of Yahuah's chosen Elect, Sha'ul referred to them as **Remnant** Israel. We must have a solid understanding of exactly "who" are the chosen sons of Yahuah who receive His inheritance. We are going to look at exactly who these chosen sons are and what Yahuah gives to His sons as "gifts".

Spiritual Israel is a subset of the physical descendants of Jacob (who was renamed Israel) called **Remnant Israel**. **Remnant Israel** are those descendants of Abraham through Isaac and Jacob who are so chosen by Yahuah and know His Name, have a heart for His Law (written on their hearts), and who accept the sacrifice made by Yahusha as the Passover Lamb. In short they are Signed, Sealed, and Delivered into **the Kingdom of Yahuah**.

Yahuah's Plan to Fulfill His Promises to Abraham

Before we can truly understand who **Remnant Israel** will be, we need at least a basic understanding of both **the Abrahamic Covenant** and **the Plan of Yahuah** to fulfill it. Once we have a firm grasp on this plan of Yahuah's to bring about the blessings of Abraham, we can begin to shed light on the Apostle Sha'ul's mission to take the gospel to the "Gentiles".

The Apostle Sha'ul's claim that he was tasked to take the gospel to the Gentiles landed him in direct conflict with the other disciples and the Pharisees of his time. The other disciples and the Pharisees knew that Yahuah's explicit revelation was that only those from the bloodline of Abraham/Isaac/Jacob were to be chosen as sons of Yahuah. The way the Christian Church teaches Sha'ul's mission also puts Sha'ul in direct conflict with Yahuah's prophets and Yahusha's **Great Commission**.

If the Christian Church's *Pauline Doctrine* is correct, then Sha'ul is a false teacher and he contradicted every aspect of **the Plan of Yahuah** for His sons. Sha'ul struggled with this accusation when faced with the Jews of his day and the other disciples. They all knew Yahuah's sons would descend exclusively from the bloodline of Jacob (Israel). In the end, however, Sha'ul was able to convince the Jews of his day and the disciples that he was not a false teacher and was, in fact, called to "the Gentiles". How did Sha'ul convince them? This chapter is going to show you exactly how Sha'ul changed their minds and prove that Sha'ul was indeed called to "the Gentiles".

Rav Sha'ul

In this chapter I am going

- to prove that the Apostle Sha'ul was unique among the disciples in his understanding of **the Plan of Yahuah**.

- to prove that Sha'ul was in fact uniquely qualified to do exactly as Yahusha commanded and "reclaim **the Lost Sheep of the House of Israel**" who were lost among the Gentile nations.

- demonstrate that Sha'ul knew exactly what he was doing taking the Gospel to the gentiles and how Sha'ul recognized **the Lost House of Israel** among the pagan societies (they lived in obedience to Yahusha's commands)

- show that Sha'ul clearly taught that **Remnant Israel** was a small remnant taken exclusively from among **the House of Israel** and **the House of Judah**.

First, we must establish the history and prophetic words of Yahuah concerning **the Nation of Israel**. Sha'ul addresses these prophecies directly and used them to justify his actions. If we are to understand Sha'ul's writing, we too must have an understanding of the prophecies he referenced to support his writings.

Sha'ul was very well versed in the Torah and Prophets and supported all of what he taught using them. So to understand the things that Sha'ul taught, we too must have a firm understanding of the Prophets he used to justify what he taught! We will go back and put Sha'ul's teaching into context and overcome the false doctrine of Replacement Theology that the "church replace Israel".

The History of the Nation of Israel

The descendants of Jacob were defined by his 12 sons. They descended into 12 tribes of peoples. These 12 tribes became a nation, **the Nation of Israel**. Israel was one nation under one King with one capital city and one Temple. That nation later was divided and went to war against each other and split into two Kingdoms. The sons of Yahuah literally went to war over the "blessings of Abraham" and established two kings, two capital cities, and even two Temples!

The Birthright Blessing vs. The Scepter Blessing

The blessings Yahuah gave to Abraham were divided by Jacob among his 12 sons. These blessings were summarized into two major blessings known as **the Scepter Blessing** and **the Birthright Blessing**.

- **The Scepter Blessing** was given to Jacob's son Judah (from whom the Jews descend).

- **The Birthright Blessing** was given to Jacob's son Joseph by proxy through Joseph's two sons Ephraim and Manasseh.

These two blessings literally created "enmity" between the 12 Tribes of Israel and they split into two houses and eventually two kingdoms:

- *The Northern Kingdom of Israel* (called in prophecy **the House of Israel**) which were 9 tribes. The "Birthright Blessing" of Abraham was given to **the House of Israel** to become many great nations.

- *The Southern Kingdom of Judah* (called in prophecy **the House of Judah** or the Jews) which were 3 tribes. The "Scepter Blessing" of Abraham was given to **the House of Judah** that through Abraham all the nations of the Earth would be blessed. A promise of the coming Messiah.

This "enmity" between the two houses angered Yahuah and it was the very reason Yahuah sent pagan empires to conquer both kingdoms and send them into captivity:

- *The Northern Kingdom of Israel* (House of Israel) was defeated and sent into Assyrian captivity. They never returned out of captivity as Yahuah divorced them completely and dispersed **the House of Israel** over the entire globe. It was through this process that Israel becomes many great nations in fulfillment of the *Birthright Blessing* Yahuah promised Abraham.

- *The Southern Kingdom of Judah* (House of Judah) was taken into Babylonian captivity, came out of captivity with the Scepter Blessing to rebuild the temple, and produce the Messiah, and were later dispersed by the Roman Empire in AD70.

Yahuah then sent His Prophets to each of the two houses to speak to them and tell what their end shall be:

> Isaiah 46
> 8 "Remember this, fix it in mind, take it to heart, you rebels. 9 Remember the former things, those of long ago; I am Yahuah, and there is no other (Elohim); I am Yahuah, and there is none like me. 10 *I make known the end from the beginning, from ancient times, what is still to come.* I say: My *purpose* will stand, and I will do all that I please.

When defining the true sons of Yahuah we must know Yahuah's purpose and "what is still to come". The Apostle Sha'ul was an expert in the Torah and Prophets (a Pharisee) and he was well aware of both and taught exactly what Yahuah prophesied.

Remnant Israel

Spiritual or Remnant Israel are those very few chosen taken from among both **the House of Israel** (who were **called** "Gentiles" because they were living among the pagan Gentiles nations and lost their identity) and **the House of Judah** (called "the Jews" who never lost their identity).

We know that the children of Israel or descendants of Abraham became many great nations and a multitude of people covering the entire globe as Yahuah promised Abraham. This fact was confirmed to Moses that all people on earth would be divided by the sons of Israel:

> **Deuteronomy 32:8**
> 8 When the Most High divided to the nations their inheritance, when he separated the sons of Adam, he set the bounds of the people according to the number of the children of Israel.

We also know from historical and archeological records the migration patterns and ancestry of many nations and peoples on Earth and that they had their beginning with Israel. The "Jews" are a very small nation and do not comprise all of "Israel" and in no way have fulfilled *the Birthright Blessing*. They are but a small subset of physical Israel. And only a small number of Jews make up His Chosen Remnant, along with a small number of "Gentiles" as they came to be called from whom a number of **the House of Israel** will be taken. Together, these two small groups, a remnant from both houses, will be called to be sons of Yahuah and they are known as **Remnant Israel** or Spiritual Israel or the "sons of Elohim" by His gracious choice.

So the fact is that Yahuah's sons are scattered among ALL nations on Earth at this time and descend from the bloodline of Abraham/Isaac/Jacob.

These Elect will be called out of all nations at the end. They will literally be physical descendants of Israel (Jacob), but THEY WILL HAVE LOST THEIR IDENTITY (and not know they are of the bloodline of Abraham/Isaac/Jacob) and they will be *"called"* Gentiles:

> **Deuteronomy 32:26**
> 26 I said, I would scatter them into (all) corners (of Earth), I would make the remembrance of them to cease from among men (no one would know they are truly Israelites):

Yahuah did divorce **the House of Israel** but only to "plant" them as seeds around the Globe to grow into many great nations. Later they would be recalled back to Him. Over the years of captivity then dispersion across the Globe, Yahuah's name was changed to "the LORD" or "Ba'al" coming out of Babylonian Captivity and His name was profaned using titles such as LORD and God:

> **Jeremiah 23:26-27**
> How long is this there in the heart of the prophets, the prophets of lies; yea, the prophets of the deceit of their own heart? They plot to cause My people to forget My name by their dreams which they tell, each one to his neighbor, even as their fathers have forgotten My name for Baal.

Even today we call Yahuah "the LORD" which means Ba'al or Master. But, Yahuah always had a plan to reclaim a small remnant from among both Houses and restore His Holy Name. This is one key as to "who" are those who make up **Remnant Israel**. Yahuah spoke through His Prophets that He would <u>CAUSE</u> them (**Remnant Israel**) to remember His Holy Name even though every effort would be made by man to delete all references to His Name even from the Bible:

> **Jeremiah 16:21**
> And, behold, I will make them know; this time I will cause them to know My hand and My might; and they shall know that My name is Yahuah.

It is only with this background in Yahuah's Plan told through His prophets concerning **the House of Israel** and **the House of Judah** that we can understand the New Testament; specifically Sha'ul's writings.

Replacement Theology? *Not in my Bible!*

The Christian Church teaches that anyone, whether they be descendants of Abraham or not, can be "grafted to the tree". Christianity teaches a very false "Greek" appropriate doctrine overturning Yahuah's choice of the bloodline of Abraham thru Jacob. This false doctrine is based on "implied doctrines" and a complete <u>rewriting of Sha'ul's teachings</u> that amount to clear violations of **sound explicit doctrine**.

This is called "Replacement Theology" where the pagan Christian Church *replaced* the bloodline of Abraham/Isaac/Jacob known as Israel as the chosen ones. In order to teach these lies, Christianity had to make all the previous covenants void and abolish the Old Testament <u>entirely</u>. Christianity teaches many false doctrines within the context of Replacement Theology such as

New Testament replaced the Old Testament

- The New Covenant replaced all other covenants
- Christmas replaced the Festival of Tabernacles
- Easter replaced Passover
- Pagan holidays replaced Yahuah's Holy Days
- The Trinity replaced the Shema
- Jesus replaced Yahusha
- Sunday replaced the Sabbath

- Rome replaced Jerusalem as "the Eternal City of Yahuah"

- Christian Priests/Preachers/Pastors replaced the Royal Priesthood of Remnant Israel

- The list goes on *indefinitely*

Replacement Theology is a lie and not at all scriptural. The Truth found in scripture is that **the House of Israel** was given a certificate of divorce and was *torn from the tree* and dispersed. That is why they had to be "grafted **back** into the tree". All the prophets of Yahuah foretell of **the House of Israel** being re-united with **the House of Judah** and "grafted back" into the family tree of Abraham/Isaac/Jacob that they descend from. These prophecies are known as **the Re-Unification of the Nation of Israel**. It is from among that re-unified Nation of Israel that a small remnant is chosen to rule the universe as sons of Yahuah. They are **Remnant Israel**.

Sha'ul Taught the Prophets and Yahuah's Plan

Sha'ul, being a Pharisee, was literally a "**LAW**yer" and expert in the Torah and Prophets. It would take just such an expert, a man uniquely trained to understand the entire revelation of Yahuah to properly teach the role of the Messiah in reclaiming the remnant sons of Yahuah from across the globe. When addressing Yahuah's sovereign choice of a remnant from the bloodline of Jacob (Israel), Sha'ul quoted the Prophet Isaiah where Yahuah foretold it would be only a very small remnant taken **only** from among the bloodline of Israel. NOT ALL physical descendants of Israel will be saved. ONLY a remnant taken from among both Houses...

> **Romans 9** - *Yahuah's Sovereign Choice of the Remnant*
> 27 Isaiah cries out <u>concerning Israel</u>: "Though the number of the Israelites (both Houses) is like the sand by the sea, **only the remnant will be saved**."

It was prophesied by Isaiah (and many other major prophets including Yahusha), and confirmed by Sha'ul; ONLY a remnant from the bloodline of Israel, the descendants of Abraham, would be saved and begotten as sons of Yahuah through transposition (resurrection).

Sha'ul also confirms that it is ONLY Abraham's descendants that the Messiah "helps" in Yahusha's role as High Priest of Israel and *no one else* and that they are all of the same bloodline or family:

Hebrews 2

10 In bringing many sons to glory, it was fitting that Yahuah, for whom and through whom everything exists, should make the author of their salvation perfect through suffering. 11Both the one who makes men holy and those who are made holy are of the same family. So Yahusha is not ashamed to call them brothers. 12 He says,

> "I will declare your name to my brothers; in the presence of the congregation I will sing your praises."
>
> 13And again, "I will put my trust in him."
>
> And again he says, "Here am I, and the children (of Israel) Yahuah has given me."

14 Since the children have flesh and blood, he too shared in their humanity so that by his death he might destroy him who holds the power of death—that is, the devil— 15 and free those who all their lives were held in slavery by their fear of death. 16 <u>For surely it is not angels he helps, but Abraham's descendants.</u> 17 For this reason he had to be made like his brothers (in the bloodline promised to Abraham) in every way, in order that he might become a merciful and faithful high priest (of Israel) in service to Yahuah, and that he might make atonement for the sins of the people (that descend from the bloodline of Abraham in context).

The Re-Unification of the Nation of Israel

The major prophecy concerning this truth; that the two houses had been divided and would be re-united in the end is found in Ezekiel Chapter 37. Ezekiel was given this vision after the Nation of Israel was divided and went to war against each other. The Nation of Israel was divided into the Northern Kingdom of Israel (**the House of Israel**) and the Southern Kingdom of Judah (**the House of Judah**). We see Yahuah's plan all along was to reclaim **the Lost Sheep of the House of Israel** and re-unite them with **the House of Judah** (the Jews).

> **Ezekiel 37** - *Reunion of Judah and Israel*
> [15] The word of Yahuah came again to me saying, [16] "And you, son of man, take for yourself one stick and write on it, 'For Judah and for the sons of Israel, his companions' (known as the House of Judah); then take another stick and write on it, 'For Joseph, the stick of Ephraim and all **the House of Israel**, his companions.' [17] Then join them for yourself one to another into one stick, that they may become one in your hand. [18] When the sons of your people (descendants of Israel) speak to you saying, 'Will you not declare to us what you mean by these?' [19] say to them, 'Thus says Yahuah your ELOHIM, "Behold, I will take the stick of Joseph, which is in the hand of Ephraim, and the tribes of Israel, his companions (the House of Israel); and I will put them with it, with the stick of Judah (the House of Judah), and make them one stick, and they will be one in My hand."' [20] The sticks on which you write will be in your

hand before their eyes. ²¹ Say to them, 'Thus says Yahuah your ELOHIM, "Behold, I will take the sons of Israel from among the (pagan Gentile) nations where they have gone, and I will gather them from every side and bring them into their own land; ²² and I will make them **one nation** in the land, on the mountains of Israel; and one king will be king for all of them; and **they will no longer be two nations and no longer be divided into two kingdoms**. ²³ They will no longer defile themselves with their idols, or with their detestable things, or with any of their transgressions; but I will deliver them from all their dwelling places (among the Gentiles) in which they have sinned, and will cleanse them. And they will be My people, and I will be their Elohim.

The House of Israel is Only *"Called"* Gentiles

When Sha'ul discusses this topic and speaks of "Israel" he is clearly referring to **the House of Judah** who was in the land of Israel at that time.   He refers to them (the Jews) the way we do today as "Israel".   But **the House of Israel** is not **the House of Judah.** We must understand this as it is critical.   **The House of Israel** had been dispersed among the nations after being sent into *Assyrian Captivity.*   **The House of Israel <u>was not</u>** in the land of Israel in New Testament times, only the Jews (**the House of Judah**) were in Israel coming out of Babylonian Captivity and they were called "Israel".   **The House of Israel** was called "Gentiles".   A little confusing, I admit, but made even more so by the false teachings of the Christian Church.

We must know prophecy and the Torah if we are to have any hope of understanding the New Testament.   Especially Sha'ul's writings as he was an expert in the Torah and Prophets.   So we must shed the proper light of Yahuah's Prophets on Sha'ul's writings to understand them especially since Sha'ul quoted them as justification for his teaching.   Sha'ul tends to write over the heads of his readers in many cases and especially in the case of the Christian Church who has denied the Plan of Yahuah foretold by His Prophets and abolished it.

When Sha'ul is describing the hardening of **the House of Judah** (Jews) "until such time as the number of Gentiles", which is what Sha'ul calls **the House of Israel,** could come in, a little wisdom is required and a little background in Yahuah's plan.   ==The word==

"Gentiles" simply means "not Jewish". So by definition ***the House of Israel*** could be and was "called" Gentiles:

Merriam Webster Dictionary

1gen·tile

noun \ˈjen-ˌtī(-ə)l\

: a person who is not Jewish

Pagan Gentiles are those **not** of the bloodline of Abraham/Isaac/Jacob. Then there are those who are *"called Gentiles"* but really aren't. Those *"called Gentiles"* are actually from ***the House of Israel*** who are not Jewish and lived among the pagan Gentiles and lost their identity. Even those who were descendents of Israel living among the Gentiles had no idea of their lineage and thought themselves to be "Gentiles":

> ### Hosea 1
> ¹⁰ Yet the number of the sons of Israel will be like the sand of the sea, which cannot be measured or numbered; And in the place (pagan Gentile lands) where it is said to them (not that it is true *it is only said of them*), "You are not My people," It will be said to them (after I reclaim them to their rightful inheritance), *"You are* the sons of the living Elohim." ¹¹ **And the sons of Judah (House of Judah) and the sons of Israel (House of Israel) will be gathered together,**

Sha'ul literally quotes Hosea 1 to justify everything he says. In Sha'ul's writing on the topic of **Remnant Israel**, Sha'ul is referring

319

to those scattered among the Gentile nations who had lost their identity, as **the Lost Sheep of the House of Israel**.   You know, the ones Yahusha exclusively said he came to reclaim in Matthew 15:24 and again in **the Great Commission** Matthew 10:6.   This is very important, **the House of Israel** by definition, not being of **the House of Judah** or Jews, are *"called"* Gentiles and it is said of them "they are not Yahuah's people" when in reality... they always were and still are just that... physical descendants of Jacob!

So the "Jews" or **the House of Judah** were hardened toward the Messiah until the remnant of **the House of Israel** from among the Gentile nations joined their number and **"in that way all of Israel, both Houses, would be saved"**.   This is what Sha'ul is teaching in his writings as we will see.   The doctrines of the Christian Church are based on **the Spirit of Error** while Sha'ul's foundation was firmly planted on the revealed Plan of Yahuah and he proved that by quoting from the Prophets concerning **the Re-Unification of the Nation of Israel**.

==We must always keep in mind that Yahuah is Elohim and Yahusha is His Messiah==.   No man, <u>not even the lofty Apostle Sha'ul</u>, or the Pope, or anyone can contradict Yahuah and Yahusha.   What Yahuah and Yahusha say and confirm **is truth**.   If Sha'ul contradicts them in any way he is to be related to the trash bin of history as a FALSE TEACHER.   Many have come to believe just that, that Sha'ul is a false teacher.   Those who believe that cannot reconcile Sha'ul's writing and have fallen for the lies told of Sha'ul by the Christian Church.   The Christian Church's *Pauline Doctrines* they teach are lies.   The Christian Church teaches Sha'ul literally created another religion to justify their pagan Babylonian lie.

This is far from true as I will prove and clearly demonstrate. Not just in regards to the Gentiles replacing Israel but also concerning the abolition of the Law and the entire Replacement Theology of the pagan church founded in Rome. Sha'ul did not teach either doctrine, but rather taught and confirmed what was declared by Yahuah and confirmed through Yahusha that **Remnant Israel** was confined to the bloodline of Jacob.

Yahusha came only for the Lost Sheep of the House of Israel

Yahusha had made it clear that he came first as *the Messiah ben Joseph,* which is the Messiah to the Lost Sheep of *the House of Israel,* not the Jews who were of *the House of Judah*. Yahusha fulfilled the prophecies of the *Suffering Servant* defined by the Spring Feast rehearsals. Messiah ben Joseph is the Messiah to the descendants of Joseph who are *the House of Israel*.

Yahusha returns as *the Messiah ben David* for *the House of Judah* or the Jews and fulfills the Fall Feasts that define, and are rehearsals, for the second coming. Yahusha did not, as Christianity teaches, come for pagan gentiles such as Canaanites, but to reclaim only *the Lost Sheep of the House of Israel* from AMONG the pagan gentiles.

> **Matthew 15**
> [21] Leaving that place, Yahusha withdrew to the region of Tyre and Sidon. [22] **A Canaanite woman** (pagan gentile not from either the House of Judah or the House of Israel) from that vicinity came to him, crying out, "Lord, Son of David, have mercy on me! My daughter is demon-

possessed and suffering terribly." ²³ <u>Yahusha did not answer a word</u>. So his disciples came to him and urged him, "Send her away, for she keeps crying out after us." ²⁴ He answered, "**I was sent only to the lost sheep of** (the House of) **Israel**." ²⁵ The woman came and knelt before him. "Lord, help me!" she said. ²⁶ He replied, "It is not right to take the children (of Abraham)'s bread and toss it to the dogs (those not chosen or pagan gentiles)."

Again, when sending out his disciples and giving **the Great Commission** we see Yahusha make it clear that he came to reconcile both houses of Israel by reclaiming **the Lost Sheep of the House of Israel** and then re-uniting them with **the House of Judah** (Jews).

Matthew 10

<u>5</u> These twelve Yahusha sent out after instructing them: "Do not go in <u>the</u> way of the (pagan) Gentiles, and do not enter *any* city of the Samaritans; ⁶ but rather **go to the lost sheep of the house of Israel**. ⁷ And as you go, preach, saying, 'the kingdom of heaven is at hand.'

What does "the way of the Gentiles" mean?

Christianity doesn't teach us anything about the true meaning of Matthew 10 because it directly contradicts Christianity's *Pauline Doctrine* that the New Covenant is now open to all pagan Gentiles outside of the bloodline of Abraham/Isaac/Jacob. Yahusha didn't seem to agree, he agreed with the Abrahamic Covenant which was and is still in effect.

What Yahusha was saying is do not go to Gentiles who outwardly display *pagan ways*. Rather do as Yahuah commanded and take the Gospel to those who by their very nature KEEP HIS LAW as Yahuah had promised He would "write the Law on the hearts" of **The House of Israel** and they would respond to the message "the Kingdom of Heaven is at hand". The Apostle Sha'ul understood this as we will see.

Was Yahusha saying "do not go the physical direction of the Gentiles?" Or, was Yahusha being consistent when he used the expression "the way" meaning **the religious example** displayed by pagan Gentiles. ==Yahusha used the term "the Way" to describe the **righteous example**== he set that we are to follow:

> **John 14:6**
> Yahusha said to him, "I am (my example is) the way, and (my example is) the truth (the true way), and (my example is) the life (it leads to eternal life); no one comes to the Father but through Me (the example I set).

This is confirmed in 1 John. My comments in parenthesis to clarify, in context, and I correct all the passive voice and personal pronouns used that confuse the topic at hand:

> **1 John 2**
> ³ By this we know that we have come to know Him (Yahuah), if we keep His commandments (Yahusha has no commandments see verse 7 below). ⁴ The one who says, "I have come to know Him (Yahuah)," and does not keep His commandments, is a liar, and the truth is not in him; ⁵ but whoever keeps His word (the Torah, the NT did not exist for another 300 years), in him the love of Yahuah has truly

been perfected (Psalm 19:7 "*the Law of Yahuah* is perfect, restoring the soul; the testimony of Yahuah is sure, making wise the simple"). By this we know that we are in (covenant with) Yahusha: ⁶ the one who says he abides (in covenant with) Yahusha ought **himself to walk in the same manner** as Yahusha walked (follow the Way set by the example of Yahusha's life by keeping Yahuah's Commandments). ⁷ Beloved, I am not writing a new commandment to you, but an old commandment which you have had from the beginning; the old commandment is the word which you have heard (the old commands which is THE WORD OF YAHUAH or THE TORAH). ⁸ On the other hand, **I am writing a new commandment to you** (ok... here is the only "new command", he restates verses 5-6 above to follow Yahusha's example in keeping the Law as the only new command) Which (keeping the Law) is true in Yahusha and in you (as you do as he did), because the darkness (of Law without Grace) is passing away and the true Light (of Law with Grace) is already shining ...
I have written to you, fathers, because you know Yahuah who has been from the beginning. I have written to you, young men, because you are strong, and the word of Yahuah (the Torah) abides in you (the Law is written in your hearts), and you have overcome the evil one.

We know **the House of Israel** was scattered among the pagan Gentile nations and Yahusha was well aware of that fact. So we can immediately dismiss the idea that Yahusha was saying "*don't go to the Gentile nations*". So how are we to understand Yahusha's statement "Do not go in the way of the Gentiles" in context of commanding us to "go to the lost sheep of the House of Israel" who were scattered among the Gentile nations?

"**The way of the gentiles**" is a term used often in the Bible and in every case it speaking of the *religious practices of the pagan Gentiles* it is not referring to a physical path or destination. Below we see the same phrase "the way of the Gentiles" referring to the religious practices or *those who display the religious practices* of pagans:

Jeremiah 10:2
New International Version
This is what the LORD says: "Do not learn the ways of the nations or be terrified by signs in the heavens, though the nations are terrified by them.

NET Bible
The LORD says, "Do not start following pagan religious practices. Do not be in awe of signs that occur in the sky even though the nations hold them in awe.

GOD'S WORD® Translation
This is what the LORD says: Don't learn the practices of the nations. Don't be frightened by the signs in the sky because the nations are frightened by them.

Jubilee Bible 2000
Thus hath the LORD said, Do not learn the way of the Gentiles, and do not fear the signs of heaven, even though the Gentiles fear them.

So, "the way of the Gentiles" means those who display "the pagan practices of the Gentiles".

Below is how Matthew 10; **The Great Commission** should read with the intent and in context of the revealed plan of Yahuah:

> ### Matthew 10
> 5 These twelve Yahusha sent out after instructing them: "Do not go to those who practice pagan religions, and do not enter *any* city of the Samaritans; 6 but rather go to the lost sheep of the house of Israel scattered among the Gentiles. These lost sheep are those who display the Way of Yahuah by keeping His Law instinctively; because Yahuah has written the Law on their hearts. 7 And as you go, preach, saying, 'the kingdom of heaven is at hand.' And those whom Yahuah has chosen will respond.

The Apostle Sha'ul was the only one to understand Yahusha's instructions properly because he understood the Torah and Prophets.

The Apostle Sha'ul's Dilemma

Sha'ul had a dilemma in that he was commissioned to take the Gospel to the pagan Gentile nations in order to call out those of **the House of Israel** lost among them. The problem Sha'ul had was that the Jews and even the disciples did not understand what Yahusha had truly said. So Sha'ul had some "explaining" to do! Explain he did and we are going to dissect his explanation in detail.

Sha'ul "called" the lost sheep *Gentiles* just as Yahuah foretold. Sha'ul couldn't identify them and the lost sheep themselves had (and even today have) no idea who they are. Yahuah <u>caused</u> them to lose all knowledge of their identity and caused their remembrance to cease from among men.

> Deuteronomy 32:26
> 26 I said, I would scatter them into (all) corners (of Earth), I would make the remembrance of them to cease from among men (no one would know they are truly Israelites):

Sha'ul "called" **the House of Judah** "Israel" because they were living in the land of Israel and citizens of the Roman province known as Israel. We must know scripture concerning who was who in order to understand what Sha'ul was saying as it gets a little confusing. But Sha'ul knew Yahuah had also promised to reverse this situation and then cause them to remember His Name and write His law on their hearts:

> **Jeremiah 16:21**
> And, behold, I will make them know; this time I will cause them to know My hand and My might; and they shall know that My name is Yahuah.

The other disciples, being common uneducated types, failed to understand these things as only Sha'ul was an expert in the Torah and Prophets. Taking the Gospel to the "Gentiles" became a major point of contention as the other disciples did not understand that **the House of Israel** was lost and "called" Gentiles. They accused Sha'ul of disobeying Yahusha's command and Yahuah's revealed Will and thought Sha'ul was literally expanding the definition of **Remnant Israel** to include truly pagan Gentiles outside of the chosen bloodline.

You see, the Jews deny there is any such thing as "Lost Tribes" among the Gentile nations. This is true even today of Judaism. Remember, they went to war with **the House of Israel** and remain, even today, in rebellion against them. This is just one of many reasons the Jews will not accept Yahusha as the Messiah. He simply hasn't come for the House of Judah (Jews) yet. To accept Yahusha as the Messiah would force the Jews to admit that most (10 out of 12 Tribes of Israel) are currently lost and considered "Gentiles" in need of a Shepherd to lead them home.

Yahuah made it clear that **the House of Israel** would be lost and without their identity among the Gentile nations.

> ### Hosea 1
> ⁶ Then she conceived again and gave birth to a daughter. And Yahuah said to him, "Name her Lo-ruhamah, for ***I will no longer have compassion on the house of Israel***, that I would ever forgive them. ⁷ ***But I will have compassion on the house of Judah*** and deliver them by Yahuah their Elohim, and will not deliver them by bow, sword, battle, horses or horsemen."
>
> ### Hosea 9
> ¹⁷ My Elohim will reject them (speaking of the House of Israel) because they have not obeyed him (broke His Laws); <u>they will be wanderers among the (pagan) nations</u> (Gentiles).

Below, Yahuah speaks through the prophet Isaiah of how His Plan was to *re-marry* **the House of Israel** and bring His estranged wife back and restore her completely. Yahuah talks about how He literally "hid His face" from **the House of Israel**:

Isaiah 54

⁵ For your Maker is your husband— Yahuah Almighty is His Name— the Holy One of Israel is your Redeemer; he is called the Elohim of all the earth. ⁶ Yahuah will call you (*the House of Israel*) back as if you were a wife deserted and distressed in spirit— a wife who married young, only to be rejected," says your Elohim. ⁷ "<u>For a brief moment I abandoned you</u>, but with deep compassion <u>I will bring you back</u>. ⁸ In a surge of anger <u>I hid my face from you for a moment</u>, but with everlasting kindness I will have compassion on you," says Yahuah your Redeemer.

Yahusha knew this was his first mission as Messiah and so did the Apostle Sha'ul.   Those lost sheep of **the House of Israel** would consider themselves pagan "Gentiles" and would not even know their own Identity.   <u>So Sha'ul had to speak to them on terms they would and could accept.</u>   Sha'ul admitted as much that he would have to become all things to all men just to win a few.

Sha'ul is speaking of how he would have to meet both houses where they were to reach them individually.

1 Corinthians 9:19-23

¹⁹ Though I am free and belong to no one, I have made myself a slave to everyone, to win as many as possible. ²⁰ To the Jews (House of Judah) I became like a Jew, to win the Jews. ... To those not having the law (the House of Israel) I became like one not having the law though I am not free from **the Law of Yahuah** but am under **the Yahushaic Covenant**; so as to win those (the House of Israel) not having the law (being lost among the Gentiles).

But Sha'ul always made it clear that Yahuah's choice of both houses of Israel stood and the Messiah was given to help the descendants of Abraham. So while Sha'ul "became all things to all men to win a few" we have to try and keep up with him and always keep in mind Yahuah's will and keep everything in context of His Prophets… especially where Sha'ul's writings are concerned.

How Did Sha'ul Know the House of Israel?

We know Sha'ul called **the House of Israel** "Gentiles" and rightfully so, by definition, they were not Jews and had lost all knowledge of their identity. But how did he know which pagans were lost sheep of the House of Israel?

> The Christian Church is <u>*critically injured*</u> in their understanding of spiritual things and the meaning of the New Testament, because they have erred... <u>*and abolished the Torah and Prophets*</u>.

He had to "become like them", as they would never have believed they were descendants of Jacob. We know Yahuah had totally divorced them and hid His Face from them. So how did the Apostle Sha'ul take the Gospel to the Gentiles in order to reclaim *only the Lost Sheep of the House of Israel* among them? Sha'ul knew the Torah and Prophets that Yahuah had forbid following "the pagan way of the Gentile nations":

> **Deuteronomy 18:9**
> "When you come into the land that Yahuah your Elohim is giving you, you shall not learn to follow the abominable practices (the way) of those nations.

Sha'ul immediately recognized Yahusha's Great Commission and knew Yahusha was again following Yahuah's command not to go to those who display the way of the pagan Gentiles. Sha'ul also knew that Yahuah would guide the effort in reclaiming that which

Rav Sha'ul

was lost in those Gentile nations.   Yahuah made Sha'ul a promise to do just that.   Sha'ul, being an expert in the Prophets, knew Yahuah prophesied that He would reclaim **the Lost Sheep of the House of Israel** and literally move on His remnant and "cause them" to remember His Name and keep His Law by writing it in their hearts.

> ### Jeremiah 16:21
> And, behold, I will make them know; this time I will cause them to know My hand and My might; and they shall know that My name is Yahuah.

==Sha'ul knew that in order to respond to the Gospel, they must be chosen, and must be of the bloodline of Jacob!==   Speaking of the time Sha'ul was being sent in obedience to Yahusha's command to go to the Lost Sheep of the House of Israel, Yahuah had made it clear how to identify them:

> ### Jeremiah 31:33
> "But this is the covenant which I will make with the house of Israel after those days," declares Yahuah, "I will put My law within them and on their heart I will write it; and I will be their Elohim, and they shall be My people.

Below, Sha'ul is speaking of how he would recognize true Israelites lost among the gentile nations.   Sha'ul makes it clear; he simply followed Yahuah's instructions in how to identify them:

> ### Romans 2
> [12] For all who have sinned without the Law will also perish without the Law, and all who have sinned under the Law (not in covenant with Yahusha to cover that sin) will be judged by (the decrees in) the Law; [13] for *it is* not the

hearers of the Law *who* are just before Yahuah, **but the doers of the Law** will be justified. (so Sha'ul was looking for LAW keepers or those who displayed "the Way of Yahuah" among the Gentiles)   ¹⁴ For when (those lost sheep among the) Gentiles who do not have the Law (being divorced by Yahuah and scattered among the Gentile nations) do instinctively the things of the Law, these, not having the Law (because Yahuah hid it from them), are a law to themselves, ¹⁵ in that they show the work of the Law written in their hearts, their conscience (the Spirit of Yahuah) bearing witness and their thoughts alternately accusing or else defending them, ¹⁶ on the day when, according to my gospel, Yahuah will judge the secrets of men through Yahusha the Messiah. (Sha'ul knew the chosen would respond to him and by that they would identify themselves as Lost Sheep of the House of Israel among the Gentiles by outwardly displaying works of the Law)

The Apostle Sha'ul was a genius!   He had to become all things to all men to accomplish the Great Commission.   He didn't go to Gentiles who displayed pagan "ways" as Yahusha forbid; he went to those who displayed works of the Law living among the Gentiles.   Sha'ul knew there were descendants of Jacob living among the Gentiles who were SEEDS!   They simply needed some Living Water (the Gospel) showered over them and they would spring up or rather stand up and be counted as sons of Yahuah. So Sha'ul set out **to seek out** those whom Yahuah had, as promised, "written His Law on their hearts" and he knew them because "**they SHOW it by outwardly keeping the Law**" verse 15 above.

Sha'ul spread the gospel as a wide net, and as a fisher of men he sat back and let Yahuah bring to him those of the bloodline of Jacob whom were lost among the Gentiles. The true bloodline from **the House of Israel** who had been lost would literally respond and come to him and demonstrate they were truly Israelites by keeping the Law and responding to the Gospel message.

Remnant Israel a subset of Israel

Unfortunately, we have to overcome 2000 years of false teachers who have taught Sha'ul's writing under **the Spirit of Error**. Unfortunately, we all approach Sha'ul's writing from the standpoint of our "teaching" in the Christian Church. I am going to go through and demonstrate that the Christian Church's doctrines attributed to the Apostle Sha'ul are in fact <u>in grave error</u>. Let's look at the letter Sha'ul wrote to the assembly in Rome.

In Romans 9 we are taught by false teachers (Christianity) that Sha'ul teaches (**in total opposition to Yahuah and Yahusha**) that you don't have to be a descendant of Abraham/Isaac/Jacob to be a son of Yahuah. We are taught that the old covenant has been abolished and replaced by the New Covenant and the pagan Greeks (Christian Church) replaced Israel. We are taught in error that it isn't blood descendants any longer but a "promise" which can be outside of that bloodline.

Romans 9 below is the justification for that false doctrine:

Romans 9

⁶ But *it is* not as though the word of Yahuah has failed. For they are not all Israel who are *descended* from Israel; ⁷ nor are they all children because they are Abraham's descendants, but: "THROUGH ISAAC YOUR DESCENDANTS WILL BE NAMED." ⁸ That is, it is not the children of the flesh who are children of Yahuah, but the children of the promise are regarded as descendants. ⁹ For this is the word of promise: "AT THIS TIME I WILL COME, AND SARAH SHALL HAVE A SON." ¹⁰ And not only this, but there was Rebekah also, when she had conceived *twins* by one man, our father Isaac; ¹¹ for though *the twins* were not yet born and had not done anything good or bad, so that Yahuah's purpose according to *His* choice would stand, not because of works but because of Him who calls, ¹² it was said to her, "THE OLDER WILL SERVE THE YOUNGER." ¹³ Just as it is written, "JACOB I LOVED, BUT ESAU I HATED."

Above, Sha'ul is saying very clearly that:

- The Word of Yahuah to Abraham that it would be through his descendants that the sons of Yahuah would be chosen "has not failed".   So Sha'ul begins proclaiming Yahuah's Plan has not failed and is still true.

- Sha'ul then states another truth proclaimed by Yahuah that not all of the descendants of Israel will be chosen but only a REMNANT will be saved among them.   So not "all Israel who descended from Israel" will be chosen as sons.

Rav Sha'ul

- Then Sha'ul clarifies that only the descendants *through Isaac* not Ishmael will be the chosen bloodline as Isaac was the promised one.

- Then Sha'ul goes on to confirm the Torah that only those who descend from Abraham thru Isaac <u>thru JACOB</u> will be chosen.

Sha'ul is building up to defining **Remnant Israel** as we will see as coming exclusively through the promised seed of Jacob. Sha'ul is saying the exact opposite of what the Christian Church teaches. Sha'ul is actually saying that ONLY those who descend from Abraham through Isaac then Jacob are considered Israel. Then among those only a <u>small remnant</u> of that bloodline will be saved and THAT Sha'ul calls **Remnant Israel**.

> The "sovereign choice" is clearly defined within the strict bloodline of Abraham/Isaac/Jacob **not** through Ishmael and not through Esau.

Let me put Sha'ul's writing in context. What Sha'ul is saying, in context with all his writings, the Torah, and Prophets, is clear. ONLY a small remnant that descended from Jacob will be saved. Abraham had other sons and so did Isaac but even though they were Abraham's descendants too, they are not from the promised bloodline.

Sha'ul is saying **Remnant Israel** <u>does not extend</u> to those seeds of Abraham but ONLY Jacobs and only a remnant from that line are chosen sons of Yahuah. The first thing Sha'ul makes clear is that Yahuah's Word to Abraham has not failed.

Below is Romans 9 with my clarification IN CONTEXT:

> **Romans 9** - *Yahuah's Sovereign Choice*
> [6] **It is not as though Yahuah's word had failed**. For not all who are descended from (physical) Israel are (Remnant) Israel (only a remnant from that bloodline). [7] Nor (just) because they are his descendants (speaking of Ishmael and Esau) are they all Abraham's children (to whom the promises belong. It is only the bloodline from Abraham that descends from Isaac through Jacob). **On the contrary, "It is through Isaac that your offspring will be reckoned**." [8] In other words (Sha'ul now makes it clear it is not all the bloodline but a chosen subset), it is not the children by physical descent who are Yahuah's children (speaking of Ishmael and Esau), but it is the children of the promise (through Isaac/Jacob) who are regarded as Abraham's offspring (in context of Yahuah's promises to Abraham. Sha'ul is simply stating that not all of the descendants of Abraham are Yahuah's Children but only the descendants of promise that went through Isaac/Jacob). [9] For this was how the promise was stated: "At the appointed time I will return, and Sarah will have a son."

Sha'ul was simply developing the proven fact spoken of by Isaiah:

> **Romans 9**
> 27 Isaiah cries out concerning Israel: "Though the number of the Israelites be like the sand by the sea, *only the remnant will be saved*."

Sha'ul was the one chosen to understand the meaning of the two comings and the true meaning of "Israel" being a Remnant from

AMONG the Jews (**House of Judah**) and from AMONG the gentiles (where **the House of Israel** had been scattered). So the fact is that Yahuah's sons are scattered among ALL nations on Earth and have no idea they are of the bloodline of Jacob. ==The Elect will be called out of all nations and will be known by the fact they have a *"heart for the Law"* and *"know Yahuah's Name"*.== They will literally be physical descendants of Israel, but THEY WILL HAVE LOST THEIR IDENTITY (and not know they are of the bloodline of Jacob). It was prophesied by Ezekiel, Hosea, Isaiah, and Yahusha then confirmed by Sha'ul that ONLY a remnant from the bloodline of Israel would be saved, **and only** that remnant from the bloodline of Israel.

The Gifts of Yahuah to Remnant Israel

Sha'ul goes on to clearly teach that to this **Remnant of Israel** or Spiritual Israel **by choice IN ADDITION to bloodline** belong the Gifts of Yahuah.   He lists these gifts to us (the Remnant sons) as belonging to the "Israelites" only not to pagan Gentiles:

> **Romans 9:4-5**
>
> To the "Israelites" (no one else) belong 7 things granted to them as gifts from Yahuah:
>
> 1.) Adoption as sons of Yahuah
>
> 2.) To be the Glory of Yahuah
>
> 3.) The "Law" which is the Torah
>
> 4.) The Temple of Yahuah and the Altar within
>
> 5.) The Promises of Yahuah (forgiveness, resurrection, eternal life, dominion, inheritance)

6.) The "fathers" - they are of the bloodline descending from Abraham, Isaac, and Jacob

7.) And the Messiah (to be partakers in the Yahushaic Covenant)

NOT to the pagan Gentiles (known today as the Christian Church)! Christianity is the modern version of the Babylonian religion of sun worship. These blessings of Yahuah belong to **Remnant Israel** alone!

Sha'ul goes on in Romans to explain that **Remnant Israel** is a chosen few from among both Houses.

Let's continue with Romans. Sha'ul defines and clarifies that it is REMNANT ISRAEL that are the true sons of Yahuah to whom these 7 things belong to. Romans 9 Verse 6 - Sha'ul declares the WORD OF YAHUAH HAS NOT FAILED. His people are still Israel that descends through Abraham/Isaac/Jacob! BUT, Sha'ul confirms the prophets that not EVERYONE born in that bloodline is a son of Yahuah. "For they are not all Israel (not everyone who descended from Jacob is part of that remnant) who are descended from Israel", but only a Chosen Remnant will be saved.

Sha'ul goes into a long explanation of how the sons of Yahuah are predestined and not determined simply based on the bloodline alone. In other words, they are from the bloodline but they are a small SUBSET of that bloodline and chosen by Yahuah. Sha'ul demonstrates that Yahuah has CHOSEN ONLY A REMNANT from the bloodline of Israel who is scattered across the globe, who have lost their identity completely, <u>but they are still chosen</u>. They just have to be reclaimed back to Yahuah.

In verse 24 below, Sha'ul then declares that **REMNANT ISRAEL** is called from "AMONG" Jews (**House of Judah**), and also from "AMONG" the Gentiles (**House of Israel**, the lost sheep had been scattered AMONG the Gentile nations).   Sha'ul understood the Messiah HAD to come twice.   The first time to restore the lost sheep and call out the Chosen lost among the Gentile nations by blinding the eyes of the Jews.   Sha'ul would know these lost descendants of Abraham by their instinctive keeping of the Law and their acceptance of the name Yahuah and Yahusha!

The second time, Yahusha would come to restore and save the House of David and call out the chosen from among **the House of Judah**.   Together, those chosen from both houses are Remnant Israel.

> **Romans 9:24**
>
> 24 even us (Remnant Israel in context), whom he also called, not only from among the Jews (the House of Judah) but also from among the Gentiles (where the House of Israel is scattered)?

Then in verse 25, Sha'ul quotes from Hosea, the first Prophet <u>to the House of Israel</u> as justification for everything he was teaching concerning *the House of Israel* and *the House of Judah*.   Sha'ul had a deep understanding of the Torah and Prophets; he was a Pharisee and teacher of the Law.

This is how we know *everything Sha'ul was discussing* in Romans 9 was in context of *the House of Israel* and *the House of Judah* and the re-unification of the Nation back together again.   We know this because Sha'ul backed up everything he said with quotes from Hosea, Isaiah, and the prophets where Yahuah's Plan to choose a small remnant from among both Houses is revealed.

Sha'ul quotes from Hosea Chapter 1. So it is within this context Romans 9 is understood. In Hosea, Yahuah is discussing this very concept that he scattered and divorced the House of Israel, yet He had compassion on the House of Judah:

> **Hosea 1**
> ⁶ Then she conceived again and gave birth to a daughter. And Yahuah said to him, "Name her Lo-ruhamah, for **I will no longer have compassion on the house of Israel**, that I would ever forgive them. ⁷ **But I will have compassion on the house of Judah** and deliver them by Yahuah their Elohim, and will not deliver them by bow, sword, battle, horses or horsemen."

Yahuah goes on then to speak through Hosea that He would, at a later date, re-unite both houses back into one as Remnant Israel:

> ¹⁰ Yet the number of the sons of Israel will be like the sand of the sea, which cannot be measured or numbered; And in the place (pagan Gentile lands) where it is said to them (not that it is true *it is only said of them*), "You are not My people," It will be said to them (after I reclaim them to their rightful inheritance), "*You are* the sons of the living Elohim." ¹¹ **And the sons of Judah and the sons of Israel will be gathered together,**

Now that is the context of Romans 9! Sha'ul is speaking of **Remnant Israel** and he knew they would come exclusively from the bloodline of Jacob but not all of that bloodline would be called **Remnant Israel**.

We see Sha'ul justify everything he was talking about concerning "Gentiles" etc. by quoting from Hosea:

> ### Romans 9:25
> "I will call those who were not My People (the House of Israel whom Yahuah had divorced) 'My People' and who were not beloved, 'Beloved' (the promise Yahuah made to restore the House of Israel through the prophet Hosea)... "
> "And it shall be in the place (Gentile nations where they were scattered) where *it is said to them* (House of Israel) 'you are not My People' (because Yahuah divorced them and their remembrance as descendants of Jacob had ceased), **there** (in those foreign countries Yahuah will call back a remnant of the House of Israel) **they** (remnant of the House of Israel) **shall be called sons of the Living Elohim** (the restoration of the House of Israel back to Yahuah)."

This was Sha'ul's commission - to follow through with what Yahusha had come to do which was **to reclaim the Lost Sheep of the House of Israel** and save a remnant from among them. And then in the next verse Sha'ul again quotes from the prophet Isaiah who also (along with every other prophet) prophesied the re-unification of the Remnant of Israel (both Houses) back to Yahuah...

> ### Romans 9:27
> And Isaiah cries out concerning (Remnant Israel to whom the 7 promises belong) "Though the number of the sons of Israel (both Houses scattered among all the nations) be as the sand of the sea (fulfilling the blessing to Abraham) ... IT IS THE REMNANT (of both houses) THAT SHALL BE SAVED"

Sha'ul was given UNIQUE revelation that Yahuah's word and promises to all Israel did not fail. Yahuah will send the Messiah TWICE, first to reclaim the lost sheep of **the House of Israel**, and then Yahusha comes again to re-unify the two houses and call out a remnant from among the Jews or **the House of Judah**. That remnant from both houses is... **Remnant Israel**. It is only to Remnant Israel or the Chosen, Elect, sons of Yahuah that belong the following Gifts of Yahuah:

Romans 9:4-5
1.) Adoption as sons of Yahuah
2.) To be the Glory of Yahuah
3.) The "Law" which is the Torah
4.) *The Temple of Yahuah* and the Altar within
5.) The Promises of Yahuah (forgiveness, resurrection, eternal life, dominion, inheritance)
6.) The "fathers" (they are of the bloodline descending from Abraham, Isaac, and Jacob)
7.) And the Messiah

As I have just demonstrated, Sha'ul knew it was a Remnant of Israel that would be saved from both Houses. Some from among **the House of Judah** (Jews) and some from **the House of Israel** from among the Gentile nations where they had been scattered in fulfillment of the Prophets. That is what Sha'ul was clearly saying in Romans. Sha'ul was clearly teaching the Torah, Feasts, Sabbath, Covenants, Temple, Promises, Bloodline, and Messiah... belong to the sons of Yahuah... Remnant Israel **and no one else**.

Sha'ul's letter to the Ephesians

Sha'ul again addressed the re-unification of the House of Israel back to Yahuah below:

Ephesians 2
[11] Wherefore remember, that you being in time past (called) Gentiles in the flesh, who are *called* Uncircumcision by that which is called the Circumcision in the flesh made by hands (the Jews called the House of Israel "Gentiles"); [12] That at that time ye were without the Messiah (lost in exile among the Gentile nations), being aliens (in strange pagan lands) from the commonwealth of Israel (descendants of Jacob to which you truly belong), and strangers from the covenants of promise (Yahuah made to His people through the bloodline of Jacob), having no hope, and without Yahuah in the world (as a result of being divorced by Yahuah, separated and dispersed for rebellion): [13] But now in Messiah Yahusha ye (House of Israel, the lost sheep) who sometimes were far off (scattered among the pagan gentiles nations) are made nigh (restored again to your inheritance, the commonwealth of Israel) by the blood of the Messiah. [14] For (Yahusha) is our (Israel's) peace, who hath made both (houses, Israel and Judah) one (again, coming as Messiah ben Joseph to reclaim the lost sheep of the House of Israel), and hath broken down the middle wall of partition between us (the breach or enmity between the two Houses); [15] Having abolished (death) in his flesh the enmity (hatred toward or rebellion against), even the law

of commandments contained in ordinances (of Yahuah that we must keep through Love, having found Grace for our transgressions); for to make in Himself of two (Houses: House of Israel and House of Judah) one new man (Remnant Israel), so making peace (between the sons of Yahuah); [16] And that he (Yahusha) might reconcile both (houses) unto Yahuah in one body (fulfilling prophecy of the Messiah to reunite Israel) by the stake (through covenant), having slain the enmity (between the two Houses) thereby: [17] And (Yahusha) came and preached peace to you (House of Israel) which were afar off (scattered among the gentile nations), and to them (House of Judah) that were near (in the land of Israel and not lost). [18] For through him (Yahusha the High Priest) we both (House of Israel and House of Judah) have access by one Spirit (of reconciliation) unto the Father. [19] Now therefore ye (the House of Israel) are no more strangers (to the commonwealth of Israel you once belonged) and foreigners (in pagan lands as lost sheep), but fellow citizens with the saints, and of the household of Yahuah (grafted back into the tree you belong called Remnant Israel);

That... is what the Apostle Sha'ul *actually* said.

Summary

The sons of Yahuah are (and have always been) primarily from the bloodline of Jacob. They are a small remnant taken from among **the House of Israel** and from among **the House of Judah** and reunited into one nation again called **Remnant Israel**. They are those chosen sons, in covenant with Yahusha, who keep His Sabbaths, who have had their minds sealed by Yahuah, who have a heart for His Law, and who will be transposed (resurrected) into an eternal life in **the Kingdom of Yahuah**.

Chapter 12

The Constitution of the Kingdom of Yahuah

Revelation 22:14 - King James Bible
Blessed *are* they that keep His commandments (the Law), that they may have the right to the tree of life, and may enter in through the gates (of **the Kingdom of Yahuah** and) into the city (of Yahuah Shammah).

Introduction

For a detailed examination of The Law and its role in our life and The Yahushaic Covenant, as well as the truth behind The Pauline Doctrine.   Please see my book The Law and The Pauline Doctrine.

The Kingdom *of Yahuah* is a government established on the "rule of law" like any human government or kingdom.   Human governments/kingdoms are but "shadows" of the true perfect Spiritual Kingdom.   In this chapter I am going to establish *Yahuah's Law* in its rightful place in His Kingdom as the governing constitution upon which His Righteousness is established and the Universe is governed.

The Kingdom *of Yahuah* is governed by a defined set of laws which clearly define:

- Our relationship with Yahuah
- Our relationship with our brothers and sisters in the Kingdom
- What is right i.e. Righteousness
- What is wrong i.e. Sin
- Penalties for breaking the law
- Mercy
- Justice
- Atonement
- The role of a King
- The role of a Judge
- The role of a Priest
- The role of the High Priest
- etc.

This chapter is of utmost importance because the false religion called "Christianity" has literally taught **an abomination** that *the Law* was abolished.

Leaving ALL CHRISTIANS without the required entries in the Book of Life:

Psalm 40:6-8

⁶ Sacrifice and meal offering You have not desired; My ears You have opened; Burnt offering and sin offering You have not required. ⁷ Then I said, "Behold, I come; **in the scroll of the book it is written of me** (having a heart for the Law of Yahuah is a witness of us in the Book of Life). ⁸ I delight to do Your will, O my Elohim; Your Law is within my heart (the foundation of the New Covenant Jeremiah 31)."

Humanity abolishing ***the Law of Yahuah*** is called *"**the Transgression of Desolation**"* which is the cause of ***the Great Tribulation***:

> **Isaiah 24: 1-6**
> The Earth is polluted by its inhabitants - They have committed *the Transgression of Desolation* (transgressed the Torah, changed the Holy Feasts to Christopagan Holidays, and broken the Everlasting Covenant of the Sabbath changing it to the pagan day of worship ... Sunday) - Therefore the Curse found in the Torah devours the whole Earth, the inhabitants of Earth will be burned up, and few men left

> **The Transgression of Desolation** (not to be confused with **the Abomination of Desolation** defined in the next chapter) is the transgression of **the Laws of Yahuah** which is the cause of the Earth's destruction. **the Transgression of Desolation** also leads those who commit it to later commit **the Abomination of Desolation;** which leads to the destruction of their body.

The Spirit of Error that permeates Christianity is the cause of **the Transgression of Desolation.** That spirit is the teaching that in the *"image of a man"* (known as Hesus Horus Krishna a.k.a **Jesus H. Christ)** the Law was abolished. In reality, the Law is the foundation of every covenant between Yahuah and mankind and **the New Covenant** is literally defined by **the Law**.

> **Jeremiah 31:31-34**
> ³¹ "Behold, days are coming," declares Yahuah, "when I will make a new covenant with **the House of Israel** and with **the House of Judah**, ³² not like the covenant which I made with their fathers in the day I took them by the hand to bring them out of the land of Egypt, *My covenant which they broke*, although I was a husband to them," declares Yahuah. ³³ "But this is the covenant which I will make with **the House of Israel** after those days," declares Yahuah, "**I will put My law within them and on their heart I will write it**; and I will be their Elohim, and they shall be My people. ³⁴ They will not teach again, each man his neighbor and each man his brother, saying, 'Know Yahuah,' for they will all know Me, from the least of them to the greatest of them," declares Yahuah, "for I will forgive their iniquity, and their sin I will remember no more."

We see above, Yahuah speaking through His Prophet Jeremiah, that Yahuah would make a new covenant with **the House of Israel** (whom He had scattered among all the nations and divorced) who had broken the Mosaic Covenant by not keeping His Law. As a result, **the House of Israel** was utterly divorced by Yahuah and rejected as being an unfaithful "wife" and violating the marriage vows (**the Law**). A new covenant would also be made with **the**

House of Judah. It would be under this "New Covenant" that Yahuah would re-unite both houses back into one nation under The Messiah Yahusha as King and choose <u>a small remnant</u> from among them known as **Remnant Israel**.

We touched on this in Chapter 10 of this book "**the Citizens of the Kingdom of Yahuah**" demonstrating that only a remnant from the bloodline of Jacob would be chosen as sons of Yahuah and they would be known by their outward keeping of His Law which was written inwardly on their hearts. Yahuah again confirmed the reality of His Law and its place in **the New Covenant** when speaking through His Prophet Ezekiel:

> **Ezekiel 36: 26, 27**
> I will give you a new heart (for my Law and write my Law on it) and put a new spirit (of loving obedience) in you; I will remove from you your heart of stone (legalistic observance of the Law without love) and give you a heart of flesh. <u>And I will put my Spirit in you and move you to follow my decrees and be careful to keep my laws</u>.

In this chapter I will cover:

- How **the Yahushaic Covenant** is "New"
- The Plan of Salvation is conditional on keeping the Law
- The Law is a gift of Yahuah to His Sons
- The Spirit of Error and the Spirit of the False Messiah
- Transgression of Desolation - the abolishment of the Law
- the Law is the governing constitution of **the Kingdom of Yahuah**
- Law Breakers are thrown out of **the Kingdom of Yahuah**
- Transposition of **the Law of Yahuah**

- o The 4 States of the Law and 3 Transpositions (transfers of position between them)
- o The Law existed prior to Adam in the Mind of Yahuah
- o First Transposition of Law - from the Mind of Yahuah to oral tradition
- o Second Transposition of the Law - the Law was transposed from oral tradition to written in the Mosaic Covenant
- o Third Transposition of the Law - the Law was transposed from written in stone to written on the hearts of His sons in **the Yahushaic Covenant**
- o Yahusha strengthened the Law
- o The Apostle Sha'ul taught the Law properly
  - o Sha'ul taught the transposition of the Law
  - o The Apostle Sha'ul – Leader of the Nazarenes, follower of Yahusha
    - o The Apostle Sha'ul's view of the Law: Abolished or not?

How is the Yahushaic Covenant "New"?

This "New Covenant" Yahuah promised to **the House of Israel** and **the House of Judah** is literally defined by one thing... the Law! It isn't abolished in any way, in fact the New Covenant is "New" in the sense that it has been **strengthened and transposed** from "written in stone" as it was in the Mosaic Covenant to literally "written on our very hearts" in **the Yahushaic Covenant**. In that way and in that way ONLY is **the Yahushaic Covenant** "New" and "not like the Covenant of Moses".

> **Jeremiah 31:31-34**
> 31 "Behold, days are coming," declares Yahuah, "when I will make a new covenant with **the House of Israel** and with **the House of Judah**, 32 not like the covenant which I made with their fathers in the day I took them by the hand to bring them out of the land of Egypt, My covenant which they broke, although I was a husband to them," declares Yahuah. 33 "But this is the covenant which I will make with **the House of Israel** after those days," declares Yahuah, "I will put My law within them and on their heart I will write it; and I will be their Elohim, and they shall be My people. 34 They will not teach again, each man his neighbor and each man his brother, saying, 'Know Yahuah,' for they will all know Me, from the least of them to the greatest of them," declares Yahuah, "for I will forgive their iniquity, and their sin I will remember no more."

What is important to note about Jeremiah's prophecy is that it is only **the House of Israel** or rather **the Lost Sheep of the House of Israel** whom Yahuah has a need to *"write it on their hearts"*. Why? Because **the House of Judah** never abandoned the Written Law (although they did add to it substantially through Takkanots which are commandments of men). It was **the House of Israel** who totally abandoned Yahuah's Law and as a result they were utterly "divorced" or separated from Yahuah.

Yahuah's Righteousness, defined by the Law, does not change; it is **the House of Israel** that comes back to His Law that leads to their "grafting back into the Family Tree" in **the Yahushaic Covenant**.

Below, is Jeremiah's prophecy with my comments in parenthesis to clarify, in context of the Word of Yahuah:

> **Jeremiah 31:31-34**
> [31] "Behold, days are coming," declares Yahuah, "when I will make a new covenant (*the Yahushaic Covenant*) with **the House of Israel** (fulfilled in the first coming defined by the Spring Feast rehearsals) and with **the House of Judah** (fulfilled in the second coming defined by the Fall Feast rehearsals), [32] not like the covenant (where the Law was written in stone defined by physical acts) which I made with their fathers (Mosaic Covenant) in the day I took them by the hand to bring them out of the land of Egypt, My covenant which <u>**they broke**</u>, although I was a husband to them (it was a Marriage Covenant, the Law is the marriage vows)," declares Yahuah. [33] "But this is (how) the covenant which I will make with **the House of Israel** after those days (is different from the Mosaic Covenant),"

declares Yahuah, "*<u>I will put My law within them and on their heart I will write it</u>*; (the Law will be fulfilled and transposed from physical act to attitude of heart i.e. Spiritual Intent) and I will be their Elohim, and they (Remnant Israel) shall be My people (because they will be faithful to the marriage vows i.e. they will have a heart for His Law). 34 They will not teach (the Law) again, each man his neighbor and each man his brother, saying, 'Know Yahuah,' for they will all know Me, from the least of them to the greatest of them," declares Yahuah, "*for I will forgive their iniquity, and their sin I will remember no more.*"

> **The New Covenant** is, in effect, **the Mosaic Covenant** transposed into the hearts of the sons of Yahuah and **the Law** strengthened from physical act to Spiritual Intent.

We see Yahuah promise to "*forgive their iniquity, and their sin I will remember no more*" in verse 34 above.   That promise itself is conditional on obedience to **the Law**.   Yahuah fulfilled this promise in <u>*one day on Passover*</u>. On that day He forgave our iniquity (contempt for His Law) and our sin (transgression of His Law) exactly as He promised.   Yahuah forgave us because of Yahusha's obedience to… **THE LAW**!   The entire plan of salvation was made conditional.   **IF** Yahusha would be obedient to the Law; **THEN** Yahuah would forgive all His sons their iniquity.   It is in Zachariah Chapter 3 that we see the terms given to fulfill the promise in Jeremiah to forgive the iniquity (the breaking of His Laws) of the sons of Yahuah.

The Plan of Salvation is *conditional* on keeping the Law

Yahuah promised in Jeremiah 31 to forgive His sons for breaking His Law (iniquity). Yahuah then gave Zachariah a vision describing exactly "how" this promise would be fulfilled in the Messiah.

We see Yahuah make the same promise to Yahusha after Yahusha was Mikveh'd by the High Priest John the Baptist. Yahusha then fled into the desert *as the scapegoat for our sin* to seek Yahuah's confirmation that he was in fact... The Passover Lamb of Yahuah as John proclaimed:

> **Zechariah 3** - *Garments for the High Priest, Yahusha*
>
> ¹ Then he showed me Yahusha **the high priest** standing before the angel of Yahuah, and Satan standing at his right side to accuse him (Matthew 4:1-11). ² Yahuah said (through the Angelic messenger) to Satan, "Yahuah rebuke you, Satan! Yahuah, who has chosen Jerusalem, rebuke you! Is not this man *a burning stick snatched from the fire*?" (Yahusha was lying on the desert floor in the blazing sun after 40 days and nights in the desert literally starving to death per Matthew 4:1-11) ³ Now Yahusha was dressed in filthy rags (a metaphor for the sin of Israel which had been laid on his shoulders by John when John Mikveh'd Yahusha as the Passover Lamb) as he stood before the angel. ⁴ The angel said to those who were standing before

him, "Take off his filthy clothes." Then Yahuah said to Yahusha, "*See, I have taken away your sin, and I will put fine garments (of the Eternal High Priest) on you*." ⁵ Then I said, "Put a clean turban on his head." So they put a clean turban on his head and clothed him, while the angel of Yahuah stood by. ⁶ The angel of Yahuah gave this charge to Yahusha: ⁷ "This is what Yahuah Almighty says (again Yahuah speaking through His proxy Angel): '**If** you will walk in obedience to me and keep my requirements (the Law), **then** you will govern my house (be seated as King) and have charge of my courts (be my Righteous Judge), and I will give you a place among these standing here (Yahusha given a seat among the Court of the Almighty). ⁸ "'Listen, High Priest Yahusha, you and your associates seated before you, **who are men symbolic of things to come** (all the sons of Yahuah will keep the Law as it will be written on their hearts): I am going to bring (you Yahusha... out of this desert) my servant, (you are) **the Branch** (Yahusha will be the Messiah, King, and Judge **IF** he will obey **the Law of Yahuah**). ⁹ See, the stone I have set in front of Yahusha! There are seven eyes on that one stone, and I will engrave an inscription on it,' says Yahuah Almighty, '*and I will remove the sin of this land in a single day*. ¹⁰ "'In that day each of you will invite your neighbor to sit under your vine and fig tree,' declares Yahuah Almighty."

So there we have it, exactly "how" Yahuah, per Jeremiah 31:34, would *"forgive their iniquity, and their sin I will remember no more."* He would send Yahusha as the Messiah and make Yahusha the High Priest of Israel who would then offer himself up as the Passover Lamb. But everything was contingent on one thing... KEEPING THE LAW! Not just Yahusha, but he would be the example (symbol of things to come) of all the future sons of Yahuah. We all are Keepers of the Law (*Nazarenes)* defenders of Righteousness against all forms of pagan influence. I explain all of this in my book **Melchizedek and the Passover Lamb**. I also cover this in much more detail in the next few books in this series.

Those who "think" they are saved in Jesus Christ who is *the lawless one* i.e. the one in whom the Law was abolished, have been deceived by the False Messiah. They are deceived because Yahuah has given them over to the Spirit of Error as they do not have the Seal of Yahuah over their frontal lobe which is the part of the brain that enables us to recognize deception.

I covered this in Chapter 8.

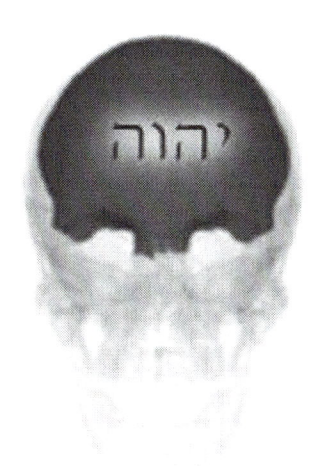

When asked if they are saved they swear they know they are. When asked "how do you know" they have no answer other than "*I just know, you know when you know*" or some type of double talk like that. ==There is an answer to the question of "how do you know you are saved" and that answer is... you <u>keep</u> **the Law of Yahuah**.== There is an answer to "how do you know you are in covenant with Yahusha" by following his example of <u>keeping **the Law of Yahuah**</u>:

1 John 2

[3] By this we know that we have come to know Yahuah, if we keep His Law. [4] The one who says, "I have come to know Yahuah," and does not keep His Law, is a liar, and the truth is not in him; [5] but whoever keeps Yahuah's Law, in him the love of Yahuah has truly been perfected. <u>By this we know that we are in covenant with Yahusha:</u> [6] the one who says he is in covenant with Yahusha ought himself to walk in the same manner as Yahusha walked (in obedience to the Law).

Christians can't give a definitive answer as to "how they know" they are saved. This is because they are not... they are following another gospel and another messiah that is false.

The Law is a gift of Yahuah to His Sons

If you buy into the **Spirit of Error** which is the very message of **the False Messiah** (that **the Law** is abolished) then you simply cannot call yourself a "son of Yahuah" because the very gifts Yahuah gives to His sons are:

Romans 9:4-5

To the "Israelites" (no one else) belong 7 things granted to them as gifts from Yahuah:

1.) Adoption as sons of Yahuah

2.) To be the Glory of Yahuah

3.) **The "Law" which is the Torah**

4.) **The Temple of Yahuah** and the Altar within

5.) The Promises of Yahuah (forgiveness, resurrection, eternal life, dominion, inheritance)

6.) The "fathers" - they are of the bloodline descending from Abraham, Isaac, and Jacob

7.) And the Messiah (to be partakers in **the Yahushaic Covenant**)

If in your heart you believe **the Law** has been abolished then you have not received Yahuah's gifts to His true sons. Yahuah has given you over to **the Spirit of Error** because you have **the Spirit of the False Messiah** governing your life not **the Law**. In this chapter we are going to cover **the Law** that has eternally existed and will eternally exist as the governing constitution of **the Kingdom of Yahuah**. First, let us define **the Spirit of the False Messiah** and **the Spirit of Error**.

The Spirit of Error and the Spirit of the False Messiah

Anyone who elevates the image of a man i.e. Hesus Horus Krishna (Jesus H. Christ) in their hearts as Elohim above Yahuah will be given over by Yahuah <u>to believe a lie</u>. That very lie is that **the Law** has been abolished. The Spirit of the Antichrist is anyone who denies that Yahusha was a mere man (came in the flesh) and believes in the doctrine of incarnation:

> **<u>1 John 4</u>**
> 1 Beloved, do not believe every spirit, but test the spirits to see whether they are from Yahuah, because many false prophets have gone out into the world (claiming to be the incarnation of God). ² By this you know the Spirit of Yahuah: every spirit that confesses that Messiah Yahusha has come in the flesh (a man) is from Yahuah; ³ and every spirit that does not confess Yahusha has come in the flesh (but says Jesus is the incarnation of God) is not from Yahuah; **this is the *spirit* of the antichrist** (or False Messiah. The False Messiah is an image of a man worshipped above Yahuah as Elohim) … ¹² No one has seen Yahuah at any time! (Because Yahusha is not Yahuah in the flesh or a demi-god).

Anyone who elevates the <u>**false**</u> image of Yahusha (Jesus) into a God in their heart has **the Spirit of the Antichrist**. **The Spirit of**

Error is given to all of those who commit this abomination and ***the Spirit of Error*** is defined as "abolishing the law" i.e. do not keep the commandments of Yahuah.

> **2 John 7** - *Beware of Antichrist Deceivers*
> 7 For many deceivers have gone out into the world <u>who do not confess Yahusha the Messiah as coming in the flesh</u> (but rather confess Jesus is the incarnation of God in the flesh). **This is a deceiver and an antichrist**. 8 Look to yourselves, that we do not lose those things we worked for, but that we may receive a full reward. 9 Whoever transgresses (*the Law of Yahuah*) and does not abide in the doctrine of the Messiah (that he <u>did not</u> come to abolish the Law) does not have (the Spirit of) Yahuah. He who abides in the doctrine of the Messiah (that not one Jot or Tittle of the Law has been abolished) has both the Father and the Son. 10 If anyone comes to you and does not bring **this** doctrine (but brings a Trinitarian lie and teaches *unrighteousness as truth* see Romans 1:18 that the Law was abolished), do not receive him into your house nor greet him; 11 for he who greets him shares in his evil deeds (breaking of the Law).

Yahuah is Elohim, He is ONE, He is Spirit, and He *is NOT A MAN*:

> **Hosea 11**
> 9 I will not carry out my fierce anger, nor will I devastate Ephraim again. For I am Elohim, **and not a man**—

Numbers 23:19
"Yahuah **is not a man**, that He should lie, **Nor a son of man**, that He should repent

Yahusha **was** exactly that... he **was** a man, and specifically called himself the son of man (which is a Hebrew idiom for human being), and he is not Yahuah "in the flesh". That is a contradiction of Yahuah's own declaration above. As I have showed clearly in this book many times already, the belief in the "incarnation" is *the Spirit of the Anti-Christ*.

We see Yahuah and Yahusha are not the same beings in any way, Yahuah has always existed, Yahusha was born human i.e. the son of man, transposed to the Spirit (resurrected) and seated by Yahuah as His Proxy King over *the Kingdom of Yahuah* as the first born son in His family:

Daniel 7
13 "I kept looking in the night visions, And behold, with the clouds of heaven One (Yahusha) like **a Son of Man** was coming, And He (Yahusha) came up to the Ancient of Days (Yahuah, they are not the same being) And was presented before Him. 14 "And to Him (Yahusha) was given (by Yahuah as an inheritance) dominion, Glory and a kingdom, That all the peoples, nations and *men of every* language Might **serve** Him (not worship Yahusha, we serve Yahusha in the Kingdom). His dominion is an everlasting dominion which will not pass away; and His kingdom is one which will not be destroyed.

Yahusha was fully human IN EVERY WAY not "God" in anyway:

> **Hebrews 2:17**
> For this reason he had to be made like them, **fully human in every way**, in order that he might become a merciful and faithful high priest in service to Yahuah, and that he might make atonement for the sins of the people.

Yahusha was fully human in EVERY WAY... It just doesn't get any clearer than that.

Sha'ul warns us **not to elevate the "image of a man" in our hearts above Yahuah** as God and teach "unrighteousness as truth" or "that the Law is abolished is true". Those who replace Yahuah with "Jesus" in their hearts will be given over to a *depraved mind.* That depraved mind is *The Spirit of Error* - Yahuah will not permit them to have any spiritual understanding whatsoever and they will be filled with unrighteousness (abolish His Law in their hearts):

> **Romans 1**
> [18] For the wrath of Yahuah is revealed from heaven against all ungodliness and unrighteousness (breaking His Law) of men **who suppress the truth in unrighteousness** (teach unrighteousness or the Law was abolished as truth), [19] because that which is known about Yahuah is evident within them (the Law is written on our hearts); for Yahuah made it evident to them... [21] For even though they knew Yahuah, they did not honor Him as Elohim or give thanks, but they became futile in their speculations (that Jesus abolished the Law), and their foolish heart was darkened (because the Torah is a light unto our path: Psalm

119:105). ²² Professing to be wise, they became fools, ²³ and exchanged the glory of the incorruptible Yahuah for **an image in the form of corruptible man** (the Messiah was a corruptible man who died)... ²⁸ And just as they did not see fit to acknowledge Yahuah any longer (pray to Jesus, invite Jesus to sit on the throne of Yahuah in their heart as God, have the mark of The Pagan Trinity on their mind), Yahuah <u>gave them over to a depraved mind</u>, to do those things which are not proper (iniquity or transgress the Law), ²⁹ being filled with <u>all unrighteousness</u> (abolishing the Law)

The Apostle Sha'ul addresses this very fact again:

2 Thessalonians 2
³ Don't let anyone deceive you in any way, for that day will not come until the rebellion (against the Law or Transgression of Desolation) occurs and the <u>man of lawlessness</u> (or man in whom the Law is abolished) is revealed (to be the False Messiah), the man doomed to destruction. ⁴ He will oppose and will exalt himself over everything that is called God or is worshiped (saying he is God in the flesh), so that he sets himself up in Yahuah's temple (in the heart/mind of man), proclaiming himself to be God (incarnate).

⁵ Don't you remember that when I was with you I used to tell you these things? ⁶ And now you know what is holding him back so that he may be revealed at the proper time. ⁷ For the secret power of lawlessness (breaking **the Law of Yahuah**) is already at work; but the one who now holds it

back will continue to do so till he is taken out of the way (because of the Transgression of Desolation). [8] And then the lawless one (the one in whom the Law was abolished) will be revealed (by Yahusha as the False Messiah), whom the Messiah Yahusha will overthrow with the breath of his mouth and destroy by the splendor of his coming. [9] The coming of the lawless one (the one in whom the Law is abolished) will be in accordance with how Satan works (the dragon gives him his power, great authority, and throne). He will use all sorts of displays of power through signs and wonders that serve the lie (that the Law was abolished), [10] and all the ways that wickedness (violating the Law) deceives those who are perishing. They perish because they refused to love the truth (of the Torah) and so be saved. [11] For this reason (because they committed The Transgression of Desolation and abolished His Law) Yahuah sends them a powerful delusion (Christianity) so that they will believe the lie (that Jesus the False Messiah abolished the Law) [12] and so that all will be condemned (by the Law not being covered by the blood of the Passover Lamb because they put their faith in Easter Jesus) who have not believed the truth (Yahusha did not abolish the Law) but have delighted in wickedness (transgression of His Law).

The reason why those who commit this transgression and believe "Jesus abolished the Law" is because that is what by definition the False Messiah does.   The False Messiah is an "image" of Yahusha that is not true.   This false image is the abominable sacrifice of Easter on **the Altar of Yahuah** (which is your heart) stopping the sacrifice of the Passover Lamb which destroys **the Temple of Yahuah** (which is your body).   This is the topic of **Chapter 14 – the Abomination of Desolation**.

The False Messiah is the one who ABOLISHES THE LAW and changes the ordained Feasts of Yahuah to pagan holidays:

> ### Daniel 7
> [25] He (the False Messiah) will speak out (in our hearts) against the Most High (proclaiming himself God) and wear down the saints of the Highest One, and he will intend to make alterations in (Yahuah's ordained) times and in the Law (of Yahuah).

> In the history of humanity, there is only one "image of a man" that we have literally elevated as "God" in His Temple (our body, we invite Jesus into our hearts), and in whose name the Feasts/Ordained Times of Yahuah were changed to pagan holidays. Only one man in whose image "causes the sacrifices made by the Eternal High Priest Yahusha to stop" changing Passover to Easter.

> ### Daniel 9:27
> He (the false Messiah) will put an end to sacrifice and offering (of the Passover Lamb, Yahusha only offers himself up as a "Lamb that has been slaughtered" for those who keep Passover in light of his sacrifice). And at the temple (your body) he will set up an abomination (the Ishtar Pig i.e. Easter.   You spiritually slaughter a pig on the altar of your heart) that causes (the) desolation (of

your body, you will die dead in your sin because you did not put your faith in Passover and there is no sacrifice left for your sin)

There is only one man in whose image the Law was abolished.... **Hesus Horus Krishna a.k.a Jesus H. Christ** the "god" created by Constantine at the Council of Nicaea. The God of the False Religion of Christianity. I deal in depth with **the Abomination of Desolation** spoken of by Daniel, fulfilled physically by Antiochus, and then fulfilled in the Spirit by Jesus in my book **the Antichrist Revealed!**

In this chapter I want to quickly address **the Transgression of Desolation** as it is the abolishment of the Law that causes the Great Tribulation and the destruction of Earth.

The *'Transgression'* of Desolation is the Abolishment of the Law

In scripture there are two events that occur among mankind that lead to the Earth's destruction and the destruction of humanity. They are **the Transgression of Desolation** and **the Abomination of Desolation**.

Very few people realize that **the Transgression of Desolation** and **the Abomination of Desolation** are two very different events and that one leads to the other.   They are both addressed in scripture and both combine as a 1, 2… punch to destroy the Earth and everyone on it.

First let us define terms:

Transgression Definition:

> Main Entry: **trans·gres·sion** 🔊
> Pronunciation: -'gre-sh&n
> Function: *noun*
> Date: 15th century
> : an act, process, or instance of transgressing : as **a**
> : infringement or violation of a law, command, or duty

Abomination Definition:

> Main Entry: **abom·i·na·tion**
> Pronunciation: &-"bä-m&-'nA-sh&n
> Function: *noun*
> Date: 14th century
> **1** : something abominable
> **2** : extreme disgust and hatred :

The Transgression of Desolation is where mankind abolishes ***the Law of Yahuah*** in the "image of the False Messiah" and changes Yahuah's Feasts to pagan holidays and Yahuah's Sabbath to a pagan day of worship. It is this transgression of the Law that leads to the desolation of Earth and everything on it.

The Abomination of Desolation is committed by those who put their faith in the False Messiah and elevate an image of him as God in their hearts. The sacrifice of the False Messiah is the most abominable animal to Yahuah defined in His Law as a pig. Those who put their faith in this abominable sacrifice are destroyed; it literally desolates/destroys their body which is ***the Temple of Yahuah***.

> One leads to the other! By committing the Transgression of Desolation and abolish His Law, we set ourselves up to be deceived by the false messiah; by keeping Easter of Passover... we commit the Abomination of Desolation.

Transgression of Desolation vs. the Abomination of Desolation

The Transgression of Desolation is humanity abolishing the Laws of Yahuah. It is this transgression that leads to the total "desolation" of planet Earth by Yahuah:

Isaiah 24: 1-6

The Earth is polluted by its inhabitants - They have committed **the Transgression of Desolation** (transgressed the Torah, changed the Holy Feasts to Christopagan Holidays, and broken the Everlasting Covenant of the Sabbath changing it to the pagan day of worship ... Sunday) - Therefore the Curse found in the Torah devours the whole Earth, the inhabitants of Earth will be burned up, and few men left.

The "curse" Isaiah is referring to that destroys the Earth is the curse for "transgressing the Laws of Yahuah"

Deuteronomy 27:26

"Cursed is anyone who does not uphold the words of this law by carrying them out."

We see in Revelation 15, the prophecy in Isaiah being fulfilled as **the Tabernacles of the Covenant Law** is opened inside **the Temple of Yahuah** to judge the Earth for committing **the Transgression of Desolation** and **the Great Tribulation** begins:

Revelation 15

⁵ After this I looked, and I saw in heaven (there is no temple on Earth at this time, it has been transposed to heaven) **the temple—that is, <u>the tabernacle of the covenant law</u>**—and it was opened (as to judge those on the Earth who have transgressed the Law). ⁶ Out of the temple came the seven angels <u>with the seven plagues</u>. They were dressed in clean, shining linen and wore golden sashes around their chests. ⁷ Then one of the four living creatures gave to the seven angels seven golden bowls <u>filled with the wrath of Yahuah</u>, who lives forever and ever. ⁸ And the temple was filled with smoke from the glory of Yahuah and from his power, and no one could enter the temple until <u>the seven plagues of the seven angels were completed</u>.

The prophet Daniel speaks of this same event where the people of Earth commit ***the Transgression of Desolation*** by transgressing ***the Law of Yahuah***. We see that ***the Transgression of Desolation*** leads later to ***the Abomination of Desolation***. Below is how the Amplified Bible translates Daniel 8 (comments in parenthesis)

Remember this is a VISION and should be understood as such and applied spiritually:

Daniel 8 – Amplified Bible

12 And the host [the body Temple] was given [to the False Messiah] together with the continual [defense provided by Michael as he is being taken away Dan. 12:1 and Rev. 12:7 and 1 Thess. 2:7] because of **the transgression of**

desolation [changing ordained feasts, changing the Holy Sabbath, and transgressing the Torah]. And righteousness and truth [of Yahuah defined by His Law] were cast down to the ground, and it [the image of the False Messiah] accomplished this [by Divine permission] and prospered [in the hearts of man as Yahuah gave those who elevated an image of the False Messiah over to a depraved mind ... *the Spirit of Error*].

13Then I heard a holy one [angel] speaking, and another holy [angel] one said to the one that spoke, "For how long is the vision concerning the continual [defense of Michael being taken away Dan. 12:1 and Rev. 12:7 and 1 Thess. 2:7], **the transgression that makes desolate**, and the giving over of both the sanctuary (*the Altar of Yahuah*/hearts of man) and the host (the human body/Temple of Yahuah...this is *the Abomination of Desolation* where the sanctuary is desolated by an abominable sacrifice and the body temple destroyed] to be trampled underfoot? 14 And he said to him and to me, For 2,300 evenings and mornings; then the sanctuary shall be cleansed and restored.

Notice above, Daniel describes the continual defense over Earth provided by the Archangel Michael literally being "taken away" because of *the Transgression of Desolation*.   Earth is left defenseless and per Isaiah 24 literally destroyed because of *the Transgression of Desolation* or transgression of *the Law of Yahuah*.

The problem is, in your English Bible it doesn't tell you it is Michael that is "removed" and "taken away", it says *sacrifices* in italics. This is just one very important example of how bad translation can literally change the meaning of the Bible completely. The word **sacrifices** in Daniel 8:12, 13 was NOT in the original Hebrew text it was ADDED by the translators in error.

What Daniel was referring to was the continual defense of the Archangel Michael as I will demonstrate next.

The reason this is extremely important is because Michael is removed or taken away from standing in our defense because humanity has abolished **the Law of Yahuah** committing **the Transgression of Desolation**. Allow me to explain...

Hebrew/Aramaic Scriptures vs. English Translations

The Meaning of Italics in the English Translations of the Bible

When the original Bible was translated from Hebrew, Aramaic, and Greek; the challenge for the translators was to correctly translate these languages into an English equivalent and make judgment calls, where in Hebrew the subject wasn't specified only implied. The problem is every translator believed that "Jesus abolished the Law"! So in their prejudice, they took liberty to ensure the truth was hidden. As I will demonstrate, these translators did not always make the correct assumptions. These translators were uninspired pagan scribes and translators not guided by **the Spirit of Yahuah**.

English Words ADDED to the Book of Daniel

In the book of Daniel, the word "*sacrifice*" was **added** to the King James Version (and every later version) in VERY important passages of scripture which define the signs and cause of the Great Tribulation and the duration between major end events.

In Daniel the word "*sacrifice*" was **added** after the Hebrew word *tamiyd* which was translated "daily" giving us "daily sacrifices". The original text did not specify what was implied by the word *tamiyd* (itself mistranslated as *daily*) so the English translators assumed the original text was implying "*sacrifice*" based on Daniel 9:27 when the proper reference is Daniel 12:1:

> **Daniel 12:1**
> "At that time Michael, the great prince who protects your people, will arise (and be removed or taken away by Yahuah because of the Transgression of Desolation). There will be a time of distress such as has not happened from the beginning of nations until then. But at that time your people--everyone whose name is found written in the book--will be delivered.

Below are the scriptures where the word *tamiyd* translated *daily* was used and the word "*sacrifice*" was **added** by the English translators assuming "sacrifice" was the proper implication of *tamiyd*. NOTE: the word "*sacrifice*" is in ITALICS in most Bibles which means the word was added and not originally in the text:

Daniel 8:11-14

¹⁰ And it (the False Messiah) waxed great, even to the host of heaven (Angelic Realm); and it cast down some of the host and of the stars to the ground, and stamped upon them. ¹¹ Yea, he magnified *himself* even to the Prince of the host (Michael the Archangel), and by Him (Yahuah) the daily *sacrifice* (sacrifice was added) was taken away, and the place of the sanctuary was cast down.

¹² And an host (Michael) was given *him* against the daily *sacrifice* (sacrifice was added) by reason of transgression (of the Law), and it cast down the truth (of Yahuah's Word) to the ground (abolished it); and it practiced, and prospered (in abolishing *the Law of Yahuah*). ¹³ Then I heard one saint speaking, and another saint said unto that certain *saint* which spake, How long *shall be* the vision *concerning* the daily *sacrifice* (sacrifice was added) and the Transgression of Desolation, to give both the sanctuary (the heart/mind of man) and the host (the body) to be trodden under foot?

Daniel 12:11

¹¹ And from the time that the daily *sacrifice* (sacrifice was added) shall be taken away, and the Abomination of Desolation set up, there shall be a thousand two hundred and ninety days.

In every case we just read, the word *sacrifice* was not in the Hebrew texts, it was added by the translators. What was taken away per Daniel 12:1 was Michael, but "daily Michael" doesn't make any sense. That is because the translators mistranslated the Hebrew word *tamiyd as" daily" when it actually means "continual" as in the continual defense Michael provides over Earth.

Hebrew Word translated "Daily" mistranslated

In Daniel, as we just reviewed, only the word "tamiyd" occurred in the original text. The word is translated "daily" and the word "*sacrifice*" was added in English to try and clarify what Daniel implied by the word *tamiyd* giving us "daily sacrifices" which is a mistranslation.

Below is the actual word translated as "daily" in English from the Strong's Concordance:

8548	tamiyd *taw-meed'*	from an unused root meaning <u>to stretch out</u>; properly, continuance (<u>as indefinite extension</u>); but used only (attributively as adjective) constant (or adverbially, constantly);

So the word "tamiyd" is an adjective used to modify a noun but the noun is missing in Hebrew. The word **tamiyd** actually means <u>to stretch out as an indefinite extension</u>, stretch out continually or constantly. It doesn't mean "daily" as translated.

The key is to try and determine what noun was implied by Daniel when he used the adjective "tamiyd". Was it the "*sacrifice*" that was implied as the English translators assumed? Or was it something else? Could it be that what was removed was the continual DEFENSE of the Holy People provided by Michael the Archangel? Yes, Daniel answered that question in Daniel Chapter 12 verse 1.

The word "tamiyd" should have been translated as "continual defense" not "daily" as it refers to Michael who **continually stretches out in defense** over the people of Earth.

The translators determined it was the "daily *sacrifice*" based on Daniel 9:27. This was a grave error on the part of the translators as we will see.

Proper Implication of "Tamiyd" is Michael not Sacrifices

EVERY verse in Daniel listed above is in context speaking of the Archangel Michael, the Prince of the Angelic Host, the Commander of the Angelic Host, being taken away by Yahuah as a result of the **Transgression of Desolation**.

The translators should have let scripture interpret scripture and, if they did so, they would have realized Daniel specifically stated it was Michael that was removed in Daniel 12:1. Daniel specifically named Michael as Israel's defender:

> **Daniel 10**
> [21] But I will tell thee that which is inscribed in the writing

of truth: and there is none that holdeth (in defense) with me against these, but Michael your prince

Therefore, the proper implication is that the **"continual defense"** of the Holy People provided by **Michael the Archangel** will be "taken away" because of *the Transgression of Desolation*... not the daily sacrifice.

Daniel 12 specifically answers this question and identifies that it is **Michael** that is taken away. Sha'ul confirmed it was **Michael** (the restrainer) that is taken away in 2 Thessalonians. John confirmed it is **Michael** that is taken away in Revelation 12 as Michael is no longer on Earth but waging a war in Heaven.

> **Daniel 12**
> 12 "At that time **Michael**, the great prince who protects your people, will arise (from providing a continual defense of Earth and go to wage war in Heaven against Lucifer, see Rev. 12). There will be a time of distress (because Earth is left defenseless because of the Transgression of Desolation) such as has not happened from the beginning of nations until then. But at that time your people—everyone whose name is found written in the book—will be delivered.

The Apostle Sha'ul discusses this exact event described by Daniel:

> **2 Thessalonians 2**
> ³ Don't let anyone deceive you in any way, for that day will not come until the rebellion (against the Law or Transgression of Desolation) occurs and the <u>man of lawlessness</u> (or man in whom the Law is abolished) is

revealed (to be the False Messiah), the man doomed to destruction. ⁴ He will oppose and will exalt himself over everything that is called God or is worshiped, so that he sets himself up in Yahuah's temple (in the heart/mind of man), proclaiming himself to be God.   ⁵ Don't you remember that when I was with you I used to tell you these things? ⁶ And now you know (it was common knowledge that Michael was the protecting angel over Israel see Daniel 10:21) what is holding him back (they knew it was Michael), so that he may be revealed at the proper time. ⁷ For the secret power of lawlessness (breaking **the Law of Yahuah**) is already at work; but the one (Michael) who now holds it back will continue to do so till he is taken out of the way (because of the Transgression of Desolation). ⁸ And then the lawless one (the one in whom the Law was abolished) will be revealed (by Yahusha as the False Messiah), whom the Messiah Yahusha will overthrow with the breath of his mouth and destroy by the splendor of his coming. ⁹ The coming of the lawless one (the one in whom the Law is abolished) will be in accordance with how Satan works. He will use all sorts of displays of power through signs and wonders that serve the lie, ¹⁰ and all the ways that wickedness deceives those who are perishing. They perish because they refused to love the truth (of the Torah) and so be saved. ¹¹ For this reason (because they committed the Transgression of Desolation and abolished His Law) Yahuah sends them a powerful delusion (depraved mind or Spirit of Error) so that they will believe the lie (that Jesus, the False Messiah, abolished the Law) ¹² and so that all will be condemned (by the Law not being covered by the blood of the Passover Lamb because they put their faith in Easter Jesus) who have not believed the truth (Yahusha did not abolish the Law) but have delighted in wickedness (transgression of His Law).

If the translators would have been true to scripture, and let scripture define itself, and used the proper meaning of *tamiyd*; then this is how Daniel should read:

Daniel 8:11-14
[10] And it (the False Messiah) waxed great, even to the host of heaven (angelic realm); and it cast down some of the host and of the stars to the ground, and stamped upon them. [11] Yea, he magnified *himself* even to the Prince of the host (Michael the Archangel), and by Him (Yahuah) the continual defense stretched out over Earth provided by Michael was taken away, and the place of the sanctuary (the mind of man) was cast down (and darkened to believe a lie). [12] Because of rebellion (against **the Law of Yahuah**), Yahuah's people and the continual defense provided by Michael were given over to it. It (the False Messiah) prospered in everything it did, and truth (Yahuah's Word) was thrown to the ground (and abolished).

[13] Then I heard one saint speaking, and another saint said unto that certain *saint* which spake, How long *shall be* the vision *concerning* the end of the continual defense of Michael and the Transgression of Desolation, to give both the sanctuary and the host to be trodden under foot?

Daniel 12:11
[11] And from the time that the continual defense provided by Michael shall be taken away (because of the Transgression of Desolation), and *the Abomination of Desolation* set up, there shall be a thousand two hundred and ninety days.

Daniel goes on to say that it is only once **the Transgression of Desolation** is complete (transgressors reach their fullness) that the False Messiah is revealed (stands up) and the Abomination of Desolation is set up:

Daniel 8
23And at the latter end of their [4th] kingdom, **when the transgressors** [the apostate people of Yahuah who committed the Transgression of Desolation causing the Great Tribulation] **have reached the fullness** [of their wickedness, taxing the limits of Yahuah's mercy], a [shadow] king of fierce countenance and understanding dark trickery and craftiness shall stand up [in the Holy Sanctuary and commit the Abomination of Desolation].

I am cover this in detail in my book *the Antichrist Revealed!* where I will fully explain in detail what I am introducing here in this chapter. I just wanted to quickly illustrate that it is the abolishment of the Law called **the Transgression of Desolation** that literally causes the Great Tribulation and the destruction of Earth.

The Law is the Governing Constitution

Yahusha is responsible for leading a "government" that is established on **the Law of Yahuah**.

> Yahusha will literally *establish* **the Kingdom of Yahuah** on <u>the Law</u> which defines justice and righteousness"

Isaiah 9:6-7
"For to us a child is born, to us a son is given, and **the government shall be on his shoulders** and he will be called Wonderful Counselor, Mighty (image of) Elohim, (for) Father of Everlasting (Life), Prince of Peace." **There will be no end to the increase of His government** or of peace, on the Throne of David and over His Kingdom, to establish it (upon **the Law of Yahuah**) and to uphold it with justice and righteousness (defined within the Law) *from then on and forevermore*.

Isaiah is saying that Yahusha brings in **the Kingdom of Yahuah** to sit on the Throne of David and govern by the Torah/Law. Daniel speaks to this very truth below:

Daniel 7
¹³ "I kept looking in the night visions, And behold, with the clouds of heaven One (Yahusha) like <u>**a Son of Man**</u> was coming, And He (Yahusha) came up to the Ancient of Days (Yahuah, they are not the same being) And was presented before Him. ¹⁴ "And to Him (Yahusha) was given (by

Yahuah as an inheritance) dominion, Glory and a kingdom, That all the peoples, nations and *men of every* language Might **serve** Him (not worship Yahusha, we serve Yahusha in the Kingdom). His dominion is an everlasting dominion Which will not pass away; And His kingdom is one Which will not be destroyed.

We see this fact stated **explicitly** by Yahuah through Isaiah Chapter 2. In this chapter, Isaiah is speaking of "the last days". Yes, the **LAST DAYS,** when Yahusha returns as conquering King to liberate Jerusalem, and reign as King on the Throne of governing by the Torah.

Let's see exactly what Yahuah says (by the mouth of His prophet Isaiah) concerning the standard of government that flows forth out of His capital city of Zion "in the last days":

> **Isaiah 2** - *The Mountain of Yahuah*
> 2 This is what Isaiah son of Amoz saw concerning Judah and Jerusalem: **2 In the last days** the mountain of YAHUAH'S temple (made up of the sum total of the sons of Yahuah, Yahusha the chief cornerstone) will be established as the highest of the mountains; it will be exalted above the hills, and all nations will stream to it. 3 Many peoples will come and say, "Come, let us go up to the mountain of Yahuah, to the temple of the Elohim **of Jacob** (the established bloodline). **He will teach us his ways, so that we may walk in his paths."** **the Torah/Law will go out from Zion, the Word of Yahuah** (the Torah/Prophets) **from Jerusalem**. 4 He will judge (by the Law) between the nations and will settle disputes for many peoples (according to the Law).

So Yahuah Himself, out of the mouth of His Prophet Isaiah, declares that in the last days He will setup the seat of His Government on His Mountain and out of that seat of government will flow **THE LAW/Torah** as the standard of government by which He will teach His Sons, His Righteousness, and judge between the nations. Yes, the Torah is the constitution of *the Kingdom of Yahuah* and that is explicitly stated by Yahuah!

So let us be careful what "we" abolish in our own minds out of ignorance of His Word and then justify by IMPLIED doctrines that contradict EXPLICIT scripture. Lest we become "workers of iniquity" or law breakers left out of (or literally kicked out of) a kingdom which is built upon the Righteousness of Yahuah defined in His Law!

> **Matthew 13:41**
> The Son of Man will send his angels, and they will gather out of his kingdom all causes of sin and all law-breakers,

Law Breakers thrown out of *the Kingdom of Yahuah*

The only sons that will exist in that Kingdom will be those who have the Law written on their hearts, not those who have disobeyed it their entire lives, abolished it in their minds, and lived a life of iniquity (lawlessness).   Yahusha made this fact crystal clear below as he casts out those who are "without the Law" or Torahless or Lawless.   That is what "iniquity" or "lawless" means in Matthew 7:23. The word in that verse is the Greek word ***anomía***:

Entry for Strong's #458 - ἀνομία

> 458. ἀνομία **anŏmia**, *an-om-ee'-ah;* from *459; illegality,* i.e. *violation of law* or (gen.) *wickedness:*—iniquity, x transgress (-ion of) the law, unrighteousness.
>
> 459. ἄνομος **anŏmŏs**, *an'-om-os;* from *1* (as a neg. particle) and *3551; lawless,* i.e. (neg.) not subject to (the Jewish) law; (by impl. a *Gentile*), or (pos.) *wicked;*—without law, lawless, trangressor, unlawful, wicked.

With that understanding in mind, hear the words of the King of **the Kingdom of Yahuah** who is the gatekeeper you must get past to enter it... the word "lawlessness" and in some translations "iniquity" or "evildoers" is the Greek word ***anomía*** defined above as '*without* **the Law of Yahuah**':

> **Matthew 7:21-23**
> "Not everyone who says to Me, King, King, shall enter the kingdom of heaven, but he who does the will of my Father (keeps His Commandments) in heaven. Many will say to Me in that day, King, King, have we not prophesied in Your name, and cast out demons in Your name, and done many wonders in Your name? And then will I (Yahusha) declare to them, <u>**I never knew you, depart from Me, you who practice lawlessness**</u>" (you who are without *the Law of Yahuah*).

The *name* they were calling on was Jesus Christ the lawless one. Yahusha does not answer to that name and denies entry to those who follow *the lawless one*.

Anomía is used 15 times in the New Testament to condemn all those who abolish **the Law of Yahuah**, have contempt for **the Law**, or break **the Law**. Those "law breakers" are literally gathered up and cast out of **the Kingdom of Yahuah**. Below is how various translations handle the word **anomía**:

> **Matthew 7:23** - *New Living Translation*
> But I will reply, 'I never knew you. Get away from me, you who **break Yahuah's laws.**'

> **Matthew 13:41**- *English Standard Version*
> The Son of Man will send his angels, and they will gather out of his kingdom all causes of sin and all ***law-breakers***,

> **Matthew 23:28** - Weymouth New Testament
> The same is true of you: outwardly you seem to the human eye to be good and honest men, but, within, you are full of insincerity and ***disregard of God's Law***.

Matthew 24:12 - *New American Standard Bible*
"Because **lawlessness** is increased (the Law defines love), most people's love will grow cold

Romans 4:7 - *GOD'S WORD® Translation*
"Blessed are those whose **disobedience** (to the Law) is forgiven and whose sins (against the Law) are pardoned.

Romans 6:19 - *International Standard Version*
I am speaking in simple terms because of the frailty of your human nature. Just as you once offered the parts of your body as slaves to impurity and to greater and greater **disobedience** (to the Law), so now, in the same way, you must offer the parts of your body as slaves to righteousness (which is keeping the Law) that <u>leads to sanctification</u>.

2 Corinthians 6:14 - *English Standard Version*
Do not be unequally yoked with unbelievers (true believers keep the Law). For what partnership has righteousness (law keepers) with **lawlessness** (law breakers)?

2 Thessalonians 2:7 - *International Standard Version*
For **the <u>secret</u> of this lawlessness** (the false doctrine that Jesus abolished the Law) is already at work

Titus 2:14 - *English Standard Version*
who gave himself for us to redeem us from all **lawlessness** and to purify for himself a people for his own possession who are zealous for good works (of the Law).

Hebrews 1:9 - *Holman Christian Standard Bible*
You have loved righteousness (kept the Law) and hated *lawlessness* (disregard for the Law); this is why Yahuah, Your Elohim, has anointed You with the oil of joy rather than Your companions.

Hebrews 8:12 - *King James 2000 Bible*
For I will be merciful to their **unrighteousness** (breaking the Law), and their **sins** (against the Law) and their **iniquities** (contempt for the Law) will I remember no more.

Hebrews 10:17 - *New International Version*
Then he adds: "Their **sins and lawless acts** I will remember no more."

1 John 3:4 - King James 2000 Bible
Whosoever commits sin transgresses also the Law: for sin is the transgression of the Law.

Crystal clear if you ask me!

> The reason those who have abolished the Law in their hearts (believing the lie told by the False Religion of Christianity) will not inherit ***the Kingdom of Yahuah*** is simple: We are being trained to govern the Universe and the foundation of that government is the Law. Yahuah simply cannot grant eternal life, and a position within ***the Kingdom of Yahuah,*** to a disobedient LAWless human being...

That would put Yahuah in a position to deal with a rebellion <u>of gods</u>!   It is that simple.   If you disobey His Law now, you cannot be trusted with eternal life, you cannot be trusted to govern, you cannot be trusted to judge, you cannot be trusted as His priest, you cannot be trusted with anything and you will die dead in your "sin" which is... **transgression of His Law**.   This cannot be over stated.

Transposition of *the Law of Yahuah*

In Chapter 1 - **Keys to studying the Kingdom of Yahuah** I defined the concept of transposition as follows:

> Transposition is the transfer of position from one state to another without changing the meaning and intent.

One of the terms I use most in this book is **Transposition**. I use this term because it is the word chosen by the Apostle Sha'ul to describe the "change" that occurred in both the physical law and physical priesthoods. Sha'ul used the Greek word *"metathesis"* in Hebrews 7:12 when explaining how the Law and the Priesthood of Levi defined by the Mosaic Covenant *"changed"* in **the Yahushaic Covenant**. Metathesis is Strong's 3331 and means *"transferred to Heaven"*... *transposition*.

3331	metathesis met-ath'-es-is	from - metatithemi 3346; transposition, i.e. transferal (to heaven), disestablishment (of a law from physical to spiritual):--change to, removing, translation.

Today the word *transposition* is used in music and the musical application beautifully and very accurately illustrates the concept as it applies to physical to spiritual transposition.

"Transposition" in music is the shifting of a melody, a harmonic progression or an entire musical piece **to another key**, while maintaining the same tone structure.

This is exactly what happened with the Law and the Priesthood from the Mosaic Covenant to **the Yahushaic Covenant** and in fact all of Yahuah's commandments and ordinances in the Mosaic Covenant.   They were first given orally, then transposed to "written in stone", and ultimately transposed to "written in our hearts" while maintaining their validity, meaning, and structure. They went through **a transfer of position** (transposition) from oral to written to spirit.

Nothing established by Yahuah has ever been "abolished" other than the decrees found within the Law for violating His commands.   Even those decrees were not "abolished" they were covered by the blood of the Passover Lamb for those who believe, and condemn those who do not put their faith in Passover.   So actually, nothing Yahuah has ever done has been "abolished" by anyone or anything.   No one has that authority.

4 States and 3 Transpositions

Keep in mind that "transposition" is the transfer of position from one state to another *without changing the structure, validity, meaning, or content*.   **the Law of Yahuah**, like **the Kingdom of Yahuah**, has always existed.   Yahuah's Righteousness is the same yesterday (eternal past), today, and forever.   Yahuah didn't just make up the Law as mankind labored along in this age to "point out his sin" as Christianity would have us believe.   No, like all other aspects of **the Kingdom of Yahuah**, the Law is a Spiritual Truth and was progressively revealed to man physically over time through covenants. We covered covenants too as an essential "key" to understanding **the Kingdom of Yahuah** in Chapter 1 of this book. That doesn't mean the Law came into existence over time; it just means that man didn't know what the Law was and had to be slowly introduced to it.

4 States of the Law

The Law has existed in 4 states over the period of progressive disclosure through covenants:

1. The Mind of Yahuah
2. Oral Tradition
3. Written in Stone
4. Written on our Hearts

3 Transpositions of the Law

In the process of progressively revealing **the Law of Yahuah** to man, the Law went through 3 distinct transpositions as it passed from one state to the next:

1. The first transposition was from the mind of Yahuah to mankind orally in small doses. Man then passed the Law down from generation to generation verbally.
2. The second transposition of the Law was from oral tradition to "written in stone" in detail defined as the physical act.
3. The third transposition was from written in stone (physical acts) to written on our hearts (Spiritual Intent).

With each transposition of the Law, it simply transferred states and remained fully intact in meaning, validity, structure, etc.

Let's take a closer look at proof that the Law existed prior to Adam and witness the transposition of that Law from the mind of Yahuah to man orally... then to man in written form... then ultimately to the hearts of His sons.

The Law existed prior to Adam

in the Mind of Yahuah

The Apostle Sha'ul clearly teaches that even though at the time Adam lived, Yahuah (through progressive revelation over time) had not yet fully communicated His Holy Law to man. The entire Holy Law was still active at the creation of man, and the penalty for disobedience which is DEATH *was imputed* to every man who violated any part of it. the fact that death existed from Adam to Moses, Sha'ul says below, is PROOF that the Law existed in its entirety at the time of Adam.

Sha'ul says below that, the fact that many died for various offenses not related to what Adam did (don't eat the apple), was proof that the Holy Law of Yahuah was a complex set of Laws and eternally valid and active. Mankind (at the time of Adam) simply was not completely aware of what the Law contained. But Yahuah's Holiness was the same at the time of Adam as it was at the time of Abraham, Moses, David, Yahusha, and you and I today. *And that Holiness is defined by His Holy Law.*

The Apostle Sha'ul addresses the reality of the Law from Adam to Moses below:

Romans 5

¹² Therefore, just as sin entered the world through one man, and death through sin, and in this way death came to all people, because all sinned.   ¹³ To be sure, sin was in the world before the law was given, but sin is not charged against anyone's account where there is no law. ¹⁴ Nevertheless, death reigned from the time of Adam to the time of Moses, even over those who did not sin by breaking a command, as did Adam, who is a pattern of the one to come.

What does all that mean?   Let me break it down to clearly demonstrate what Sha'ul is talking about below:

Romans 5

¹² Therefore, just as through one man sin (sin is disobedience to the Law *1 John 3:4*) entered the world (Adam disobeyed Yahuah's commands bringing sin into the world), and death through sin (the Law of Sin and You Die), and thus death spread to all men (as Death is the penalty of sin which is breaking the Law.   *Original Sin*, another false doctrine, did not spread to all men, genetic DEATH did), because all man sinned (and therefore die for their own sin, not because they are born with Original Sin, the Law clearly states that no man is to be punished for another's sin including Adam's)

¹³ To be sure, sin (breaking the Law) was in the world before the (written) law was given (to Moses), but sin (breaking the Law) is not charged against anyone's account **where there is no law**. (so the fact that sin was in the

world before the written law is proof the Law existed all the way back to Adam)

> NOTE: Keep all of Sha'ul's writings in context; Sha'ul is proving that because there was transgression since Adam that the Law was alive and active. Because if the Law did not exist, neither would transgressions and death could not reign:
>
> **Romans 4:15**
>
>> 15 Because the law worketh wrath *(death for disobedience)*: <u>for where no law is, there is no transgression</u>.

Continuing with Romans 5... (so Sha'ul is saying there must have been the Law at the time of Adam because there was transgression...) ¹⁴ Nevertheless (now Sha'ul says death is the proof of the Law), **<u>death reigned from the time of Adam to the time of Moses</u>**, (and DEATH is the penalty of "sin" or breaking the Law. So transgression and death is PROOF the Law existed from Adam to Moses) even over those who did not sin by breaking a command, as did Adam (the Law was a lot more complex than anyone knew because people were dying for all types of sin not just "eating the apple")

So, we see that the Law existed in the mind of Yahuah all the way back to Adam, they just weren't aware of what all the Law required. Mankind was still held to account for the Law from Adam to Moses as made evident by death. Death being the

Rav Sha'ul

penalty of transgressing the Law reigned from Adam to Moses and therefore is proof **the Law of Yahuah** is eternal both past and future.

Man was in the initial stages of **progressive disclosure**. But rest assured, the Law still governed Yahuah's Creation and death was still the penalty for violating it and sin was still being charged against EVERYONE who transgressed any part of His Holy Law. That is what Sha'ul is saying.

I needed to bring this to our attention because **the False Religion of Christianity** teaches us that "Sha'ul" said the Law came into existence 430 years after the Abrahamic Covenant.

> **Galatians 3** – *The written Law introduced*
> The law, introduced 430 years later, does not set aside the covenant previously established by Yahuah and thus do away with the promise. [18] For if the inheritance depends on the law, then it no longer depends on the promise; but Yahuah in his grace gave it to Abraham through a promise.

Well, "if" Sha'ul actually said *what Christianity teaches he said*; he wasn't much of a Pharisee and expert in the Torah; because not only did Sha'ul say the Law existed at creation, but Sha'ul knew Abraham was given the Law orally in detail!

> **Gen 26:5** – *Abrahamic Covenant*
> 5 Because that Abraham obeyed my voice, and kept my charge, my commandments, my statutes, and my laws.

Don't worry, I will cover Galatians and explain it all along with every other false teaching of the Christian Church concerning the Law. We are going to address all of it in my upcoming book **the**

Law of Yahuah. Sha'ul seems to contradict himself and contradict every other prophet and Yahusha concerning the Law (if you believe the Pauline Doctrine of the Christian Church that is).

In order to understand Sha'ul's writing we must know what Sha'ul knew... the Torah and Prophets! We must understand **the Yahushaic Covenant** as it pertains to faith vs. righteousness. We will put Sha'ul *into context* (something Christianity fails to do) of all his writings and the Torah and the Prophets and see exactly what Sha'ul actually said, believed, and lived in my book '**the Law of Yahuah'**. To stay on point in this chapter, I am establishing the Law as the governing constitution of **the Kingdom of Yahuah**.

Transposition of the Law is what Sha'ul taught in all his writings. In teaching the transposition of the Law Sha'ul can be brought into agreement with Yahuah, Yahusha, the Prophets, and all the other commentators in the New Testament concerning the Law. Sha'ul was first and foremost... a Pharisee and lived a life of strict obedience to the Law:

> **Acts 24:14** – *Sha'ul declaring his belief in the Law and Prophets*
> "But this I admit to you: I worship the Elohim of our fathers in accordance with the Way (which they call a sect). **I continue to believe everything that accords with the Torah (the Law) and everything written in the Prophets.**"
>
> **Philippians 3: 4-6**: *Sha'ul was a Pharisee, a Jewish Rabbi blameless in keeping the Law until he died*
> 4. Though I might also have confidence in the flesh. If any

> other man thinketh that he hath whereof he might trust in the flesh, I more: 5. Circumcised the eighth day, of the stock of Israel, of the tribe of Benjamin, an Hebrew of the Hebrews; **as touching the law, a Pharisee**;
> 6. Concerning zeal, persecuting the church; **touching the righteousness which is in the Law**, *blameless*.

If the way Christianity teaches Sha'ul's writings is true, then the Apostle Sha'ul is not only a colossal hypocrite but he is a false teacher for directly contradicting Yahuah's prophets and the Messiah. Yahusha was a Torah Observant Jewish rabbi who "didn't come to abolish the Law and the Prophets".

Christianity has been bearing false witness against the Apostle Sha'ul for 2,000 years. It is time we honor the Apostle Sha'ul and treat his writings with respect in light of his lifelong commitment to the Law. But like I said, Sha'ul properly taught the transposition of the Law and taught that the Law was active all the way back to Adam.

First Transposition of Law

from the Mind of Yahuah to oral tradition

Now we know the Law was alive and active all the way back to Adam. We clearly see below, the Law was communicated verbally to our forefathers and defined the "terms and conditions" of every covenant **long before the covenant with Moses**. Each covenant between Yahuah and his sons are literally *Marriage Covenants* and the Law defines the *Marriage Vows*.

> **Note:** *It is through keeping these vows that we become one with Yahuah (the two shall become one through marriage covenant). The human marriage covenant is a physical to spiritual parallel of the covenants between Yahuah and His sons. In the Yahushaic Covenant, Yahusha is the bridegroom and the rest of Yahuah's sons are the bride. The covenant was consummated with blood; the 144,000 chosen from among the 12 tribes of Israel called Remnant Israel are "virgins" and so forth.*

In the Abrahamic Covenant **the Law of Yahuah** was transposed from the Mind of Yahuah to our forefathers verbally as we read below, "Abraham obeyed **my voice**" and kept *the Law of Yahuah*:

Gen 26:5 – KJV – *Abrahamic Covenant*
5 Because that *Abraham obeyed my voice* (Yahuah communicated the Law verbally transposing it from His

> mind to oral tradition), and kept my charge, my commandments, my statutes, and my laws.

So obviously in Galatians Sha'ul was talking about "**the Written Law**" came 430 years after the promise to Abraham.

> **Galatians 3** – *Law transposed to stone 430 years earlier*
> The (written) Law, introduced (in stone) 430 years later, does not set aside the covenant previously established by Yahuah and thus do away with the promise.

We see below that ***the Law of Yahuah*** was passed down orally to Jacob through his father Isaac who received the Law from Abraham who received it from Yahuah's voice:

> **Ps 147:19-148:1** – KJV – *the Law passed down orally to all our forefathers*
> 19 He sheweth His Word (the Torah) unto Jacob, his statutes and his judgments (the Law) unto Israel. 20 He hath not dealt so with any nation: and as for his judgments, they have not known them.

Second Transposition of the Law

The *Law was transposed from oral to written in the Mosaic Covenant*

In the Mosaic Covenant, the Law was transposed from oral tradition to written in stone.   Let me clearly establish that the commandments of Yahuah are <u>eternal</u> to Israel (His chosen sons) - the bloodline of Abraham/Isaac/Jacob. They are for "all time" eternal past and future, they are an everlasting covenant, forever.

> **Deut. 4**
> 39 Acknowledge and take to heart this day that Yahuah is Elohim in heaven above and on the earth below. There is no other. 40 <u>Keep his decrees and commands</u>, which I am giving you today, so that it may go well with <u>you and your children after you</u> (perpetual no end) and that you may live long (Eternal Life - ***physical to spiritual parallel***) in the land Yahuah your Elohim gives you (the Promised Land - Kingdom of Yahuah - ***physical to spiritual parallel***) <u>for all time</u> (eternal permanent ordinances).

Isaiah declares that it is the disobedience to **the Laws of Yahuah**, the violation of these statutes, and the breaking of the <u>EVERLASTING</u> covenant (which is the Sabbath Covenant), that the earth is defiled and falls under a curse and is utterly destroyed at the end.

> **Isaiah 24** - Yahuah's *Devastation of the Earth*
> [1] See, Yahuah is going to lay waste the earth and devastate it; he will ruin its face and scatter its inhabitants....

³ The earth will be completely laid waste and totally plundered. Yahuah has spoken this word. ⁴ The earth dries up and withers, the world languishes and withers, the heavens languish with the earth. ⁵ The earth is defiled by its people; **they have disobeyed the laws**, violated the statutes and broken the everlasting covenant (the Sabbath). ⁶ Therefore (because we have abolished His Law and changed His Sabbath to Sunday) a curse consumes the earth; its people must bear their guilt.   Therefore earth's inhabitants are burned up, and very few are left.

I don't know about you, but as for me and my house… we will study His Law and keep His Sabbath.   I for one want to enter His Kingdom and be one of the "very few left" after Yahuah purges the Earth of those who deny His Law. I don't want to be told "depart from me you law breaker" by Yahusha and I don't want to be rounded up and kicked out of the Kingdom for disobedience!

> **Matthew 13:41**
> The Son of Man will send his angels, and ***they will gather out of his kingdom*** *all causes of sin and* <u>*all law-breakers*</u>,

When you understand that the Law is the governing constitution of **the Kingdom of Yahuah** and literally the marriage vows of His covenants, you realize only those who have it "written on their hearts" will be qualified to govern.   If you truly love Yahuah, that love is demonstrated by keeping His Law:

1 John 5:3
In fact, this is love for Yahuah: to keep his commands. And his commands are not burdensome

Only those with a "heart for His Law" and lovingly keep the marriage vows will be found trustworthy of Eternal Life. Yahuah can't have a bunch of lawless unfaithful eternal beings running around trying to govern the Universe in unrighteousness now can He?   Those who abolish the Law (Law breakers) will not make it past the "gatekeeper" Yahusha.   They will be told "depart from me, I know you not, you who practice disobedience to the Law".

Third Transposition of the Law

The *Law was transposed from written to Spiritual Intent in the Yahushaic Covenant*

Once the Law was gradually introduced to man over time orally from Adam through Abraham until Moses, then written in stone in detail, it was transposed to spiritual intent in **the Yahushaic Covenant**. Sha'ul was well aware of this fact:

> **Hebrews 10:16** – *the Law the foundation of New Covenant*
> This is the covenant I will make with them after that time, says Yahuah. I will put my laws in their hearts, and I will write them on their minds.

Yahusha's primary mission was to fulfill (transpose) **the Law of Yahuah**, especially as it related to the Spring Feasts of Passover/Unleavened Bread/First Fruits/Shavuot.

> **Matthew 5** - *The Fulfillment of the Law*
>
> 17 "Do not think that I have come to abolish the Law (Torah) or the Prophets (the Torah and Prophets are what we in error call the Old Testament. So, Yahusha said Yahuah's Word wasn't abolished and is not "old" after all); I have not come to abolish them but to fulfill them (bring them to their fullest meaning and Spiritual application through transposition). 18 For truly I tell you, until heaven and earth disappear, not the smallest letter, not the least stroke of a pen (all 613 Laws remain), will by any means *disappear from the Law until everything is accomplished*. 19 Therefore anyone who sets aside one of the least of these commands and teaches others accordingly will be

called least in the kingdom of heaven (that is if such a person even enters the Kingdom), but whoever practices and teaches these commands (the Law) will be called great in the kingdom of heaven. 20 For I tell you that unless your righteousness (defined as obedience to the Law) surpasses that of the Pharisees and the teachers of the law, **you will certainly not enter the kingdom of heaven**. (by this he meant the Law would be strengthened to attitude not the act.   By applying the Law to Spiritual Intent, we can surpass the outward righteousness of the Pharisees)

Ezekiel prophesied the same transposition of the Law in the New Covenant:

Ezekiel 36: 26, 27

I will give you a new heart (for my Law and write my Law on it) and put a new spirit (of loving obedience) in you; I will remove from you your heart of stone (legalistic observance of the Law without love) and give you a heart of flesh. And **I will put my Spirit in you and move you to follow my decrees and be careful to keep my laws**.

Yahusha *Strengthened* the Law

Matthew 19
[16] And someone came to Him and said, "Teacher, what good thing shall I do that I may obtain eternal life?" ... **if you wish to obtain eternal life, keep the commandments** (of Yahuah, Eternal Life is the promise for obedience to the Law)."

As I pointed out in my book "***Melchizedek and the Passover Lamb***", Yahusha was a student of John the Baptist who was Yahusha's prophesied mentor. John was also the rightful High Priest of Israel as the first male heir to the High Priest Yahusha III (John's Grandfather) who oversaw the rebuilding of the Second Temple.

Yahusha was the next male heir to Yahusha III after John (Yahusha III was the Messiah's great grandfather) and was consecrated High Priest of Israel to succeed John through Mikveh. John was the leader of the true sons of Yahuah and they were known as Nazarenes. Yahusha assumed the position of leader of the Nazarenes followed later by the Apostle Sha'ul. They all were Hebrew Notsri or Nazarenes. Notsri or Nazarenes were prophesied in the Torah as guardians of the Law, Prophets, and Messiah.

It is a mistranslation in our Bibles where it says "Jesus of Nazareth" that should read "Yahusha the Nazarene". Yahusha was from Judea, but the terms "sect of the Nazarenes" and "Yahusha of Nazareth" both employ the adjective *nasraya* (or

Notsri) meaning **branch**. It is referring to the prophecy in Isaiah concerning **the Branch** and prophecy of Zachariah concerning **the Branch**.

Yahusha the Nazarene

The English word "Nazarene" (Greek "Nazaraios," Aramaic "Natsraya," or Hebrew "Notsri") comes from the Hebrew word *netser* (branch), which itself is derived from the verb natsar which means *'to guard, watch, keep, or preserve'* in context speaking of **the Torah, Prophet, and the Messiah**. the Torah and Prophets are the true Word of Yahuah. Yahusha was indeed a Notsri and keeper of the Torah and Prophets. That is why he was called Yahusha the Notsri (mistranslated as Jesus of Nazareth), keeper and guardian of the Torah and Prophets.

Yahusha came to restore the Torah and Prophets

Yahusha did not come to abolish the Law and Prophets but to guard and protect them from human traditions elevated as "laws" called **Takkanots**. Takkanots had invaded and polluted **the Law of Yahuah** among the Jews coming out of Babylonian Captivity. Classical Jewish law granted rabbinic sages wide legislative powers. Meaning, Rabbis could add to **the Law of Yahuah** at will. There are two powerful legal tools within the halakhic system given to Rabbis:

- *Gezeirah*: "preventative legislation" of the classical rabbis instituted as Laws, intended to prevent violations of the commandments of Yahuah

- *Takkanah*: "positive legislation", practices instituted as Laws by the rabbis not based (directly) on the commandments of Yahuah as such

Together both the Gezeirah and Takkanah are called *"**Takkanots**"* or commandment of men elevated as Laws in Jewish society. the Torah was no longer the standard of righteousness with the Jews but rather the **Talmud** was. The Talmud is a massive collection of "rabbinical traditions" that were added as "laws". The Talmud is a collection of Takkanots.

The Talmud consists of 63 tractates, and in standard print is over **6,200 pages long**. In comparison, **the Law of Yahuah** contains 613 commands. The Talmud contains the teachings and opinions of thousands of rabbis on a variety of subjects, including Hadaka (law), Jewish ethics, philosophy, customs, history, lore and many other topics. **The Talmud is the basis for all codes of Jewish law**.

The Talmud is utterly impossible to understand and even more so to "obey". Yahusha's message to the Jews was one more of "keep it simple", and stick with the Commandments of Yahuah and not the commandments of men. Yahusha came to RESTORE the Torah and Prophets not abolish them. You might imagine how this put Yahusha at odds with the "establishment". He was literally overturning the Rabbinical System of Takkanots.

The Rabbis had made it very complex in the Talmud as literally thousands of "human laws/Takkanots" were added to Yahuah's Law. As a result, enmity toward **the Law of Yahuah** grew up among the Jews out of total frustration. The people were being held to account <u>to the Talmud</u> not ***the Law of Yahuah*** and it became a burden; too heavy to bear.

This is the environment Yahusha was sent to confront. Yahusha was **the prophet** that Moses said would "properly teach the Torah" and restore it. The Jews were badly in need of a correction and needed to get back to the Torah. Yahusha <u>did come</u> to "abolish Rabbinical Law" and that didn't go over very well with the establishment.

With each new generation of rabbis, the Talmud just kept (and is still today) growing and growing and getting all the more complicated and complex. Yahuah expressly forbids such things as Takkanots as we are not to add to or subtract from the Law:

> **Deuteronomy 4:2**
> You shall not add to the word which I am commanding you, nor take away from it, that you may keep the commandments of Yahuah your Elohim which I command you.

Yahusha confronted these human traditions and commands called Takkanots:

> **Matt 15:1**
> Then the scribes and Pharisees who were from Jerusalem came to Yahusha, saying, 2 "Why do Your disciples **transgress the tradition of the elders** (they transgressed the Takkanots not the Torah)? For they do not wash their hands when they eat bread (a Takkanoh not a command of Yahuah)." 3 He answered and said to them, "Why do you also transgress the commandment of Yahuah (the Law) because of your tradition (Takkanots)? ... 9 '(Yahusha then

quoted them Isaiah 29:13 where Yahuah said) 'And in vain they worship Me, Teaching [as] doctrines <u>the commandments of men (Takkanots)</u>.' "

On the topic of the Torah and Prophets, Yahusha is crystal clear:

Matthew 5 - *The Fulfillment of the Law*

17 "<u>Do not think that I have come to abolish the Law</u> (Torah) or the Prophets; ***I have not come to abolish them but to fulfill them*** (bring them to their fullest meaning and Spiritual application through transposition). 18 For truly I tell you, until heaven and earth disappear, <u>not the smallest letter, not the least stroke of a pen, will by any means disappear from the Law until everything is accomplished</u> (all 613 Laws remain active and valid). 19 Therefore anyone who sets aside one of the least of these commands and teaches others accordingly will be called least in the kingdom of heaven (that is if such a person even enters the Kingdom), but whoever practices and teaches these commands (the Law) will be called great in the kingdom of heaven (the Law will be alive and active in **the Kingdom of Yahuah**). 20 **For I tell you that unless your righteousness** (defined as obedience to the Law) **surpasses that of the Pharisees and the teachers of the law, <u>you will certainly not enter the kingdom of heaven</u>.**

I am going to go much deeper into Yahusha's mission among the Jews as he literally confronted the scribes and Pharisees at every turn and literally "overturned" the Rabbinical System. This is why he fell out of favor with the Jewish elite and found much favor among the Jewish masses.   This is just one of the many topics of my next book **the Yahushaic Covenant**.

The point I want to make here is that Yahusha came to fulfill the Law and Prophets not abolish them.   Fulfill means to "make whole" or "to fill to the fullest measure" spiritually.   Yahusha then went on to give us an example of what exactly he meant by "fulfill" and it definitely is not "abolish" in any way.   Yahusha went on to strengthen the Law and elevate it (transpose it) to a higher standard.   No longer is committing the physical act the sin, it is just "thinking it" that is truly sin.   The act is just the result of the Spiritual Intent of the heart.

Yahusha didn't go into all 613 Laws and layout the **physical to spiritual parallel** for us of each one.   He did, however, go through a few of the commandments.   He demonstrated to us as an example of "how" he fulfilled the Law and transposed it from "written in stone" or rather physical act to "written on our hearts" or Spiritual Intent.   <u>It is up to us now</u> to use those examples and apply them to all of Yahuah's commandments.   I will cover all 613 Laws in my book '**the Law of Yahuah**'.

Just after declaring he didn't come to abolish the law but to fulfill it in Matthew 5, Yahusha laid out the concept of transposition of the Law and **physical to spiritual parallel**s:

Murder – Transposed from physical act/letter of law to Spiritual Intent

> 21 "You have heard that it was said to the people long ago, 'You shall not murder, and anyone who

murders will be subject to judgment.' 22 But I tell you that anyone who is angry with a brother or sister will be subject to judgment.

Adultery – Transposed from physical act/letter of law to Spiritual Intent

27 "You have heard that it was said, 'You shall not commit adultery.' 28 But I tell you that anyone who looks at a woman lustfully has already committed adultery with her in his heart.

Divorce – Transposed from physical act/letter of law to Spiritual Intent

31 "It has been said, 'Anyone who divorces his wife must give her a certificate of divorce.' 32 But I tell you that anyone who divorces his wife, except for sexual immorality, makes her the victim of adultery, and anyone who marries a divorced woman commits adultery.

Oaths – Transposed from physical act/letter of law to Spiritual Intent

33 "Again, you have heard that it was said to the people long ago, 'Do not break your oath, but fulfill to Yahuah the vows you have made.' 34 But I tell you, do not swear an oath at all

Eye for Eye – Transposed from physical act/letter of law to Spiritual Intent

> 38 "You have heard that it was said, 'Eye for eye, and tooth for tooth.' 39 But I tell you, do not resist an evil person. If anyone slaps you on the right cheek, turn to them the other cheek also

Love for Enemies – Transposed from physical act/letter of law to Spiritual Intent

> 43 "You have heard that it was said, 'Love your neighbor and hate your enemy.' 44 But I tell you, love your enemies and pray for those who persecute you

Yahusha transposed the Law from written in stone (physical act) to written on our hearts (spiritual intent).

The Apostle Sha'ul Taught the Law Properly

In my book **the Law of Yahuah** I am going to dive deep into the mind of the Apostle Sha'ul. I will explain exactly how false doctrines have crept into, and have become the very foundation of, the Christian Church called "the Pauline Doctrine".

Much of the misunderstanding comes in the way our English Bibles were translated. They were translated very poorly to put it mildly. Concerning **the Law of Yahuah,** the translators failed to distinguish when Sha'ul was talking about "the law of the land" which was the (6,200 page) Talmud and when Sha'ul was referring to **the (613) Laws of Yahuah.** They translated both as 'the law' leaving those reading the English Bibles totally in the dark as to what Sha'ul was saying.

When speaking of **the Law of Yahuah**, the Apostle Sha'ul used the Greek phrase "ho nomos" or THE Law. The word "nomos" or just "law" is *any law whatsoever* or *the law of the land*. When Sha'ul added the article "ho" before "nomos" he was speaking of **the Law of Yahuah**.

We see that "nomos" without the article "ho" is not referring specifically to **the Law of Yahuah** but to "any law whatsoever" or law of the land.

Νomoß - **Strong's Number:** 3551

Definition

1. *anything established, anything received by usage, a custom, a law, a command*
   a. *of any law whatsoever*

This is not translated in our English Bibles and we are not taught these things in our Christian Churches and learning centers that train our pastors. Therefore, many times when Sha'ul is speaking against the Takkanots or Talmud, it is mistranslated as **the Law** and we are taught he is speaking against **the Law of Yahuah**. When he is actually, like Yahusha, overturning the Rabbinical System of Takkanots.

In my upcoming book **the Law of Yahuah**; I am going to cover this and much more concerning the writing of the Apostle Sha'ul and show he was very much a Notsri or Nazarene, a keeper and protector of the Law, the Prophets, and the Messiah. Sha'ul carried forward the banner that both John the Baptist and Yahusha carried to re-establish the Torah and overturn Rabbinical Judaism. That battle with the establishment, like John and Yahusha, cost Sha'ul his life at the hands of those who benefited from the established system in Jerusalem.

Sha'ul taught the transposition of the Law

In Hebrews 7:12, when speaking about the change in the Law from the Abrahamic Covenant to *the Yahushaic Covenant*; Sha'ul used the word "metathesis" that was translated "***change***". The word translated "***change in the Law***" in Hebrews 7:12 is a Greek word #3331 in Strong's. If you look this word up, the proper translation and meaning of this word is NOT "***change***" as in "abolished" as taught by Christianity but rather it is "***transferred to Heaven***"... ***transposition***.

| 3331 | metathesis met-ath'-es-is | from - metatithemi 3346; transposition, i.e. transferal (to heaven), disestablishment (of a law from physical to spiritual):--change to, removing, translation. |

Sha'ul is speaking of ***physical to spiritual parallel***s as he illustrates that the Levitical Priesthood was given to help us understand physically what Yahusha would do spiritually as High Priest before Yahuah. Given the final High Priest has come and taken His position as Melchizedek... the human priesthood of Levi was TRANSFERRED over to Melchizedek and so was the Law by which the priesthood has authority to make sacrifices and offerings! Neither was abolished.

Below is how Hebrews 7:12 should have been translated:

Hebrews 7:12
"for when there is a transfer of the priestly office (of Levi to Melchizedek), out of necessity there is ALSO A TRANSFER of the LAW of the priesthood (by which the Priesthood has authority)"

In other words, Sha'ul is explaining that the Law that defines the priesthood and sacrifices had to be transferred with Yahusha "out of necessity". Yahusha would have no authority as High Priest without the Law that defines the High Priesthood. the Law was not abolished, it was **transposed**. That is what Sha'ul is teaching in all his writings.

Now Yahusha is the Spiritual High Priest and has all the duties and authority provided him by *the Law of Yahuah* concerning sacrifices and atonement. Both the High Priesthood and the Law were "transferred to heaven" or transposed spiritually from the physical realm to the Spiritual Realm as *the Kingdom of Yahuah* had arrived in *the Yahushaic Covenant*.

Sha'ul was demonstrating that Yahuah had progressively revealed the role Yahusha would play as High Priest by first giving us the Levitical Priesthood in the Mosaic Covenant. By studying the physical sacrifices and atonement required of the Levitical Priesthood we could come to a better understanding of the spiritual sacrifices and atonement made by Melchizedek before *the Altar of Yahuah* in the spirit. Then after progressively disclosing the role of Melchizedek and teaching us Spiritual Truths of the role of Melchizedek using the physical priesthood of Levi...

the Law which gives the priesthood authority and the priesthood itself was TRANSPOSED to *the Kingdom of Yahuah*.

> The next time a "Christian" condemns you for keeping *the Law of Yahuah,* because you have *a heart for it,* and makes the accusation *"why don't you perform animal sacrifices"*, as if to condemn you for not keeping the WHOLE LAW... be sure and let them know that <u>**Yahusha is performing the sacrifices**</u> and offerings prescribed by the Law in *the Kingdom of Yahuah* as our *Eternal High Priest.*

"We" are not under the Law of the Priesthood as the priesthood has been transposed over to Yahusha; we have an Eternal High Priest <u>very much performing those very duties on our behalf.</u>   I'll cover this in detail in my upcoming book *the Law of Yahuah*.

The Apostle Sha'ul – Leader of the Nazarenes, follower of Yahusha

The Apostle Sha'ul was a Nazarene or Notsri who are those who guard, protect, and preserve the Law and the Prophets and the Messiah.   After Sha'ul was arrested in Jerusalem; he was escorted to Caesarea to appear before the governor, Felix. Under the authority of Ananias, the "unauthorized" high priest, Tertullus brought the charges before Felix. Notice his accusation:

Acts 24:5-6
"For we have found this man a pestilent fellow [a plague], and a mover of sedition among all the Jews throughout

the world, and a <u>ringleader of the sect of the Nazarenes</u>: Who also hath gone about to profane the temple: whom we took, and would have judged according to our (Rabbinical) law".

The Apostle Sha'ul's view of the Law: Abolished or not?

I know, what about what Sha'ul said?   He clearly said the Law has been abolished.   He said "Jesus" nailed it to the "cross". He said the Torah, which came 430 years after the promise of the seed to Abraham (Gal 3:17), was given at SINAI, and was not a permanent set of binding ordinances!   Sha'ul said the new ministration of the spirit **has in fact done away with the Law!** Sha'ul said the Law was nothing more than a "tutor" that we no longer need.   Sha'ul said a man is justified by faith apart from the Law! and so on and so forth go the lies of the Pauline Doctrine of the Christian Church.

Don't worry! I will answer all of those objections in my book ***the Law and the Pauline Doctrine***.   In that book I put Sha'ul's writing back into context, and I properly teach Sha'ul's writings.   I demonstrating that every one of the above statements <u>is a lie</u>.

I demonstrate that the Christian Church has taken Sha'ul's writings <u>out of context</u>, translators have mishandled the Greek manuscripts, and Christianity has done everything possible to use Sha'ul to justify abolishing ***the Law of Yahuah***.

Rav Sha'ul

> The Apostle Sha'ul was, in fact, a devout Jew, a Torah Master (Pharisee), a **LAW**yer, who loved **the Law of Yahuah** and proclaimed that fact over and over and is found TEACHING others to be obedient to the Law:

Acts 21:23-24 – *Sha'ul praising those who "live in obedience to the Law"*
23 so do what we tell you. There are four men with us who have made a vow. 24 Take these men, join in their purification rites and pay their expenses, so that they can have their heads shaved. Then everybody will know there is no truth in these reports about you, but that you yourself are <u>living in obedience to the law</u>.

Romans 2:13 – *Sha'ul declaring obedience to the Law is the definition of Righteousness*
13 For it is not those who hear the law who are righteous in Yahuah's sight, <u>but it is those who obey the Law who will be declared righteous</u>.

Acts 24:14 – *Sha'ul declaring his belief in the Law and Prophets*
"But this I admit to you: I worship the Elohim of our fathers in accordance with the Way (which they call a sect). <u>I continue to believe everything that accords with the Torah and everything written in the Prophets</u>."

Acts 28:17 – *Sha'ul declaring he is a Torah Observant Jew*
Brothers, (speaking to the local Jewish leaders) although <u>I have done nothing against either our people or the traditions of our fathers</u> (the Torah and Prophets)...

Acts 20:16 – *Sha'ul going out of his way to celebrate the giving of the Torah*
For Sha'ul had decided to bypass Ephesus on his voyage, in order to avoid losing time in the province of Asia, because he was hurrying to get to Jerusalem, if possible in time to celebrate Shav'uot. (Celebrate WHAT? Sha'ul went out of his way to celebrate Shav'uot which is THE CELEBRATION OF THE GIVING OF THE TORAH!)

Acts 22:12 – *Sha'ul going to a Torah observant Jew to be healed*
A man named Hananyah, an observant follower of the Torah (why would he add that statement?) who was highly regarded by the entire Jewish community there, came to me, stood by me and said "Brother Sha'ul, see again!".

Philippians 3: 4-6: Sha'ul was a Pharisee, a Jewish Rabbi blameless in keeping the Law until he died
4. Though I might also have confidence in the flesh. If any other man thinketh that he hath whereof he might trust in the flesh, I more: 5. Circumcised the eighth day, of the stock of Israel, of the tribe of Benjamin, an Hebrew of the Hebrews; as touching the law, a **Pharisee**; 6. Concerning zeal, persecuting the church; touching the righteousness which is in the Law, **blameless**.

Sha'ul, being frustrated with the Spiritual Immaturity of believers and their total lack of knowledge of the Torah/Law, said this:

Hebrews 5:12 - *Spiritual Immaturity*
12 For though by this time you ought to be teachers (of the Torah, there was no such thing as the New Testament

when he wrote this), you need someone to teach you again the first principles of the oracles of Yahuah (the Torah); and you have come to need milk and not solid food. 13 For everyone who partakes only of milk is **unskilled in the word of righteousness** (Righteousness is Keeping the Law so "word of righteousness" is the Torah), for he is a babe. 14 But solid food belongs to those who are of full age (mature Saints with minds set on Spiritual Law), that is, those who **by reason of use** (keeping the Feasts/Torah/Sabbaths) have their (Spiritual) senses exercised (trained through *physical to spiritual parallel*s) to discern both good and evil (which is defined by the Law of Yahuah, good is obedience to His Commands, evil is breaking them).

Sha'ul encouraged the church in Colossae whom he properly taught to keep the Torah. It was a pagan community and province of Rome and they were being "judged" by their pagan neighbors for keeping the Torah. Sha'ul encouraged the keeping of the Kosher Laws/Feasts/New Moons/Sabbaths because in doing so they would learn Spiritual Truths through physical rehearsals and metaphors. Sha'ul is literally teaching the reality of learning through *Physical to spiritual parallel*s below:

Colossians 2
[16] Therefore do not let anyone judge you by what you eat or drink (as they kept Kosher Laws), or with regard to a religious festival (as they kept the Feast Cycles), a New Moon celebration (as they celebrated each month) or a Sabbath day (as they kept the 4th Commandment and celebrated weekly). [17] These (things Sha'ul taught them to

do, <u>remember they were pagans not Jews</u>) are a shadow (physical rehearsals) of the things that were to come (Spiritual Truths); the reality, however, is found in **the Yahushaic Covenant**.

The Christian Church (for 2,000 years) has taught the scripture above as though Sha'ul was chastising the church for following "Judaizers", who came after him teaching the church to keep the Torah. Like Sha'ul, was somehow mad they were keeping the Law.

> That is ridiculous! Jews could have cared less about what they considered "pagan gentiles", or what Sha'ul was doing.

They were only upset with Sha'ul, because he was a high ranking Pharisee <u>who abandoned them to follow Yahusha</u>! They were already condemning Sha'ul for going to the gentiles to begin with. Why would they then go after him, and take the time to follow Sha'ul around "judaizing" a bunch of pagans. Jews do not proselytize!

These were **the Lost Sheep of the House of Israel** living among the Gentiles, who had converted, and were taught by Sha'ul to keep the Torah that they, in their hearts, longed to keep. They were already displaying outwards sign of living it as it was "written on their hearts". They were being condemned by their pagan neighbors for their "foreign behavior". Sha'ul clearly said do not let anyone judge them for DOING these things. It is amazing how we are blinded to what is actually said in scripture as we approach it from the bias of our "teaching".

> Either Sha'ul is a liar for saying one thing and, teaching another; and a false teacher for teaching doctrines that directly contradict <u>explicit declarations made by Yahusha and Yahuah</u>... or maybe... perhaps we have been misled about what Sha'ul said by the Christian Church.

Could it be that the Christian Church stands in rebellion against Yahuah and His Law and has twisted scripture to justify their lawlessness? Be sure and read my upcoming books **the Yahushaic Covenant** and **the Law of Yahuah** as I explain the Law in **the Yahushaic Covenant** and deal directly with the writings of the Apostle Sha'ul.

Let us reveal the REAL Apostle Sha'ul, he...

- Actually celebrated the giving of the Law on Shav'uot.

- Went to a Torah observant Jew to be healed from blindness

- Pleaded with his fellow Jews that he continued to believe everything written in the Law and had done nothing to undermine it (or teach it to be abolished).

- Said only those who obey the Law will be declared righteous before Yahuah.

- Said obedience to the Law leads to sanctification

- Took the Nazarite Vow (defined in the Law) and lived in obedience to the Law.

- Remained until his death a Torah Observant Jew

- Was blameless in keeping the Law

- Was a Jewish Rabbi who studied under the famous Rabbi Gamaliel

- Was a Pharisee which today would be the equivalent of a Lawyer

Summary

We have all been taught (in Christianity) "another gospel" that "Jesus abolished the Law".

> ### Galatians 1
> [6] I am astonished that you are so quickly deserting the one who called you to live (by the Law, writing it in your heart) in the grace (forgiveness for transgressing the Law) of the Messiah (the Passover Lamb whose blood covers the decrees in the Law that demand your death for sin) and are turning to a different gospel (that the Law is abolished, the Spirit of Error) — [7] which is really no gospel at all (because all the promises, gifts, righteousness, kingdom, bloodline, and eternal life are all given in the Torah. If you abolish the Law, you abolish the foundation of His Kingdom, which gives "the Gospel of the Messiah" meaning and purpose). Evidently some people (Christians) are throwing you into confusion and are trying to pervert the gospel of the Messiah (who did not come to abolish the Law). [8] But even if we or an angel from heaven should preach a gospel other than the one we preached to you, **let them be under Yahuah's curse!** [9]
>
>> #### Deuteronomy 27:26
>> "Cursed is anyone who does not uphold the words of this law by carrying them out."

That "other gospel" is **the Spirit of the False Messiah** (Antichrist) which leads to **the Spirit of Error** in those who believe that false gospel. The true gospel of Yahusha the Messiah is that he did not come to abolish the Law. the Law is the "terms and conditions" of every covenant in the Bible. The Law is the "marriage vows" between Yahuah and His true sons. The Law is the governing constitution of *the Kingdom of Yahuah*. Obedience to the Law is righteousness:

> **Romans 2:13**
> 13 For it is not those who hear the law who are righteous in Yahuah's sight, **but it is those who obey the Law who will be declared righteous**.

Only those who are obedient to the Law will inhabit *the Kingdom of Yahuah*.

> **Matthew 13:41**
> The Son of Man will send his angels, and they will gather out of his kingdom all causes of sin and all law-breakers,

It is (literally) the lie that "Jesus abolished the Law" or *the Transgression of Desolation* that leads to the total destruction of Earth:

> **Isaiah 24**
> 1 See, Yahuah is going to lay waste the earth and devastate it; he will ruin its face and scatter its inhabitants... ³ The earth will be completely laid waste and totally plundered. Yahuah has spoken this word. ⁴ The earth dries up and withers, the world languishes and withers, the heavens languish with the earth. ⁵ The earth is defiled by its people; they have disobeyed the laws (committed the Transgression of Desolation), violated the statutes and broken the everlasting covenant (the Sabbath is the everlasting covenant, and it has been broken and changed to Sunday or Dies Solis the "day of the sun god").

429

> ⁶ Therefore (because of the Transgression of the Law the Earth is desolated i.e. the Transgression of Desolation or rebellion against the Law) a curse consumes the earth; its people must bear their guilt (for transgressing His Law). Therefore, earth's inhabitants are burned up, **and very few are left**. (Those left are like Yahusha; Torah Observant son's of Yahuah faithful to the marriage vows known as Remnant Israel)

Again, the curse that devours the Earth is...

> **Deuteronomy 27:26**
> "Cursed is anyone who does not uphold the words of this law by carrying them out."

The Law is the governing constitution of **the Kingdom of Yahuah** that defines the role of Yahusha as King and High Priest.   It is upon **the Law of Yahuah** that the universe is properly governed. the Law is the marriage vows in **the Yahushaic Covenant** whereby we become one in the family of Yahuah.   There simply is no room in **the Kingdom of Yahuah** for those who break His Law.

Those who break His Law are denied entry into the Kingdom by Yahusha and are rounded up and thrown out by the Angels of Yahuah.

> **Matthew 19**
> ¹⁶ And someone came to Him and said, "Teacher, what good thing shall I do that I may obtain eternal life?" ¹⁷ And He said to him, "Why are you asking Me about what is good? There is *only* One who is good; **but if you wish to enter into life, keep the commandments** (the Law)."

I'll end this chapter with this last verse in Revelation 12. Those of us who keep **the Law of Yahuah** have been under attack for 2,000 years by the false religion of Rome. The Spirit behind Christianity is Dagon... **the Dragon** (see my book *Christianity the Great Deception*). We are **Remnant Israel** from the seed of Jacob, those who obey His Law and have our sin forgiven in covenant with Yahusha:

> **Revelation 12**
> [17]And the dragon was wroth with the woman, and went to make war with the remnant of her seed, which keep the commandments of Yahuah, and have the testimony of the Messiah Yahusha.

Chapter 13

Days Set Aside for Celebration in the Kingdom of Yahuah

Introduction

For more information on The Spring Feast Cycle, please read my free book The Narrow Gate.

In **the Kingdom of Yahuah** there is established <u>by Yahuah</u> days of celebration or festivals. We are commanded to keep these most holy days of celebration as they define Yahuah's Plan of Salvation. These holy days were "shadows of things to come" and literal rehearsals of future events <u>when they were commanded</u>. Some of these events have occurred already at this point in history and those holy days are now commemorations of major events fulfilled in the past. The holy days are called the Ordained Times of Yahuah, and Festivals of Yahuah. In Hebrew they are called **moedim**. The moedim were given by Yahuah as rehearsals to teach the sons of Yahuah what the Messiah would come and accomplish in order to provide salvation. Yahusha's role as Messiah was defined by these holy days and it is in keeping them that we know the true Messiah and are able to identify **the false Messiah**. All of them are holy convocations, meaning they are to be observed in the fellowship of true believers. These moedim are not "Jewish Festivals" and they are not "the Festivals of Moses" as the false religion of Christianity would paint them. They are Yahuah's Festivals and are commanded to be kept by His true sons. In this chapter I will define these celebration days in **the Kingdom of Yahuah** and provide a general explanation for what they mean to us today. Keeping in mind that faith without works is dead, it is in keeping these festivals that our faith is demonstrated in them and what they mean to us. Faith expressed through actions of obedience makes us perfect. We see that we are justified not by faith alone, but by faith combined with works.

James 2:14-26

[14] What *does it* profit, my brethren, if someone says he has faith but does not have works? Can faith save him? [15] If a brother or sister is naked and destitute of daily food, [16] and one of you says to them, "Depart in peace, be warmed and filled," but you do not give them the things which are needed for the body, what *does it* profit? [17] **Thus also faith by itself, if it does not have works, is dead.** [18] But someone will say, **"You have faith, and I have works." Show me your faith without your works, and I will show you my faith by my works.** [19] You believe that there is one Elohim. You do well. Even the demons believe—and tremble! [20] **But do you want to know, O foolish man, that faith without works is dead?** [21] Was not Abraham our father justified by works when he offered Isaac his son on the altar? [22] Do you see that faith was working together with his works, and **by works faith was made perfect**? [23] And the Scripture was fulfilled which says, "Abraham believed Yahuah, and it was accounted to him for righteousness." And he was called the friend of Yahuah. [24] **You see then that a man is justified by works, and not by faith only.** [25] Likewise, was not Rahab the harlot also justified by works when she received the messengers and sent *them* out another way? [26] **For as the body without the spirit is dead, so faith without works is dead also.**

We must keep these Festivals of Yahuah because He gave them to us to teach us very valuable spiritual Truths. If humanity had kept the Festivals of Yahuah they would never have fallen for the False Messiah.

Yahuah's Appointed Festivals

These holy days in **the Kingdom of Yahuah** are defined by Yahuah below:

> **Leviticus 23** - *The Appointed Festivals*
> ¹ Yahuah said to Moses, ² "Speak to the Israelites and say to them: 'These are my appointed festivals, **the appointed festivals of Yahuah**, which you are to proclaim as sacred assemblies.
>
> ## *The Sabbath*
>
> > ³ "'There are six days when you may work, but <u>**the seventh day**</u> (not the first day Sunday and not "one day in seven") is a day of Sabbath rest, a day of sacred assembly. You are not to do any work; wherever you live, it is a Sabbath to Yahuah.
>
> ## *The Passover and the Festival of Unleavened Bread*
>
> > ⁴ "'**<u>These are Yahuah's appointed festivals</u>**, the sacred assemblies you are to proclaim at their <u>appointed times</u>: ⁵ <u>Yahuah's Passover</u> begins at twilight on the fourteenth day of the first month (this is when Yahusha kept what is called the Last Supper). ⁶ On the fifteenth day of that month <u>Yahuah's Festival of Unleavened Bread</u> begins; for seven days you must eat bread made without yeast. ⁷ On the first day hold a sacred assembly and do no regular work. ⁸ For seven days present a food

offering (cook meet, not pork, on the grill and have a feast) to Yahuah. And on the seventh day hold a sacred assembly and do no regular work.'"

Offering the First fruits

⁹ Yahuah said to Moses, ¹⁰ "Speak to the Israelites and say to them: 'When you enter the land I am going to give you and you reap its harvest, bring to the priest a sheaf of the first grain you harvest. ¹¹ He is to wave the sheaf before Yahuah so it will be accepted on your behalf; the priest is to wave it on the day after the Sabbath. ¹² On the day you wave the sheaf, you must sacrifice as a burnt offering to Yahuah a lamb a year old without defect, ¹³ together with its grain offering of two-tenths of an ephah of the finest flour mixed with olive oil—a food offering presented to Yahuah, a pleasing aroma—and its drink offering of a quarter of a hin of wine. ¹⁴ You must not eat any bread, or roasted or new grain, until the very day you bring this offering to your Elohim. **This is to be a lasting ordinance for the generations to come, wherever you live** (hasn't been done away with, it is an eternal ordinance wherever you live).

The Festival of Weeks

¹⁵ "'From the day after the Sabbath, the day you brought the sheaf of the wave offering, count off seven full weeks. ¹⁶ Count off fifty days up to the

day after the seventh Sabbath, and then present an offering of new grain to Yahuah. ¹⁷ From wherever you live, bring two loaves made of two-tenths of an ephah of the finest flour, baked with yeast, as a wave offering of first fruits to Yahuah. ¹⁸ Present with this bread seven male lambs, each a year old and without defect, one young bull and two rams. They will be a burnt offering to Yahuah, together with their grain offerings and drink offerings—a food offering, an aroma pleasing to Yahuah. ¹⁹ Then sacrifice one male goat for a sin offering and two lambs, each a year old, for a fellowship offering. ²⁰ The priest is to wave the two lambs before Yahuah as a wave offering, together with the bread of the first fruits. They are a sacred offering to Yahuah for the priest. ²¹ On that same day you are to proclaim a sacred assembly and do no regular work. **This is to be a lasting ordinance for the generations to come, wherever you live.** (hasn't been done away with, it is an eternal ordinance wherever you live).

²² "'When you reap the harvest of your land, do not reap to the very edges of your field or gather the gleanings of your harvest. Leave them for the poor and for the foreigner residing among you. I am Yahuah your Elohim.'"

The Festival of Trumpets

²³ Yahuah said to Moses, ²⁴ "Say to the Israelites: 'On the first day of the seventh month you are to have a day of Sabbath rest, a sacred assembly commemorated with trumpet blasts. ²⁵ Do no regular work, but present a food offering (cook some meet, not pork, on the grill and have a feast) to Yahuah.'"

The Day of Atonement

²⁶ Yahuah said to Moses, ²⁷ "The tenth day of this seventh month is the Day of Atonement. Hold a sacred assembly and deny yourselves, and present a food offering to Yahuah. ²⁸ Do not do any work on that day, because it is the Day of Atonement, when atonement is made for you before Yahuah your Elohim. ²⁹ Those who do not deny themselves on that day must be cut off from their people. ³⁰ I will destroy from among their people anyone who does any work on that day. ³¹ You shall do no work at all. **This is to be a lasting ordinance for the generations to come, wherever you live**. ³² It is a day of Sabbath rest for you, and you must deny yourselves. From the evening of the ninth day of the month until the following evening you are to observe your Sabbath."

The Festival of Tabernacles

³³ Yahuah said to Moses, ³⁴ "Say to the Israelites: 'On the fifteenth day of the seventh month **Yahuah's Festival of Tabernacles** begins, and it lasts for seven days. ³⁵ The first day is a sacred assembly; do no regular work. ³⁶ For seven days present food offerings to Yahuah, and on the eighth day hold a sacred assembly and present a food offering to Yahuah. It is the closing special assembly; do no <u>regular</u> work.

³⁷ ("'These are **Yahuah's appointed festivals**, which you are to proclaim as sacred assemblies for bringing food offerings to Yahuah—the burnt offerings and grain offerings, sacrifices and drink offerings required for each day. ³⁸ These offerings are in addition to those for Yahuah's Sabbaths and in addition to your gifts and whatever you have vowed and all the freewill offerings you give to Yahuah.)

³⁹ "'So beginning with the fifteenth day of the seventh month, after you have gathered the crops of the land, celebrate the festival to Yahuah for seven days; the first day is a day of Sabbath rest, and the eighth day also is a day of Sabbath rest. ⁴⁰ On the first day you are to take branches from luxuriant trees—from palms, willows and other leafy trees—and rejoice before Yahuah your Elohim for seven days. ⁴¹ Celebrate this as a festival to

Yahuah for seven days each year. **This is to be a lasting ordinance for the generations to come; celebrate it in the seventh month**. ⁴² Live in temporary shelters for seven days: All native-born Israelites are to live in such shelters ⁴³ so your descendants will know that I had the Israelites live in temporary shelters when I brought them out of Egypt. I am Yahuah your Elohim.'" ⁴⁴ So Moses announced to the Israelites the appointed festivals of Yahuah.

The Meaning of the Fall and Spring Festivals

Yahuah gave His sons prophetic "shadow pictures" of the role the Messiah would play in Yahuah's Plan of Salvation. Yahuah laid out for us the weekly Sabbath and two sets of Festivals; spring and fall. They are literally rehearsals that we are to keep each year that teach us through physical examples the greater Spiritual Truth that would be fulfilled in Yahusha the Messiah.

The two sets of Spring and Fall festivals are portraits of the first and second coming of the Messiah.

The Spring Festivals – Fulfilled in the First Coming

It is outside the scope of this book to go into the great detail by which Yahusha fulfilled the Spring Festivals. I highly recommend anyone reading this book watch the following video series by Michael Rood: Prophecies in the Spring Festivals of Yahuah. The extreme detail by which these were fulfilled in Yahusha is living proof that Yahusha is truly the Messiah foretold by the prophets.

PASSOVER AND FEAST OF UNLEAVENED BREAD (Leviticus 23:4-8)

Historical Meaning prior to Yahusha's fulfillment

Prior to the Messiah's coming to fulfill the Spring Festivals, Israel celebrated the Spring Festivals to commemorate the saving power of the 'blood of the lamb' that saved Yahuah's people from the

Angel of Death as Moses delivered the Israelites from Egyptian slavery and into the Promised Land.

The celebration of the Spring Festivals included the slaughter of the Passover lamb, which typified the Lamb of God, who would cover the sins of the world. Those who demonstrated their faith in Passover by keeping these festivals had the equivalent of the blood of the lamb on the doorposts of their heart.

Messianic Fulfillment

Yahusha fulfilled the Spring Festivals in great detail as the Passover Lamb of Yahuah. Yahusha kept Passover on Tuesday the 14th of Abib as Yahuah commanded. This is what Christianity calls "the Last Supper" to avoid admitting the obvious truth that Yahusha kept *the Law of Yahuah*. As Yahusha kept the meal that begins the Spring Festivals the evening (Yahuah's days begin at sunset) that began Passover, he commanded us to keep Passover as well. Yahusha instructed us to keep Passover now in "remembrance" of his sacrifice for us. It is **in keeping Passover** that we express our faith in the true Messiah:

> **James 2:18**
> But someone may well say, "You have faith and I have works; show me your faith without the works, and I will **show you my faith by my works**."

> **1 Corinthians 11:23-26** – *Sha'ul teaches the transposition of Passover*
> 23 For I received from Yahusha that which I also delivered to you (that Yahusha fulfilled the Passover), that Yahusha

the Messiah in the night in which He was betrayed (on Passover) took bread; [24] and when He had given thanks, He broke it and said, "This is My body (the Passover Lamb), which is (sacrificed) for you; do this (keep Passover) in remembrance of Me." [25] In the same way *He took* the cup also after supper, saying, "This cup (is the bloodshed to consummate the marriage covenant of Yahusha) **is the new covenant in My blood**; (Passover is the proper sacrifice in the New Covenant... not Easter) do this (put your faith in Yahusha's sacrifice by keeping Passover), as often as you drink *it*, in remembrance of Me (expressing your faith in Yahusha is in keeping Passover in light of his sacrifice)." [26] For as often as you eat this bread and drink the cup (each year on the 14th of Abib, the Passover), you proclaim (express your faith in) Yahusha's death (as the Passover Lamb) until He comes.

Yahusha's sacrifice as the Passover Lamb is only offered to those who, in obedience to Yahuah's Law and Yahusha's instruction, keep Passover and in that keeping of Passover the blood of the Lamb is Spiritually poured on **the Altar of Yahuah** (our hearts).

Luke 22:19

And when Yahusha had taken some bread and given thanks to Yahuah, He broke it and gave it to his disciples, saying, "This (bread) is My body which is given for you (as the Passover Lamb of Yahuah); do this (keep Passover) in remembrance of Me (my sacrifice for you)."

FIRSTFRUITS (Leviticus 23:9-14)

Historical Meaning

This day was like the American Thanksgiving holiday. It was not observed on a particular date but always on a particular day. Just as Thanksgiving is always observed on the fourth Thursday in the month of November, the presentation of the First fruits was always celebrated on the first day of the week, during the Feast of Unleavened Bread.

Messianic Fulfillment

Yahusha came as the Anointed King of Israel, the Messiah, nearly 2,000 years ago; and with that are associated the festivals the Israelites observed around the spring harvest. When he was crucified, Yahusha died as the Passover Lamb; Yahusha was raised 3 days and 3 nights after Passover on the weekly Sabbath. Yahusha then "ascended" to his Father the next day and presented to Yahuah the first fruits from the grave.

FEAST OF WEEKS (Leviticus 23:15-22)

"From the day after the Sabbath, the day you brought the sheaf of the wave offering, count off seven full weeks. Count off 50 days up to the day after the seventh Sabbath, and then present an offering of new grain to Yahuah."

Historical Meaning

The Feast of Weeks was to be observed on the day after the seventh Sabbath--the seven full weeks (seven Sabbaths) from the presentation of the first fruits. Thus, the Feast of Weeks was always on the first day of the week. Further, it was to be observed 50 days from the presentation of first fruits, which indicates that the first fruits were always presented on the same day of the week as well--the first.

Messianic Fulfillment

On the 50th day from Yahusha's resurrection, the Holy Spirit came on the apostles on the Day of Pentecost (the Feast of Shavuot). On that day, 3,000 believed the words of the apostles and received salvation (Acts 2). The Feast of Weeks is also a portrait of the divine timeline which is celebrating the 7th Sabbath representing the 7th Millennium.

The Fall Festivals – Fulfilled in the Second Coming

It is outside the scope of this book to go into the great detail by which Yahusha will fulfill the prophetic picture of the Fall Festivals. I highly recommend anyone reading this book watch the following video series by Michael Rood: <u>Prophecies in the Fall Festivals of Yahuah</u>.

FEAST OF TRUMPETS (Leviticus 23:23-25)

Historical Meaning

Observed on the first day of the seventh Jewish Holy month (September on our calendar). The purpose of the Feast of Trumpets is not clearly stated in the Bible, but according to Jewish tradition, it was to warn the people of the impending Day of Atonement, which came nine days later. The 10 days between the Feast of Trumpets (shofars) and the Day of Atonement are called the 10 Days of Awe when we solemnly reflect inwardly on our lives and identify all sin in preparation for atonement.

Messianic Fulfillment

The first of the autumn festivals described in Leviticus 23 is the Feast of Trumpets. Again, though Leviticus doesn't tell us much about the purpose of this day, Jews understand it to be the warning of the approaching Day of Atonement, by which all sin must be dealt with. I believe the Feast of Trumpets is fulfilled by the seven trumpets of Revelation 8-9, 11. Study indicates that the sounding of the trumpets coincides with the messages of the three angels--Worship the Creator Yahuah, Babylon is fallen, and Do not worship Babylon. The Second Coming occurs at the last trumpet of the Feast of Trumpets. The 10 Days of Awe between the Feast of Trumpets and the Day of Atonement, is the timeframe between the return of Yahusha and the army of Yahuah (His sons), and when we liberate creation and Yahusha makes atonement. This timeframe is specifically mentioned as the duration of the greatest tribulation on earth:

> **Revelation 2:10**
> 'Do not fear what you are about to suffer. Behold, the devil is about to cast some of you into prison, so that you will be tested, and you will have tribulation for ten days. Be faithful until death, and I will give you the crown of life.

DAY OF ATONEMENT (Leviticus 23:26-32)

Historical Meaning

Observed on the 10th day of the seventh month. This was the day when the people were to be cleansed of sin. All sin was to have been confessed and transferred into the sanctuary by this time, and the high priest ministered on the Day of Atonement to remove the sins from the sanctuary and have them born into the wilderness by the scapegoat (Leviticus 16).

Messianic Fulfillment

The second of the autumn festivals is the Day of Atonement. This day was the only day on which the ministry of the high priest directly included the ark of the covenant. At no other time was the ark to be seen by human eyes. Revelation 11:19 is the first and--if memory serves--only time the ark is specifically mentioned; and I believe that it refers to the time by which all sin must be confessed and repented of. Notice, in the last few verses of Revelation 11, that the ark is revealed very shortly after the seventh trumpet is sounded.

FEAST OF TABERNACLES AND CLOSING ASSEMBLY (Leviticus 23:33-36)

Historical Meaning

The Feast of Tabernacles celebrated the autumn harvest, just as the Feast of Weeks celebrated the spring harvest.

Messianic Fulfillment

The third of the autumn festivals is the Feast of Tabernacles. This was the celebration of the harvest at the end of the year, just as the Feast of Weeks was the celebration of the spring harvest. The difference is that the Feast of Tabernacles was a much bigger celebration (see Leviticus 23). Revelation 14:14-16 describes the harvest; and Revelation 7:9-15 is another reference to those who are harvested from the earth.

The Feast Cycle is Based on the Message Written in the stars!

Psalm 19 – *The Zodiac proclaims the Wedding!*
19 The heavens (*'shamarym'* or Zodiac) declare the glory of Yahuah, and the sky above (shamarym/Zodiac) proclaims his handiwork. 2 Day to day pours out speech, and night to night reveals knowledge. 3 There is no speech, nor are there words, whose voice is not heard. 4 Their voice goes out through all the earth, and their words to the end of the world. In them he has set a tent for the sun, 5 **which comes out like a bridegroom leaving his chamber**, and, like a strong man, runs its course with joy. 6 Its rising is from the end of the heavens, and its circuit (Zodiac means circuit of the sun) to the end of them, and there is nothing hidden from its heat.

In my first book in this series; ***Creation Cries Out! 2nd Edition – The Mazzaroth***, I explain in great detail the Original Gospel of Yahusha the Messiah written into the star at creation.

This message in the stars, the Heavenly Scroll, concerning the bridegroom redeeming his bride was then further elaborated in the Feasts of Yahuah.

In this Heavenly Scroll, as David pointed out in Psalms, the Sun is a metaphor of the Messiah and the story told by the Mazzaroth is that of a wedding! The Feast Cycle is an annual rehearsal of this wedding as the Plan of Salvation is carried out in context of a wedding. This wedding cycle is the "path/course/line" the bridegroom/strong man who is the Messiah is foretold to take each year as King David proclaimed in Psalms 19. It is outside the scope of this book to go any further into the contents of the Heavenly Scroll, please refer to my book *Creation Cries Out! 2nd Edition – The Mazzaroth*.

This fundamental message written into the stars by the Creator as a witness to all mankind is further revealed in covenants made between the Creator and mankind. Each and every covenant in the Bible is a "marriage covenant" and the Law are the "marriage vows". This Plan of Salvation through a wedding was further revealed to us in parables and idioms.

- Parable of the Wedding Banquet in Matthew 22
- Parable of the Faithful Servant in Matthew 24
- Parable of the 10 Virgins in Matthew 25
- Revelation 19

We find that Yahusha, who is the bridegroom, constantly taught the same message written in the stars, giving us more and more insight into the Plan of Salvation... the plan of the bridegroom redeeming his bride.

The Annual Wedding Portrait

The Appointed Times (or the Feast of Yahuah) each year are a literal rehearsal of this divine wedding. This message and meaning behind the annual feasts is hidden knowledge revealed only to those "invited to the wedding". Like Sha'ul said, it was not understood by the leaders of Israel in the second temple period, or by those who lead us in this age even now. Yet, we follow these same leaders (Pharisees i.e. modern day Rabbinical Judaism) and their "way of doing things" and in doing so we err in our responsibility to rehearse them properly as His Bride!

We have missed the most basic understanding of the Feasts, and we all have become ritualistic in our adherence to these appointed days. We have missed the point and meaning of these rehearsals! We just go through the motions; we are not really rehearsing the events of the wedding.

The Physical Shadow of Greater Truths

Hebrew/Jewish weddings were pre-arranged marriages. They consisted of the father choosing a qualified groom, the groom paying the dowry or "ransom" for the bride, the groom introducing himself to her father, the bride presenting herself to the bridegroom, the bridegroom going away to prepare a place for her in his father's estate, the bridegroom returning for his bride, the wedding, and finally the wedding banquet.

With this in mind, let me show how perfectly the Feasts Cycle or Appointed Times of Yahuah reflect the physical marriage process. Keeping in mind that a marriage between a man and a woman is a physical to spiritual parallel that should help us understand our roles in the Fall and Spring Feasts:

- ***The father choosing a qualified Groom*** – this is reflected in Yahuah's choice of the Messiah Yahusha as proclaimed through the prophets.

- ***The Rehearsal Dinner*** – the Chagigah meal on the 14th of Abib is a "remembrance meal" where we are to discuss the upcoming wedding rehearsal and what each day represents. This is called "The Last Supper" in our twisted English Bibles. I explain all this in my upcoming book The Narrow Gate.

- **The Groom paying the dowry or "ransom" for the Bride** – this is a shadow of Passover as Yahusha "paid the debt to the Father of the Bride" and redeemed us from our prior lives into a new life in covenant with Yahuah. He paid the dowry, or ransom, owed to our Father - **Matthew 20:28** *"just as the Son of Man did not come to be served, but to serve, and to give his life as a ransom for many."*

- **The Groom introducing himself to the Father of the Bride** – Feast of First fruits. **John 20:17** *"Yahusha said, "Do not hold on to me, for I have not yet ascended to the Father."*

- **The Bride presenting herself to the Bridegroom and agreeing to the marriage vows** – Shav'uot. On Shav'uot we are to follow the example set by Yahusha during Passover. We are to mikveh ourselves, bring our own lives as an offering at the altar of Yahuah (a lamb without blemish), and then present ourselves properly to our Bridegroom on Shav'uot. We agree to the wedding vows (the Law) by saying "this we will do" or "I do" as they did at the foot of Mt. Sinai. It is a celebration of the giving of the Wedding Vows and our accepting them. Sha'ul expressed the way we are to present ourselves in following Yahusha's example of Mikveh, circumcision, and bringing an offering. Again we see ==the Plan of Salvation is a MARRIAGE:==

    ### Ephesians 5
    25 Husbands, love your wives, just as the Messiah loved the assembly and gave himself up for her (as the Passover Lamb paying the dowry) 26 to set her apart, (ritually) cleansing her by the washing with

water according to the commandments (of Mikveh), 27 and to present her (consecrated) to himself (with a circumcised heart) as a radiant assembly, without spot or wrinkle or any other blemish (as we offer our lives as living sacrifices), but holy and blameless (as the spotless Bride of Yahuah).

- **The bridegroom going away to prepare a place for the bride in his father's estate** - <u>John 14</u> Yahusha says "<u>2</u> "*In My Father's house are many dwelling places; if it were not so, I would have told you; for I go to prepare a place for you. <u>3</u>"If I go and prepare a place for you, I will come again and receive you to Myself, that where I am, there you may be also. <u>4</u>"And you know the way where I am going.*" Here Yahusha is speaking in the Mystery Language a parable and idiom confirming the wedding.   Yahusha goes and prepares a place for us in the Kingdom of Yahuah.   He is not referring to a physical place (because we reign with him on Earth), he is referring to a place in the family of Yahuah.   Yahusha is going to perform the duties of High Priest and offer the proper gifts and sacrifices before the throne of Yahuah required to grant us adoption as sons/daughters.   Then he says he is returning for us as a Bridegroom returns for his Bride.

- **The Bridegroom returning for his Bride** – Feast of Trumpets or Yom Teruah.   This is a portrait of the second coming of the Bridegroom to receive his Bride.   Yahusha returns and the Bride is resurrected to meet him.   This occurs on the Feast of Trumpets (Yom Teruah) which is celebrated over a two-day period at the beginning of the

7th month because it is the only feast based on the timing of the new moon.   Yom Terauh became known therefore as the idiom "**the feast of which no man knows the day or hour**" because we don't know the exact timing of the new moon.   Yahusha confirmed his return on the Feast of Trumpets when he used an idiom for this feast in **Matthew 24:36** ""*But about that day or hour no one knows, not even the angels in heaven, nor the Son, but only the Father.*"   Here Yahusha was both confirming his return on the Feast of Trumpets and the arranged marriage using another idiom "*no one knows, not even the angels in heaven, nor the Son, but only the Father*".   You see, the marriage was arranged by the father unknown to the son.

- **The wedding** – Yom Kippur or Day of Atonement.   I am going to address this in more detail in a minute.

- **The wedding banquet** – Sukkot or the Feast of Tabernacles.   This feast is known as the Wedding Banquet as portrayed in Revelation 19 and was the meaning behind the Parable of the Wedding Banquet in Matthew 22.

The Festivals of Yahuah are Kept in the Future Kingdom of Yahuah

Isaiah 66

19 "I will set *a sign* (the Sabbath is the sign see vs. 23 and keep this in context) among them, and I will send some of those who survive to the nations—to Tarshish, to the Libyans and Lydians, to Tubal and Greece, and to the distant islands that have not heard of my fame or seen my glory. They will proclaim my glory (as Creator) among the nations (how? By displaying THE SIGN to them). 20 And they will bring all your people, from all the nations, to my holy mountain in Jerusalem as an offering to Yahuah... 22 "For just as the new heavens and the new earth that I am making will continue in my presence (the Sabbath is an eternal sign)," says Yahuah, "so will your descendants and your name continue. 23 "Every month on Rosh-Hodesh (from month to month) and **every week on Shabbat** (from week to week), ***everyone living*** will come to worship in my presence," says Yahuah. 24 "As they (who bear His Sabbath Sign) leave (from worshipping Yahuah on the Sabbath), **they will look on the corpses of the people who rebelled against me** (in context rebelled against His Sabbath) for their worm will never die, and their fire will never be quenched; but **they will be abhorrent to all humanity**."

Zechariah 14:16-19

And it shall come to pass, that every one that is left of all the nations which came against Jerusalem shall even go up from year to year to worship the King (who sits on the throne of creation), Yahuah of hosts, (we don't worship Yahusha who sits at Yahuah right hand as King of His Kingdom) **and to <u>keep the feast of tabernacles</u>**. And it shall be, that whoso will not come up of all the families of the earth unto Jerusalem to worship the King, Yahuah of hosts, even upon them shall be no rain. And if the family of Egypt go not up, and come not, that have no rain; there shall be the plague, <u>wherewith</u> **<u>Yahuah will smite the heathen that come not up to keep the feast of tabernacles</u>. This shall be the punishment of Egypt, and the punishment of all nations that come not up <u>to keep the feast of tabernacles</u>.**

Luke 22:7-19

Then came the day of unleavened bread, when the Passover Lamb must be killed (and eaten). And he sent Peter and John, saying, Go and prepare us the Passover, that we may eat… And he said unto them, With desire I have desired to eat this Passover with you before I suffer: For I say unto you, I will not any more eat thereof, **<u>until it be fulfilled in the kingdom of Yahuah</u>**. And he took the cup, and gave thanks, and said, Take this, and divide it among yourselves: For I say unto you, I will not drink of the fruit of the vine, **<u>until the kingdom of Yahuah shall come</u>** (Yahusha clearly declares he will keep Passover in *the*

Kingdom of Yahuah). And he took bread, and gave thanks, and brake it, and gave unto them, saying, This is my body which is given for you: **this do in remembrance of me.**

The Meaning of the Weekly Sabbath

The Sabbath is a weekly celebration of Yahuah's Plan for His Sons. That plan is 6,000 years of "labor" then a 1,000 year "Sabbath Rest".

The Day of Yahuah (which is the day of Yahuah's wrath) when, due to the **Transgression of Desolation,** Yahuah destroys the Earth just before the beginning of the 1,000 year Sabbath Rest:

> **Isaiah 24: 1-6**
> The Earth is polluted by its inhabitants - They have committed the Transgression of Desolation (transgressed the Torah, changed the Holy Feasts to Christopagan Holidays, and broken the Everlasting Covenant of the Sabbath changing it to the pagan Sunday) - Therefore the Curse found in the Torah devours the whole Earth, the inhabitants of Earth will be burned up, and few men left.

Speaking of the Day of Yahuah, the author of 2 Peter explains that in the prophetic language of Yahuah a day is a thousand years. He frames the timeframe for *this age* from creation until the end of the Plan of Yahuah when this Earth is destroyed.

That plan defined by the Sabbath Covenant:

> **2 Peter 3**
> [3] Know this first of all, that in **the last days** mockers will come with *their* mocking, following after their own lusts, [4] and saying, "Where is the promise of His coming? For *ever* since the fathers fell asleep, all continues just as it was

from the beginning of creation." ⁵ For when they maintain this, it escapes their notice that by the word of Yahuah *the* heavens existed long ago and *the* earth was formed out of water and by water (Genesis 1:1), ⁶ through which **the world at that time was destroyed** (when Lucifer fell leading a rebellion on Earth), being flooded with water (beginning boundary – creation when, after flooding the Earth after the fall of Lucifer, Yahuah started over and established the 7-Day Sabbath Covenant). ⁷ But by His word the present heavens and earth are being reserved for fire, **kept for the day of judgment** and destruction of ungodly men (ending boundary when after the 1,000 year Sabbath Rest Yahuah destroys the Earth by fire).

⁸ But do not let this one *fact* escape your notice, beloved, that with Yahuah **one day is like a thousand years, and a thousand years like one day**. ⁹

What Peter is saying is in response to mockers who mock the second coming because it hasn't occurred yet. Peter is saying if you understood Yahuah's Plan you would never mock it because the second coming doesn't occur until the 6,000[th] year to setup the Sabbath Kingdom. Peter is explaining that from Genesis 1 through Revelation 22 the 7-Day Sabbath Covenant is a *physical to spiritual parallel* with each day being a thousand years. 6,000 years we work as Yahuah did (labor under the curse of Adam) and the last 1,000 years we enter into Yahuah's Rest (when the curse of Adam is lifted and creation liberated.

God's Master Timeframe
The Everlasting Covenant

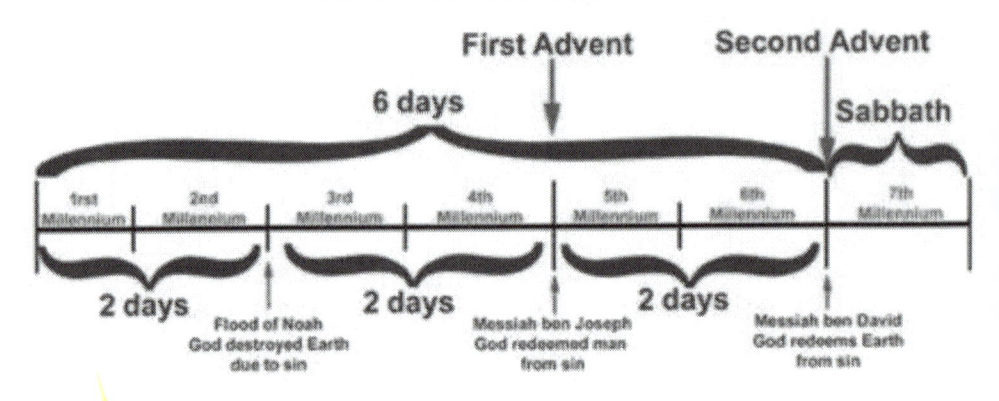

First Advent — Second Advent

6 days | Sabbath

1st Millennium | 2nd Millennium | 3rd Millennium | 4th Millennium | 5th Millennium | 6th Millennium | 7th Millennium

2 days — Flood of Noah, God destroyed Earth due to sin

2 days — Messiah ben Joseph, God redeemed man from sin

2 days — Messiah ben David, God redeems Earth from sin

We enter into Yahuah's Rest, the Sabbath Kingdom, only if we keep the 7th Day Sabbath as Yahuah did:

> **Hebrews 4** - *A Sabbath-Rest for the People of Yahuah*
> 1 Therefore, since the promise of entering his rest still stands (the Sabbath Covenant is still in effect), let us be careful that none of you be found to have fallen short of it (by failing to Keep the Sabbath). 2 For we also have had the gospel preached to us, just as they did; but the message they heard was of no value to them, because those who heard <u>did not combine it with faith</u> (by keeping the Sabbath we are expressing our faith in the Plan of Yahuah and His coming Kingdom that Yahusha will establish that Kingdom in the 6,000th year). 3 Now we who have believed (in Yahusha, King of the Sabbath) enter that rest, just as Yahuah has said,
>
> "So I declared on oath in my anger, 'They shall never enter my rest.' "And yet his work has been finished since the (re)

creation of the world (<u>Yahuah Himself kept the Sabbath and commanded we do to, the 4th Commandment</u>). 4 For somewhere he has spoken about **the seventh day** (not Sunday and not 1 day in 7 but THE 7th day) in these words: "And on **the seventh day** Yahuah rested from all his work." 5 And again in the passage above he says, "**They** (who do not keep My Sabbath) **shall never enter my rest**."

6 It **still remains that some (the remnant sons of Yahuah) will enter that rest**, and those who formerly had the gospel preached to them did not go in, because of their disobedience (to the Sabbath). 7 Therefore Yahuah again set a certain day, calling it Today, when a long time later he spoke through David, as was said before:

"Today, if you hear his voice, do not harden your hearts. (against His Sabbath)" 8 For if Joshua had given them (Israelites) rest (entering the promised land), Yahuah would not have spoken later about another day (the Sabbath Rest is yet to come verse 1). 9 **There remains, then, a Sabbath-rest for the people of Yahuah**; 10 **for anyone who enters Yahuah's rest also rests from his own work, just as Yahuah did from his** (You must keep the Sabbath just as Yahuah did on the 7th Day). 11 Let us, therefore, make every effort to enter that rest (by being obedient to the Sabbath), so that no one will fall by **following their example of disobedience** (to the Sabbath set by the False Religion of Christianity).

12 For the word of Yahuah is living and active. Sharper than any double-edged sword, it

> penetrates even to dividing soul and spirit, joints and marrow; it judges the thoughts and attitudes of the heart. 13Nothing in all creation is hidden from Yahuah's sight. Everything is uncovered and laid bare before the eyes of him to whom we must give account (for why, in context, we did not keep the Sabbath)

So each week, we celebrate the Sabbath looking forward to Yahusha's return and the establishment of **the Kingdom of Yahuah.** It is the sign we display back to Yahuah as He looks down upon mankind looking for those who truly believe His Word and take the time to celebrate with Him the coming Kingdom of Yahuah.

If you don't keep the Sabbath you are a law-breaker (worker of iniquity) by breaking the 4th Commandment. Those who break the Sabbath Covenant will die and their corpses will be an eternal reminder as those who keep the Sabbath step over their dead bodies to enter **the Kingdom of Yahuah.** Only those who bear the Sign to the nations (ensigns) and proclaim Yahuah's glory as Creator (the Sabbath is Yahuah's stamp on creation) will enter **the Kingdom of Yahuah**:

> ### Isaiah 66
>
> 19 "I will set *a sign* (the Sabbath is the sign see vs. 23 and keep this in context) among them, and I will send some of those who survive to the nations—to Tarshish, to the Libyans and Lydians, to Tubal and Greece, and to the distant islands that have not heard of my fame or seen my glory. They will proclaim my glory (as Creator) among the

the Kingdom

nations (how? By displaying THE SIGN to them). 20 And they will bring all your people, from all the nations, to my holy mountain in Jerusalem as an offering to Yahuah... 22 "For just as the new heavens and the new earth that I am making will continue in my presence (the Sabbath is an eternal sign)," says Yahuah, "so will your descendants and your name continue. 23 "Every month on Rosh-Hodesh (from month to month) and **every week on Shabbat** (from week to week), ***everyone living*** will come to worship in my presence," says Yahuah. 24 "As they (who bear His Sabbath Sign) leave (from worshipping Yahuah on the Sabbath), **they will look on the corpses of the people who rebelled against me** (in context rebelled against His Sabbath) for their worm will never die, and their fire will never be quenched; but **they will be abhorrent to all humanity**."

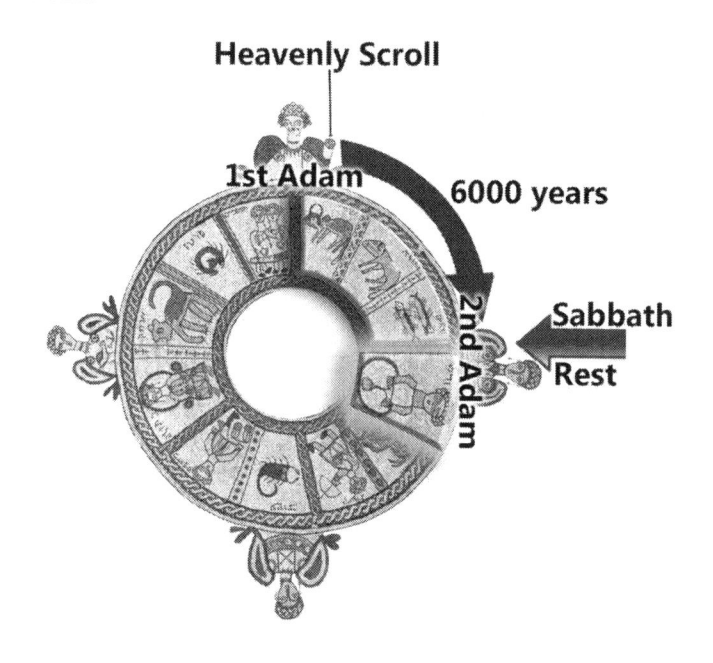

Heavenly Scroll

1st Adam — 6000 years — 2nd Adam — Sabbath Rest

Yahusha and His Disciples Kept the Festivals of Yahuah

John 2:23
²³ Now when **He was in Jerusalem at the Passover**, during the feast, many believed in His name, observing His signs which He was doing.

John 7:2-10
² Now the feast of Yahuah, **the Feast of Booths** (Tabernacles), was near...¹⁰ But when His brothers had gone up to the feast, then He Himself also went up, not publicly, but as if, in secret.

Acts 18:20-21
When they desired him to tarry longer time with them, he consented not; But bade them farewell, saying, **I must by all means keep this feast** (of Passover/Unleavened Bread) that cometh in Jerusalem:

Acts 2:1
And when the day of Pentecost (the Feast of Shavuot) was fully come, they were all with one accord in one place.

Acts 20:16
For Sha'ul had determined to sail by Ephesus, because he would not spend the time in Asia: **for he hasted, if it were possible for him, to be at Jerusalem the day of Pentecost** (the Feast of Shavuot).

Luke 22:1
Now the **feast of unleavened bread** drew nigh, which is

called the Passover (because that is when the Passover Lamb was eaten, Passover is actually the night before).

Luke 22:7-19
Then came the day of unleavened bread, when the Passover Lamb must be killed (and eaten). And he sent Peter and John, saying, Go and prepare us the Passover, that we may eat... And he said unto them, With desire I have desired to eat this Passover with you before I suffer: For I say unto you, I will not any more eat thereof, **until it be fulfilled in the kingdom of Yahuah**. And he took the cup, and gave thanks, and said, Take this, and divide it among yourselves: For I say unto you, I will not drink of the fruit of the vine, **until the kingdom of Yahuah shall come** (Yahusha clearly declares he will keep Passover in *the Kingdom of Yahuah*). And he took bread, and gave thanks, and brake it, and gave unto them, saying, This is my body which is given for you: **this do (keep Passover) in remembrance of me**.

1 Corinthians 11:23-26 – Sha'ul teaches the transposition of Passover
[23] For I received from Yahusha that which I also delivered to you (that Yahusha fulfilled the Passover), that Yahusha the Messiah in the night in which He was betrayed (on Passover) took bread; [24] and when He had given thanks, He broke it and said, "This is My body (the Passover Lamb), which is (sacrificed) for you; do this (keep Passover) in remembrance of Me." [25] In the same way *He took* the cup also after supper, saying, "This cup (is the blood shed to consummate the marriage covenant of Yahusha) **is the**

==new covenant in My blood==; ==(Passover is the proper sacrifice in the New Covenant… not Easter)== ==do this (put your faith in Yahusha's sacrifice by keeping Passover)==, as often as you drink *it*, in remembrance of Me (expressing your faith in Yahusha is in keeping Passover in light of his sacrifice)." ²⁶ For as often as you eat this bread and drink the cup (each year on the 14ᵗʰ of Abib, the Passover), you proclaim (express your faith in) Yahusha's death (as the Passover Lamb) until He comes.

1 Corinthians 5:6-8 – Sha'ul teaches the transposition of The Feast of Unleavened Bread

⁶ Your boasting is not good. Do you not know that a little leaven leavens the whole lump *of dough*? ⁷ Clean out the old leaven so that you may be a new lump, just as you are *in fact* unleavened. For Yahusha is our Passover Lamb who also has been sacrificed. ⁸ **Therefore let us celebrate the feast**, not with old leaven, nor with the leaven of malice and wickedness, but with the unleavened bread of sincerity and truth.

The Apostle Sha'ul addressed the Feast Cycle and the Plan of Yahuah below:

Romans 8

²⁰ For the creation was subjected to futility (when Adam fell), not willingly, but because of Yahuah who subjected *it* in hope (of a coming Messiah); ²¹ because **the creation itself also** (like the sons of Yahuah during the Spring Feasts) **will be delivered** (in the fulfillment of the coming Fall Feasts) from the bondage of corruption into the glorious liberty of the children of Yahuah (on the **DAY OF**

ATONEMENT). **22** For we know that the whole creation groans and labors (for 6,000 years per the Sabbath Covenant) with birth pangs together until now (the 7th Millennium, the Sabbath). **23** Not only *that,* but we also who have the Firstfruits (the Passover Lamb/Feast of First Fruits/Spring Feasts) of the Spirit (Given on the Feast of Weeks, the guarantee/Spring Feasts), **even we ourselves groan within ourselves** (along with creation because we have not yet been resurrected and delivered), **eagerly waiting for the adoption** (as elohim, into the Family of Yahuah), the redemption of our body (deliverance on the Feast of Trumpets, Resurrection/Fall Feasts). **24** For we were saved (during the Spring Feasts by the Passover Lamb) in **this** hope (that He will return again and fulfill the Fall Feasts, resurrect our bodies and liberate creation), but hope that is seen is not hope; for why does one still hope for what he sees (we have not yet witnessed the fulfillment of the Fall Feasts, so Hope for our deliverance endures)? **25** But if we hope for what we do not see, we eagerly wait for *it* (our deliverance during the Fall Feasts) with perseverance (those who persevere until the end shall be delivered).

Chapter 14

Conclusion

In this book I have, in obedience to Yahusha's command, properly taught *the Kingdom of Yahuah;* as that is the central theme of the Bible:

> **Mark 1:15 -** New American Standard Bible
> "The time is fulfilled, and the kingdom of Yahuah is at hand; repent and believe in the gospel."
>
> **Matthew 4:17 -** Aramaic Bible in Plain English
> From then on, Yahusha began to preach and to say, "Return to Yahuah, for the Kingdom of Heaven has come near."
>
> **Matthew 10:7**
> Go and announce to them that the Kingdom of Heaven is near.
>
> **Matthew 3** - GOD'S WORD® Translation
> "Turn to Yahuah and change the way you think and act, because the Kingdom of Yahuah is near."

In this book I have defined what it means that *"the Kingdom of Yahuah is within you"*:

> **Luke 17**
>
> [20] Now when Yahusha was asked by the Pharisees when the Kingdom of Yahuah would come, He answered them and said, "the Kingdom of Yahuah does not come with observation; [21] nor will they say, 'See here!' or 'See there!' For indeed, **the Kingdom of Yahuah is within you.**"

Within you is the transposition of the Kingdom of Yahuah into the spiritual realm:

- His Temple is your body
- His Altar is your heart
- His Sacrifices on the altar of your heart is your spiritual worship and obedience to the Truth found in the Torah. We worship in "spirit and in truth"
- The Law of Yahuah is written on your heart
- Our bodies are living stones
- We are living Arks of the Covenant

In the next book in this series, **the Yahushaic Covenant Volume 1 – The Mediator,** I will further define the covenant we are in, our rights within that covenant, and our responsibilities to Yahuah as members of His household… through the *Yahushaic Covenant*.

The 'Battle of the Ages' continues...

This is "the battle of the Ages" in scripture; the battle for the message contained in the "Zodiac" ... **The Heavenly Scroll**:

- Jerusalem vs. Rome/Babylon
- Yahuah vs. Sol Invictus/Ba'al
- The Shema vs. Incarnation
- Yahusha vs. Jesus/Tammuz
- The son of God vs. God the Son
- The Sabbath vs. Dias Solis/Sunday
- The Passover Lamb vs. Easter/The Ishtar Pig
- The Holy Days vs. Holidays
- The Law vs. Lawlessness
- The Spirit of Truth/Torah vs. The Spirit of Error/Law abolished
- The Spirit of Yahuah vs. the Spirit of the False Messiah/Incarnation
- The Nazarene vs. Christianity/Christopaganism found in all pagan religions whose roots go back to Babylon.

In my book series, I established that there was **Original Revelation** to man from Yahuah that was corrupted into Sun Worship. I then begin to define **The Mystery Religion of Babylon**. It is important we understand exactly what religion evolved out of Babylon because it is that religion that is condemned in the Bible as the religion that leads humanity astray at the end. It is THE religion that The Messiah returns to destroy with his testimony.

The Babylonian religion is the formal religion built around the "other Gospel" of the corrupted Zodiac as taught by the watchers. The religion that evolved out of Babylon was dispersed throughout the Earth when Yahuah scattered humanity and confused the languages at The Tower of Babel. That Mystery Religion was Sun Worship, and it was passed down from Babylon to Egypt to Rome and survives even today. Christianity is identical to the Mystery Religion of Babylon which is proven in my book series.

Book 1: Creation Cries Out!

In this book I trace the great deception back to its origin and explain how the "Gospel message in the stars" was corrupted into another gospel. I re-establish the message contained in the Heavenly Scroll and give Yahuah the Glory He deserves as the Creator of all things. In this book, the original revelation found written in the stars is broken down, defined, and glorified. I explain how the watchers corrupted the true message and taught mankind to worship the creation over the Creator. Creation Cries Out! Reveals the secrets preserved in the Heavens, and provides clear instruction so that the Great Seal over the Bible and the books of prophecy can be opened. Every prophet of Yahuah based their predictions on the Heavenly Scroll and described it in great detail.

Book 2: Mystery Babylon the Religion of the Beast

In this book I explain how that corrupted message was formulated into a formal religion in Babylon and define that religion as it existed then. We will go back to the very beginning of "paganism" and examine the gods and rituals that define this false religion. We will trace this religion, show how it evolved, who created it, and how it came to dominate all mankind. This information is vital as there is prophesied to be, at the end, a religion on Earth based on Mystery Babylon that deceives all humanity. The only way to properly identify that religion today that has fulfilled this prophecy is to fully understand Mystery Babylon.

Book 3: 'Christianity and the Great Deception'

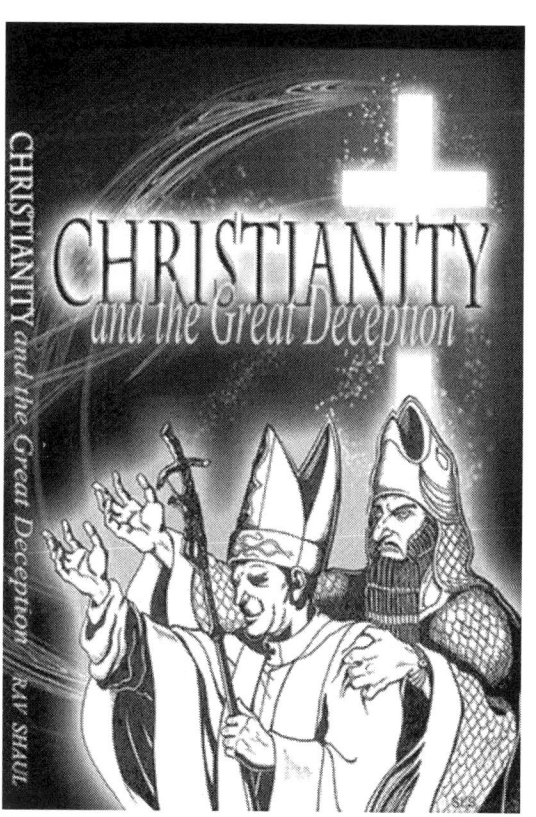

I compare Christianity to Mystery Babylon and prove that it is a carbon copy and is the prophesied false religion. Every description of "God" is taken directly from Babylon. From the Trinity to calling the Creator "The LORD" are all based on sun worship. I explain where Jesus H. Christ came from, who created that false image, and how that false messiah is a carbon copy of the second member of the Babylonian Trinity named Tammuz. From the false sacrifice of a pig on Easter, to Sunday worship, to Christmas… every aspect of the Christian Religion is a carbon copy of Mystery Babylon! I document everything carefully from historical sources, the Catholic Church documents, and the Bible. No one who has read this book has remained a "Christian" after finishing it.

Book 4: 'The Antichrist Revealed!'

In this book I prove that Jesus H. Christ is the false image of the true messiah, and I demonstrate how he meets every prophecy of the "Antichrist". I define in great detail such things as the Abomination of Desolation, the Spirit of the Antichrist, the Spirit of Error, the other Gospel, and much more. In this book, I demonstrate through Biblical prophecy that the false messiah is an "image" of the true Messiah not an actual person. This book is 500 pages of solid proof that the "god" of this Earth, Jesus Christ is the "Abominable Beast" foretold by name, sacrifice, and rituals. I prove that "Jesus" is not the name of the Messiah in any language much less Hebrew. We dissect that name and prove how the name of the Messiah was intentionally altered to give glory to Zeus over Yahuah. The true name of the Messiah is Yahusha.

Book 5: 'The Kingdom'

With the false religion, the false messiah, the false sacrifice, the false rituals clearly defined in the first 4 books, I begin to relay a firm foundation in what is true. In this book I define The Kingdom of Yahuah in great detail. I explain how all previous 6 covenants were transposed into the final 7th Covenant of Yahusha. I breakdown every aspect of the Kingdom using physical to spiritual parallels of a kingdom on Earth. What is this Kingdom, what is its purpose, what is its domain, who is its King, what is its constitution, who are its citizens, and what responsibility to the citizens who gain citizenship? All answered in this book.

Book 6: 'The Yahushaic Covenant Volume 1 - The Mediator'

In this book I break down The New Covenant and explain who Yahusha is in relation to Yahuah, what our roles are in the covenant of Yahusha, and much more. The Yahushaic Covenant is the "Salvation of Yahuah Covenant". I explain the role the Law plays in our lives under covenant with Yahusha. I explain the effects of Hellenism and blending the truth with paganism. I breakdown the scripture in context, shedding light on the writings in the Renewed Covenant with the original scriptures (Old Testament if you must). I re-teach the scriptures in light of the ancient language and cultural matrix of the 1st Century people of Yahuah living in the land of Israel.

Book 7: 'The Yahushaic Covenant Volume 2 - The Law and the Pauline Doctrine'

In this book, I explain the role the Law plays in our lives and re-teach Sha'ul's writings from the standpoint of intent. I overcome the Christian lie that Sha'ul taught against the Torah. We go in and take a hard look at how Sha'ul's writing were translated and "twisted" by the Greeks into another Gospel called The Paulne Doctrine. In this book, I introduce us all to Rav Sha'ul the leader of the Nazarenes! What does that mean, and what does that one fact say about the way his writings have been translated today? I explain the various aspects of The Law, how it was transposed over time from the Mind of Yahuah, to written in the stars at creation, to given orally, to written in stone, to finally written on our hearts. I explain the various jurisdictional aspects of the Law, look at the Law from the standpoint of intent, and provide solid instruction to the Nazarene today in how to approach the Law of Yahuah.

Book 8: 'The Yahushaic Covenant Volume 3 - Melchizedek and the Passover Lamb'

What does Melchizedek really mean? In this book I explain how Yahusha became the King of Kings and the Eternal High Priest by blood lineage to King David and the ordained Zadok Priesthood. We travel back 2,000 years to the time of the Messiah's birth to fully understand the mindset of that time. A time of great expectation toward the coming Messiah. We look back into historical documents surrounding that time period to identify the lineage of Yahusha. Lineage that was lost to antiquity when Rome burned the original manuscripts. Who were Yahusha's "other grandparents" that contributed equally to his bloodline, we have just never been introduce to? How is Yahusha "King of Israel". How is Yahusha the "High Priest of Israel". The Bible declares Yahusha inherited those titles. If so, how and from whom? This book is a must read and introduction to the REAL Messiah in a way you have never known him.

Book 9: 'The Narrow Gate'

In this book I explain how keeping the Feasts of Yahuah properly is a pre-requisite of entering the Kingdom. The Feast Cycle is the "Narrow Gate" of a wedding and we must rehearse these events from the standpoint of "a Bride". What is the true meaning of the feasts, what are they rehearsing, how do we keep them? All these questions are answered and more in the final book in this series, The Narrow Gate.

Please visit my website www.sabbathcovenant.com for in depth teachings, audio lessons, links to these books, and much more. If this book has been a blessing to you, please support this ministry. Email info@sabbathcovenant.com for more information or you can donate or become a Sponsor on our website.

All Glory belongs to Yahuah. He is our Creator, Author of the Heavenly Scroll, and Father of the called out ones (Nazarenes). And to Yahusha the Nazarene, the Messiah and Royal High Priest of Israel, I say...

"WORTHY IS THE LAMB! TO RECEIVE HONOR, AND GLORY, AND POWER, AND PRAISE"

HALLELUYAHUAH

LET IT BE SO DONE, ON EARTH AS IT IS WRITTEN IN THE HEAVENLY SCROLL.

Kingdom blessings, and much love...

Rav Sha'ul

If this book has been a blessing to you, please support this ministry and keep these books free! Please visit www.sabbathcovenant.com and also visit my YouTube Channel for further video teachings and presentations. The Sabbath Covenant Channel...

https://www.youtube.com/channel/UCVLZgChmeSa78Mo7b228sjQ

Made in the USA
Lexington, KY
02 April 2017